EMILE ANTOINE

BOURDELLE

PIONEER OF THE FUTURE

24 MAY - 29 OCTOBER 1989

"If you want my opinion on Bourdelle's sculpture, I am very happy to give it, because Bourdelle is one of those men and artists who must be talked about. He is a "pioneer of the future". I love his sculpture because it is very personal and it corresponds to his sensitive nature and his passionate and fiery temperament".

Auguste Rodin

THIS SECOND EDITION OF THE CATALOGUE INCLUDES A SUPPLEMENT AT THE BACK WITH ADDITIONAL MATERIAL AND ILLUSTRATIONS OF THE EXHIBITION AT THE YORKSHIRE SCULPTURE PARK.

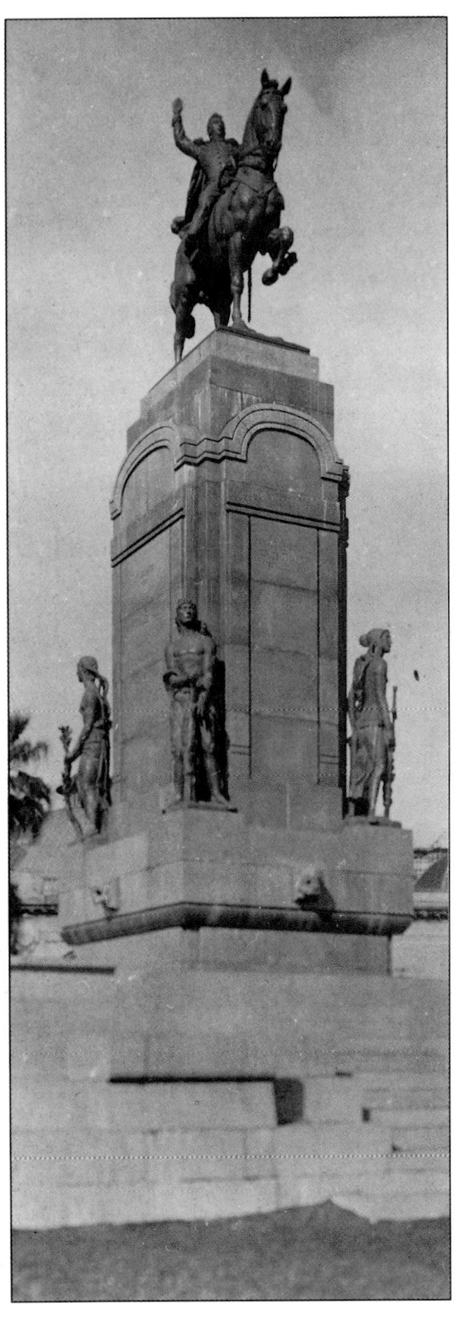

The Alvear Monument
Plaza de la Recoleta, Buenos Aires
unveiled in 1926

Grand Cheval sans Cavalier
Monumental Horse without Rider
1914-1917
4.60m x 4.30m x 2.25m

YORKSHIRE
SCULPTURE PARK
BRETTON HALL
WEST BRETTON
WAKEFIELD
WEST YORKSHIRE
WF4 4LG
ADMINISTRATION: 0924 830579
INFORMATION: 0924 830302

ISBN 1 871480 03 5

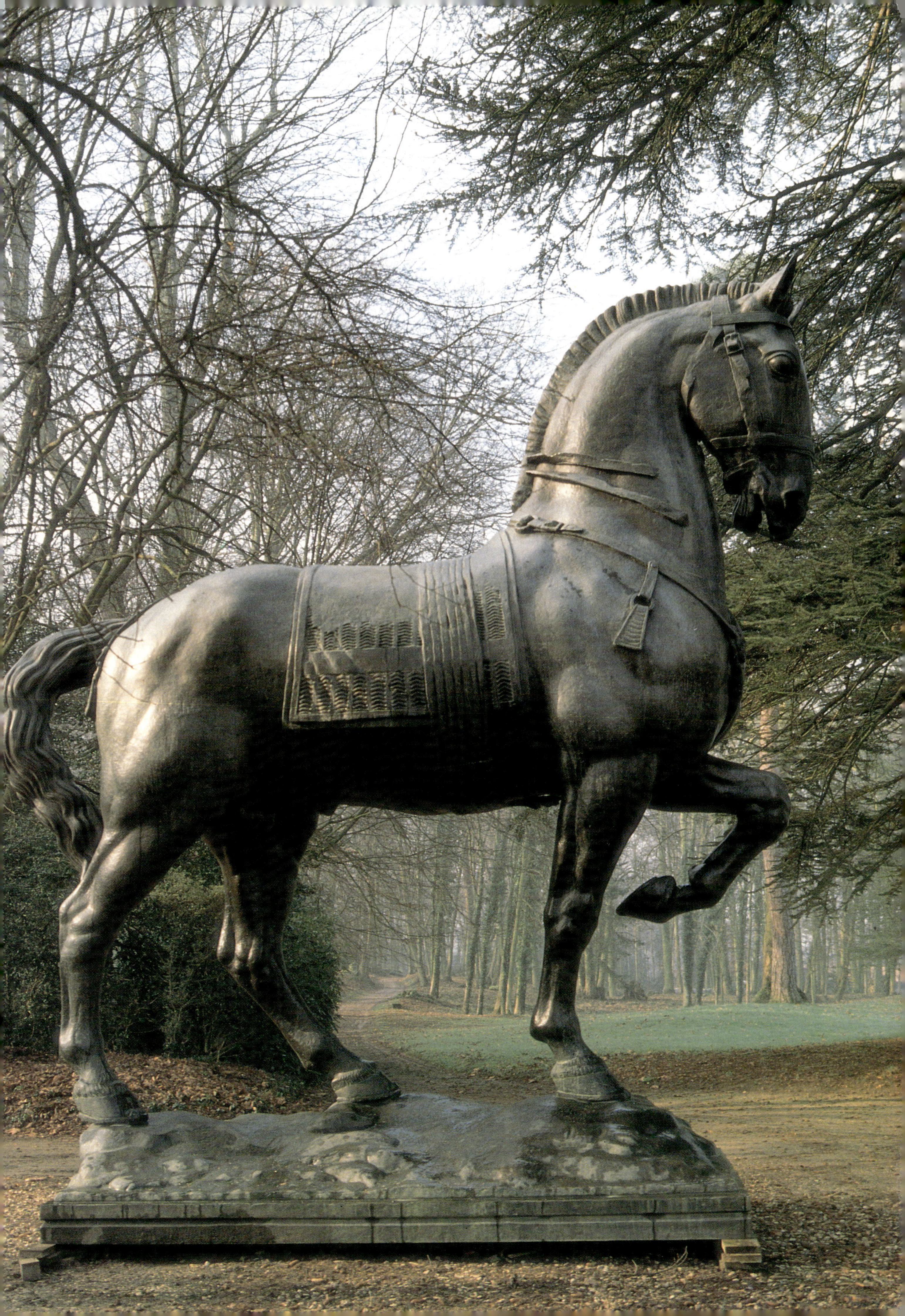

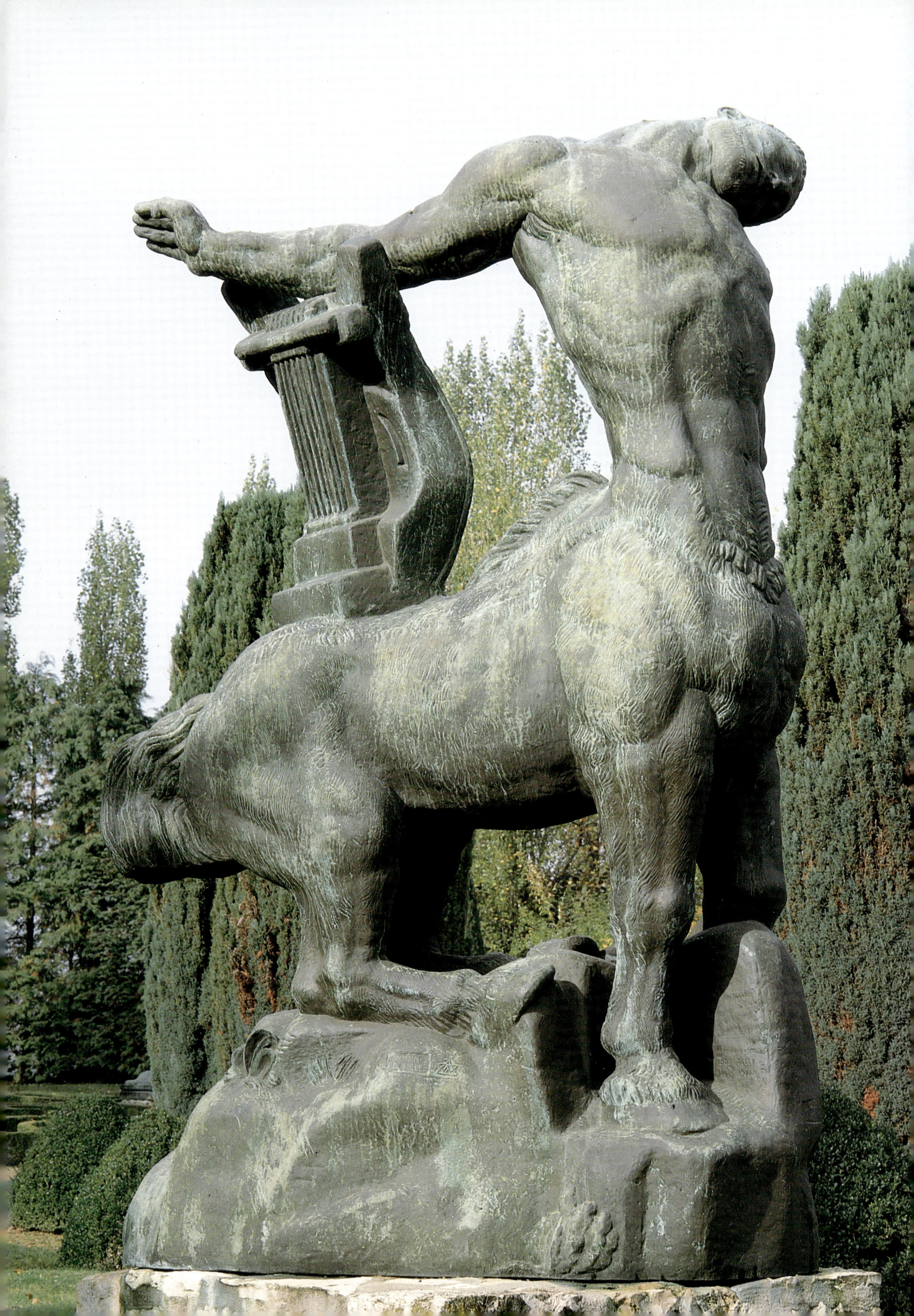

Grand Centaure Mourant
Monumental Dying Centaur
1914
2.88m x 0.80m x 1.85m

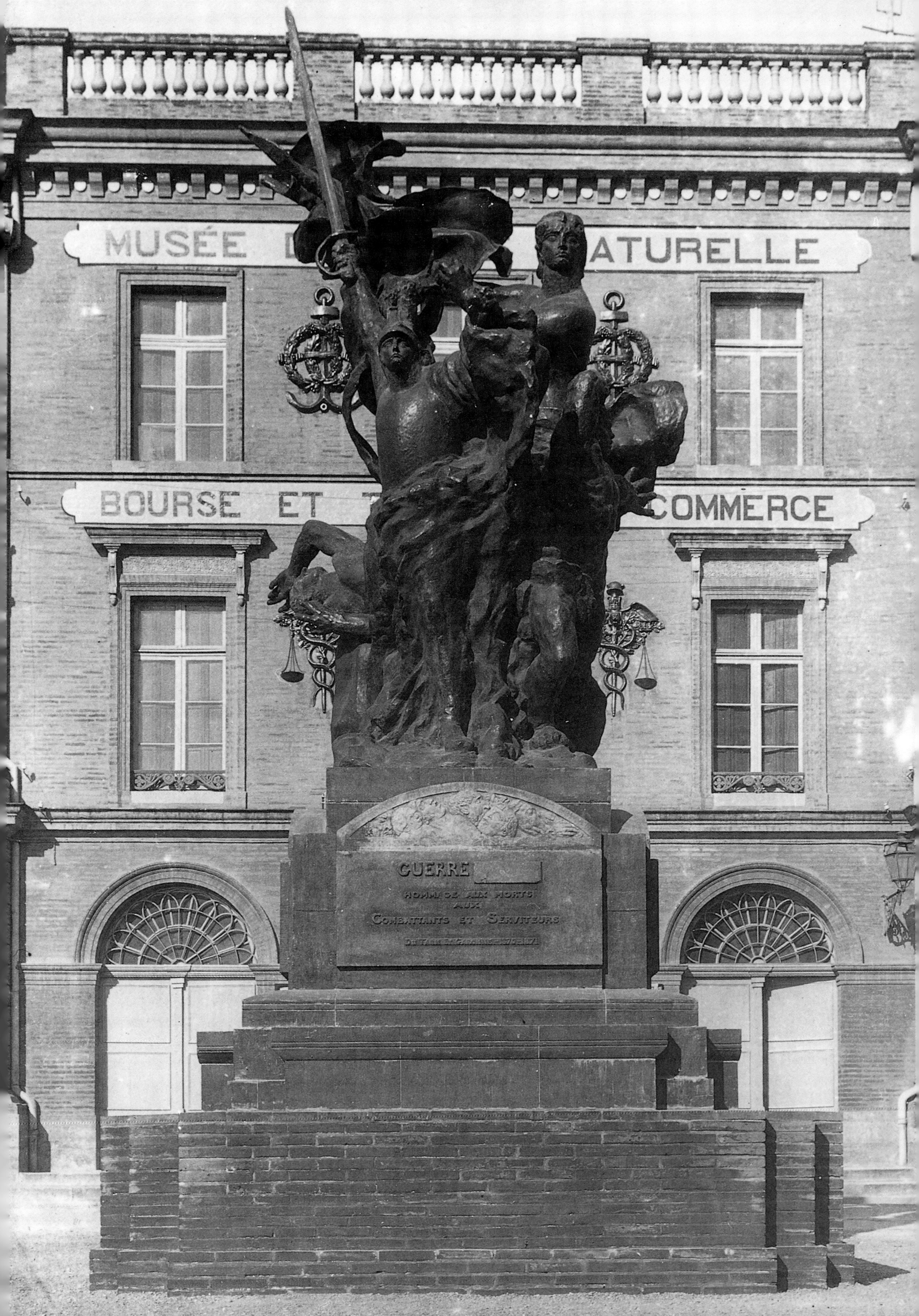
MUSÉE
ATURELLE
BOURSE ET
COMMERCE
GUERRE
HOMMAGE AUX MORTS
AUX
COMBATTANTS ET SERVITEURS

MICHAEL LE MARCHANT

INTRODUCTION

"This work was as much criticised in Paris as in Montauban. It is nevertheless true to say that it is a work of epic character, one of the best initiatives in today's sculpture. Such grandeur and such unity, when the work is examined in its entirety especially from a distance, are remarkable owing to the distribution of essential values. This monument reminds one of the work of the finest epochs, by its freshness, its spontaneity of vision and execution. By doing this Bourdelle did not fail to offend all those who, having been taught in the spirit of the times, sought to reach easy and quick success by satisfying the conventional taste, which was also their own. It is also true that Bourdelle contributed to the regeneration of today's sculpture as much as could be done for the present time".

Auguste Rodin

Monument to the Dead of 1870 in Montauban

There is a tiny hamlet, close to the banks of the Aveyron river, which is named *"Bourdelle"*: in all probability the family has its origins there in south west France. Emile Antoine Bourdelle was born nearby in Montauban, as was the great French painter Ingres. Bourdelle's paternal grandfather was a goatherd and his father a cabinet maker. In their monograph Jianou and Dufet quote the artist as recalling,

"Quercy is the most beautiful country in the world. I used to spend my holidays there, running after the goats, carving rough pieces of wood and sometimes enjoying myself by making clay figures and baking them in the oven with the bread. Although I had not yet learned to read I sang strange songs to my goats, played tunes on my flute under the oak-trees and told fantastic stories to my friends the shepherds".

It was the rugged beauty of the landscape and the purity of the Romanesque architecture of the region that combined to form Bourdelle's taste and his future style. The simplicity and spirituality of the man were also formed there. It is enough to be confronted by these great works gathered under the Yorkshire sky to realise that Bourdelle was a builder, an architect, and yet also a poet. It was he who celebrated the reunion of art and architecture in a charming depiction in one of the reliefs for the Théâtre des Champs-Elysées. If Bourdelle's roots are in the archaic, and if his subjects are heroic, his sculpture is conceived and constructed for all time. His love of nature and his lyricism maintain a balance with the epic quality of his work.

He was a tireless worker undaunted by the massive scale of great works such as the *Alvear Monument* and the reliefs of *Apollo* and his muses. The Musée Bourdelle is where you must go to see the great range of Bourdelle's work. Elsewhere in Paris the *Mickiewicz Monument,* while impressive as it stands adjacent to the Seine near the Place d'Alma, is not well placed for public accessibility. *La France* surveys with evident horror the building works outside the old Musée d'Art Moderne. While at the new Musée d'Orsay the heroic figures *Force* and *Victory* appear to guard the back entrance! However the Théâtre des Champs-Elysées and its reliefs have been beautifully restored. Surely now the great *Centaur,* or *Pénélope,* should be placed in the Tuileries Gardens as a homage.

Bourdelle is however valued for his work and his teaching throughout the world. Giacometti and Richier were amongst his many pupils. He has been a formative influence on many Japanese artists and amongst them are Takata Kaheiji Kaneko, Takashi Shimizu and Takei. His lectures at the Grande Chaumière were attended by many famous individuals including Krishnamurti and Lenin. The influence, the *"rayonnement de Bourdelle",* lives on.

On a personal note, it was perhaps fifteen years ago that I sat down with Rhodia Dufet Bourdelle and her husband Michel Dufet, together with our dear friend Arnold Haskell, for the first of many conversations *en famille.* Not a little work was to follow through which Bruton Gallery has helped to spread afar Bourdelle's great works.

Recently I have had the pleasure of acting as the catalyst to unite friends from the Yorkshire Sculpture Park with those from Paris (still sculpture's centre for me). There was magic in agreeing that we would bring about *the* definitive Bourdelle exhibition, the greatest of any time and any place. One year later, or maybe two - *voila!*

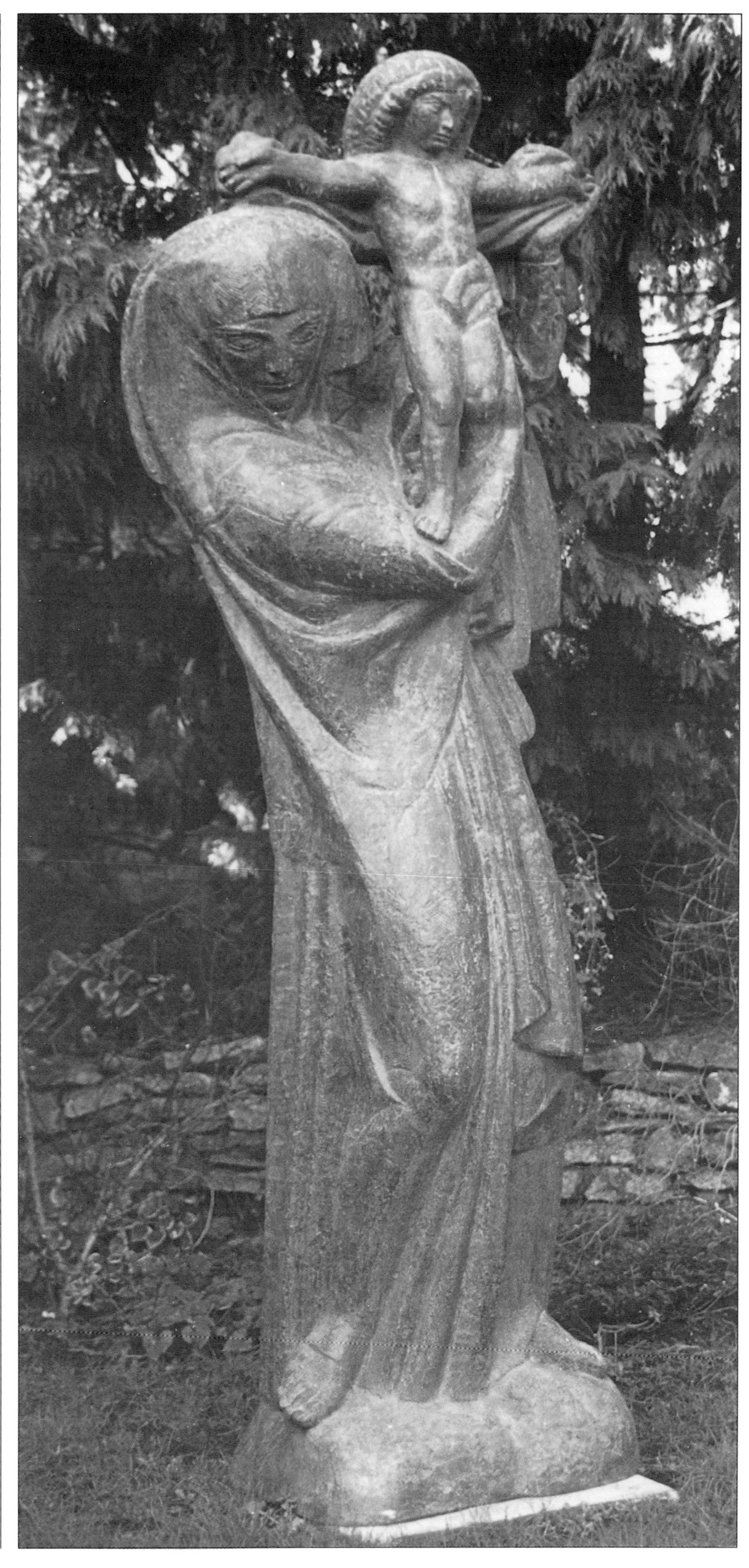

Vierge à l'Enfant
Virgin and Child
1921
2.50m x 0.90m x 0.70m

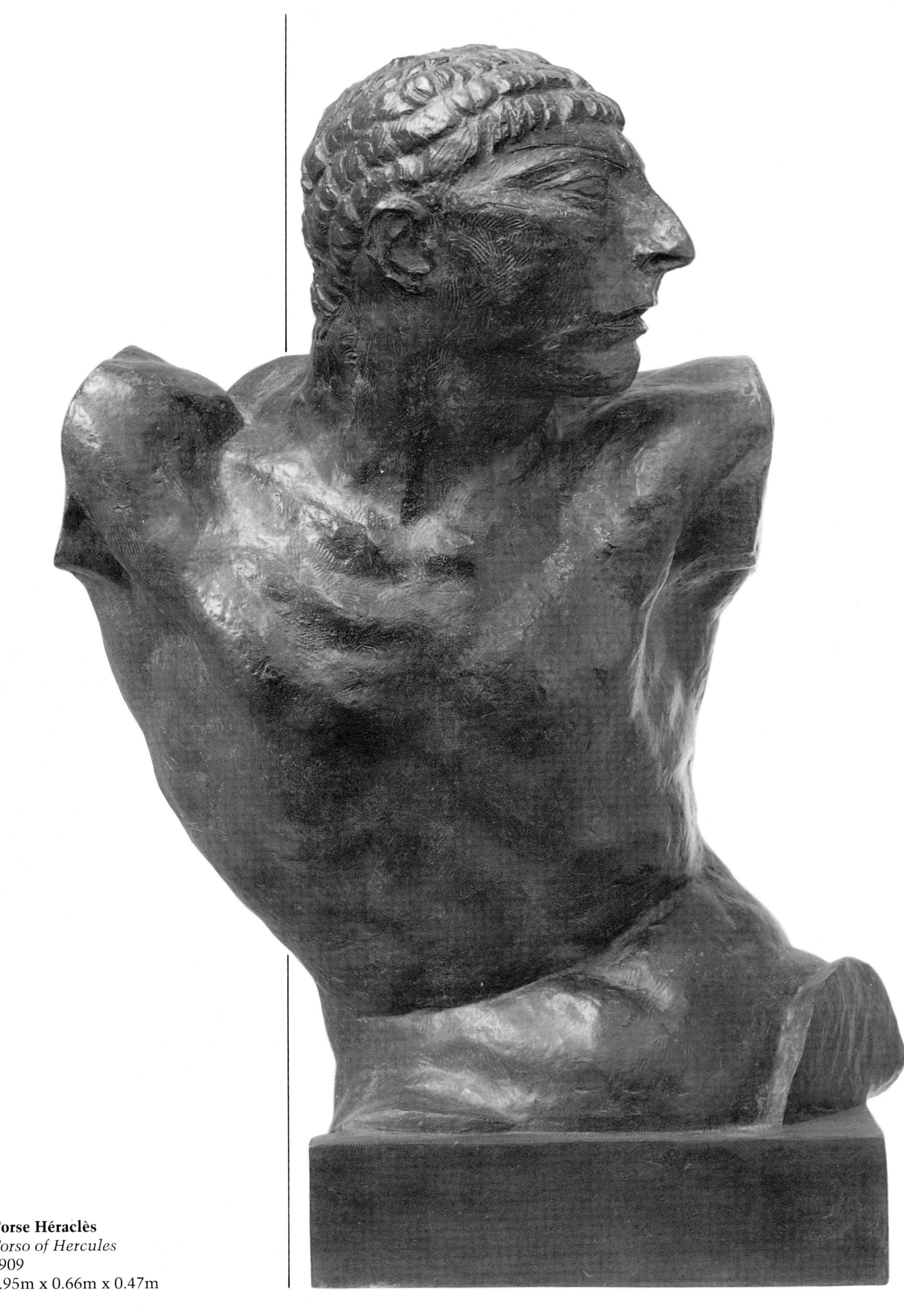

Torse Héraclès
Torso of Hercules
1909
0.95m x 0.66m x 0.47m

PETER MURRAY

EMILE ANTOINE BOURDELLE 1861-1929

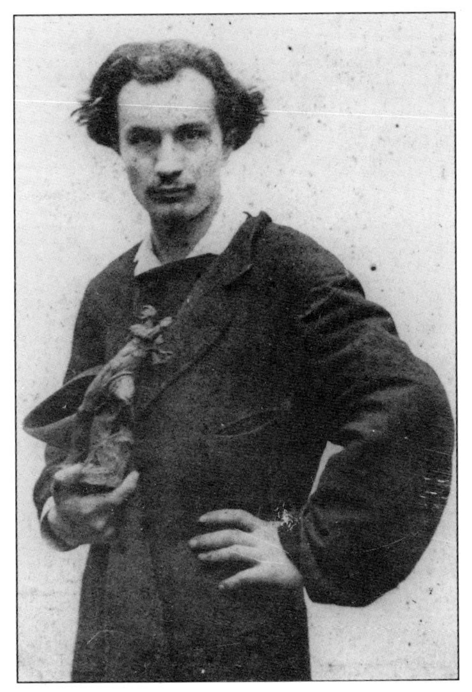

Emile Antoine Bourdelle shortly after settling in Paris in 1884

It has been suggested by the French art historian, Ionel Jianou, that Emile Antoine Bourdelle is the most French sculptor of the School of Paris. Certainly Rodin was a great admirer, *"I love his sculpture because it is very personal and it corresponds to his sensitive nature and his passionate and fiery temperament"*. In 1909 he referred to Bourdelle as a *"pioneer of the future"*.

It is true to say that on this side of the Channel Bourdelle's work has not been given the attention it warrants. Apart from the notable exhibition organised by Peter Cannon-Brookes in 1983 at the National Museum of Wales there has not been an opportunity to study the full breadth of his sculpture from the intimate, often tender, small pieces to the monumental.

This exhibition in 1989 at the Yorkshire Sculpture Park salutes a great sculptor. Bourdelle, consumed by idealism and a belief in the eternal nature of sculpture, produced through discipline, conviction and his audacious talent a prodigious body of work which helped to regenerate sculpture as a significant art form in the twentieth century.

Bourdelle thought of sculpture in monumental terms. He had a real understanding of scale and was deeply committed to art in public places. André Suarès, the French writer and poet, said that Bourdelle was an architect who has *"... given back to the world monumental form"*. It is sadly ironic that such a supreme monumental sculptor had so few opportunities to site his work in the open air.

Grande Force
Monumental Strength
1914-1917
3.72m x 1.20m x 1.10m

Grande Victoire
Monumental Victory
1914-1917
3.72m x 1.30m x 1.10m

Bourdelle was a perfectionist. Although this exhibition cannot illustrate the volumes of sketches, designs, models, plans and the smaller and medium sized sculptures required to produce such masterpieces as the Alvear Horse it does confirm André Suarès' view that Bourdelle is,

"...the artist who sees all in monumental terms, who can calculate how best to use space, and how to relate every detail to the whole, so as to finally create in reality an object animated by his spirit, in harmony with the earth, the sky and the light".

Emile Antoine Bourdelle was born in 1861 in Montauban into a poor artisan family and for much of his life knew real poverty and hardship. His grandfather was a goatherd and as a child he helped his relatives to tend the animals. Throughout his life he made frequent references to his peasant origins and his respect and understanding of the order and the forces of nature's energies. He once wrote,

"With nature one must be at once humble, tenacious and ardent, if one wishes to discover her laws. An artist must be all these things if he is to return to the immortal objects which a shepherd of genius has daily within reach of his mind and hand. As the grandson of a weaver and a goatherd, I have constantly striven to remember their lives, as one remembers a spring".

At the age of thirteen Bourdelle decided to leave school to help his father support the family. The experience of carving ornaments and other objects in his father's cabinet making business enabled him to win a scholarship to the Ecole des Beaux-Arts in Toulouse, a city which the distinguished designer and art historian, Michel Dufet, suggests, *"...prides herself with the finest achievements of Romanesque architecture".*

It was there that Bourdelle lived and studied for nine years, and first discovered architecture and Romanesque art which had such a profound and lasting influence on the development of his sculpture. Much later in 1921 he reflected, *"Romanesque art is organic, logical art; it is concerned with universal features. It was in this cradle of the absolute that French genius was rocked".*

A great admirer of the skills of medieval builders and architects he was also highly sensitive to the spirituality he sensed in French Romanesque art and the poetry of architecture. His writings reveal the pervasive influence of Romanesque churches on the philosophy and construction of his work. For example he described the church in the village of Trôo as admirably simple in its *"...planes and execution. This is ordered art. This is unanimity in all the quietude and in all the vitality of sculpture and architecture...".* The collegiate church in Lavardin he said was made of *"sacred cubes"* and he described Notre Dame in Paris in the following poetic manner, *"You are pure and you are young, splendid in your abandonment, equalled by none in timeless Paris; you are proud solitude".*

In his sculptures he wanted the expressive elements to be

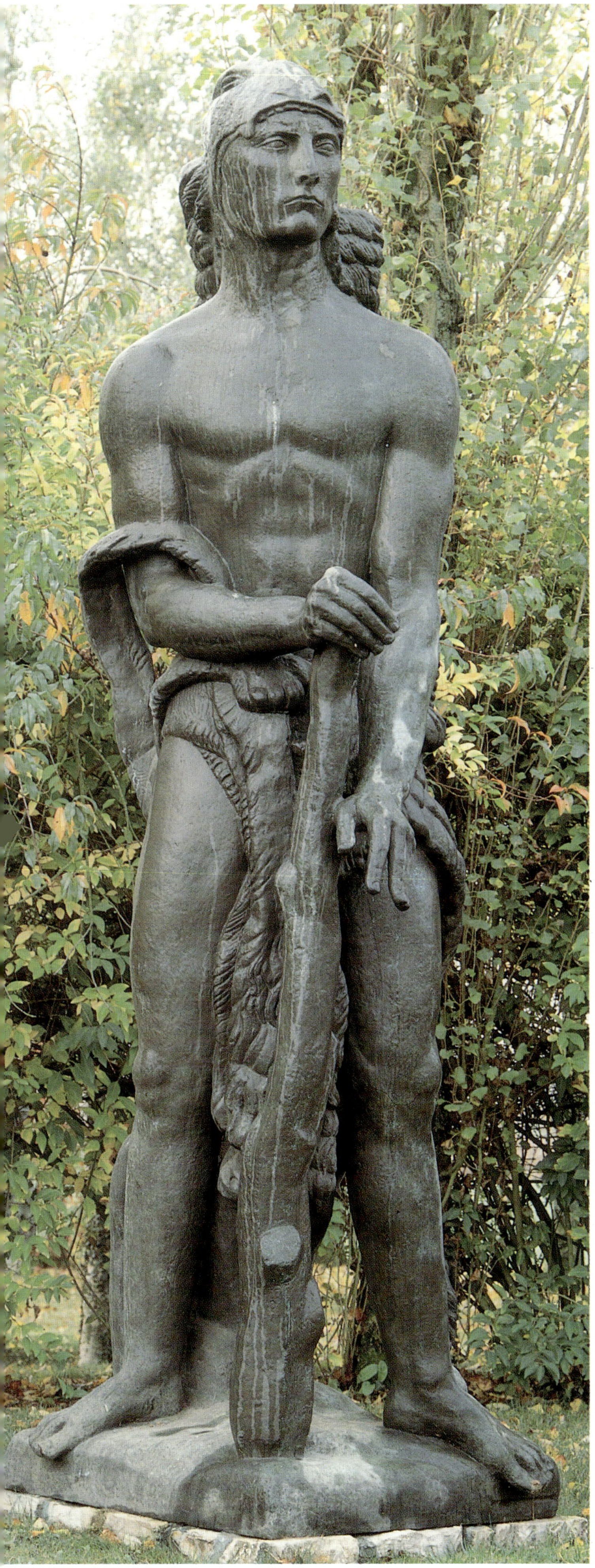

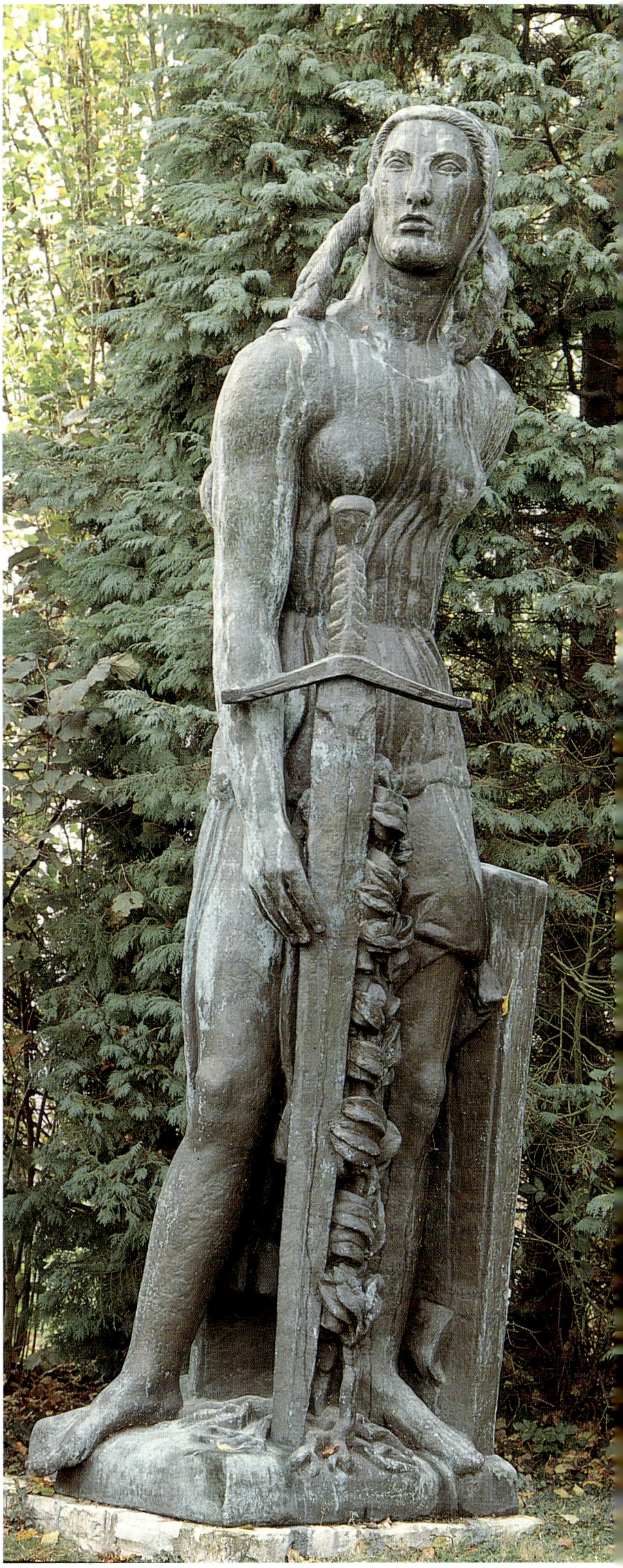

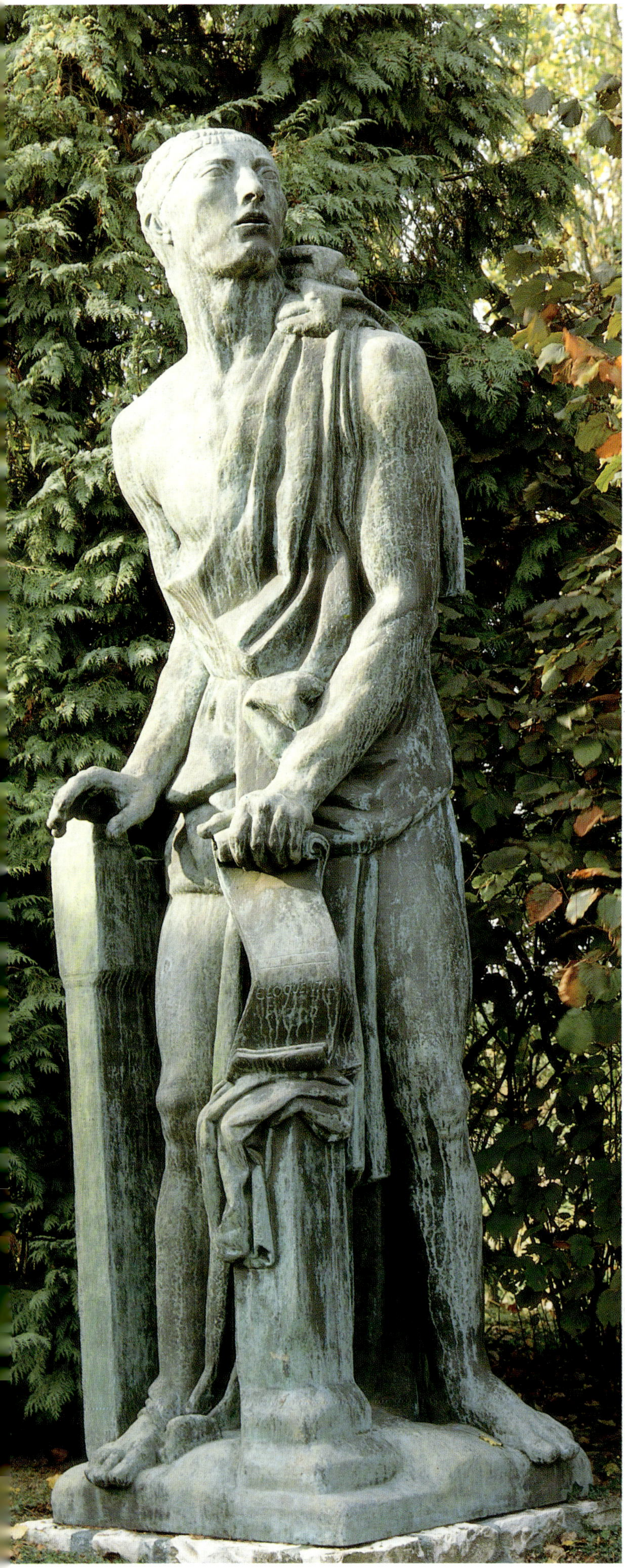

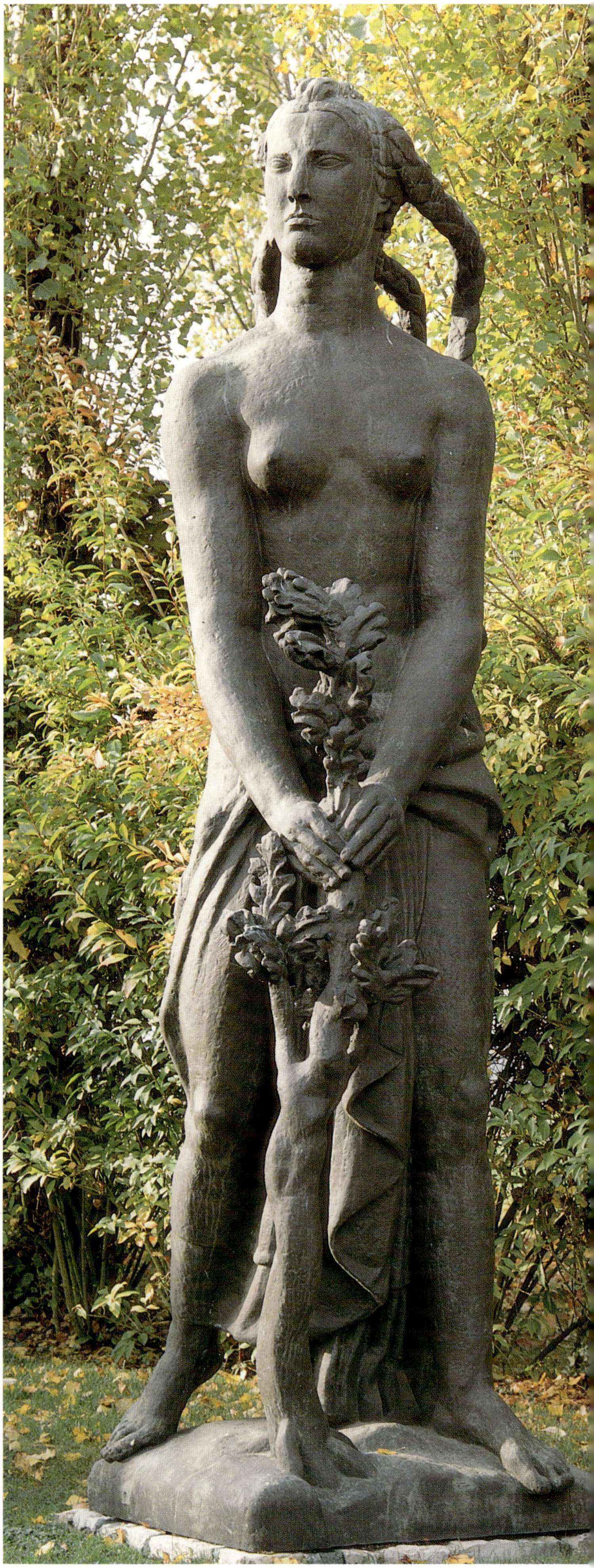

inseparable from the order and harmony of the whole. Like architecture, his sculptures were built; rigorously constructed from the inside outwards. *"All sculpture"*, he said, *"must be architectural even the most delicate"*. The relationship of sculpture to architecture was also a major concern, as illustrated in his ambitious carving of the high reliefs for the Théâtre des Champs-Elysées (1910-13), *"...sculpture should blossom from the wall like fruit from the trees"*.

In 1884, however, Bourdelle who was still a student was a long way from these concerns. In the entrance examination for the Ecole des Beaux-Arts in Paris he was awarded second place. So at the age of twenty-three he moved to Paris with high hopes of becoming a successful artist and established himself in a small studio in the impasse du Maine where he stayed for the rest of his life. Impasse du Maine is now the centre of bustling Montparnasse. When Bourdelle moved there it was surrounded by fields with flocks of sheep. It is now called rue Antoine Bourdelle and his old home is the Musée Bourdelle from which all the works for this exhibition have come.

During his first year in Paris he made his debut at the Salon des Artistes Français. Although heartened by this immediate success he was disillusioned with the teaching; immediately rebelling against what he considered to be the oppressive nature and emptiness of an exhausted academicism. Fate intervened in the form of a serious illness and, upon returning to Paris after a period of convalescence in Montauban, he boldy left the Ecole des Beaux-Arts in 1885.

"...I have had enough. I do not understand a thing in their system of prizes and competitions. By the age of thirty I must have shown that I am worthy; work for me means the street, it means life itself".

Rejecting the *"corpses"* of academic sculpture, and with an unshaken belief in his own destiny, he set about the task of becoming a full time artist. The problem of earning a living from his chosen vocation became more acute when his grandfather and aunt came to live with him followed, after his mother's death, by his father. It did, however, provide the young sculptor with firm family support.

Emotionally moved by his mother's death he immersed himself in work. For Bourdelle this became an intense and fertile period of creativity. In 1888 he embarked upon his first sculptures of Beethoven; a theme which was to fascinate and tantalise him for the rest of his life resulting in many drawings, sculptures and proposals for monuments.

When he was eighteen Bourdelle saw an engraving of Beethoven and was struck by what he considered to be a visual resemblance with himself. Upon hearing his music he identified closely with the great composer, recognising the same spiritual power as in his own sculpture, stating that he *"heard"* sculptures in

Grande Eloquence
Monumental Eloquence
1914-1917
3.72m x 1.20m x 1.20m

Grande Liberté
Monumental Liberty
1914-1917
3.72m x1.30m x 1.10m

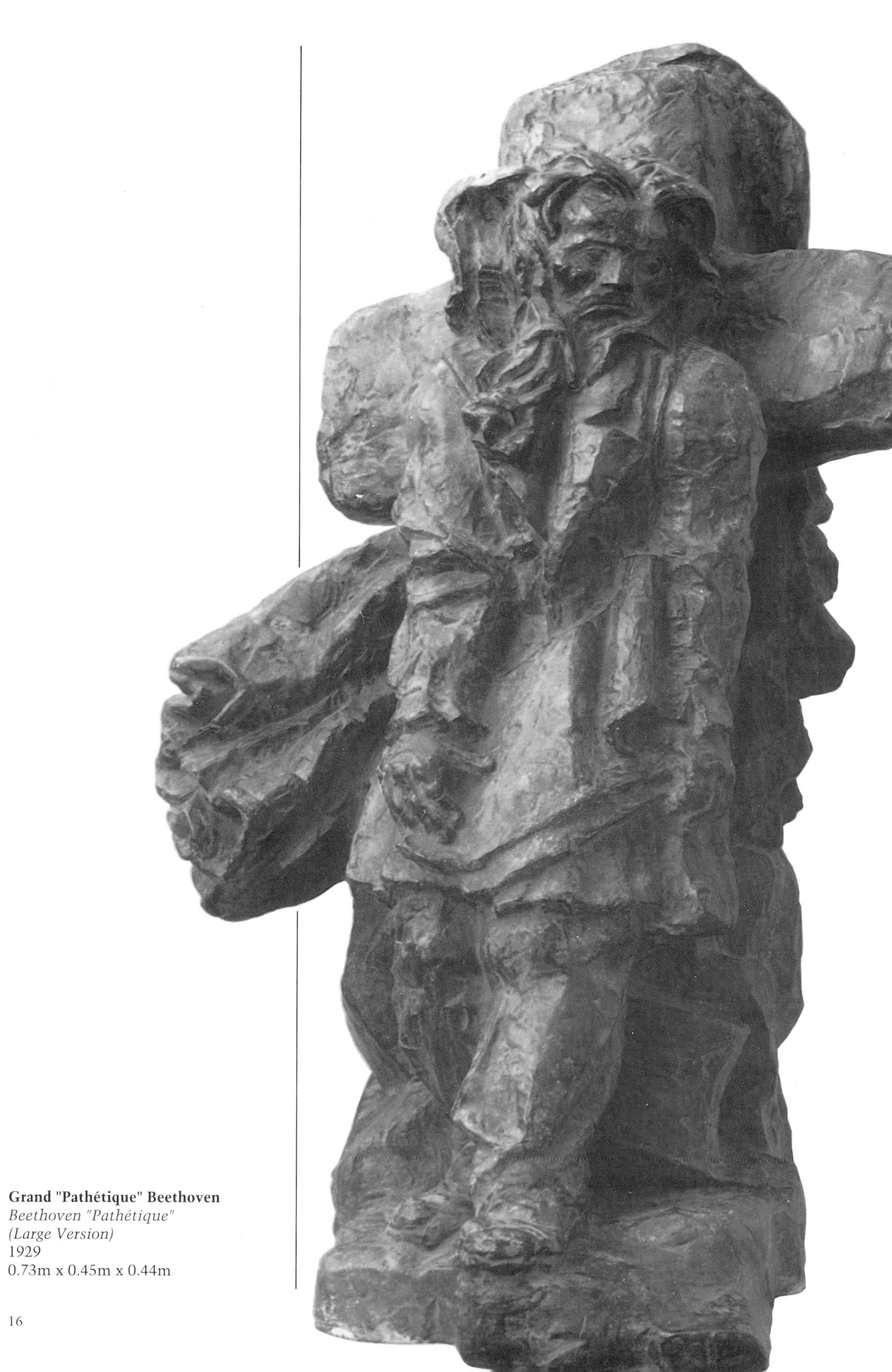

Grand "Pathétique" Beethoven
Beethoven "Pathétique"
(Large Version)
1929
0.73m x 0.45m x 0.44m

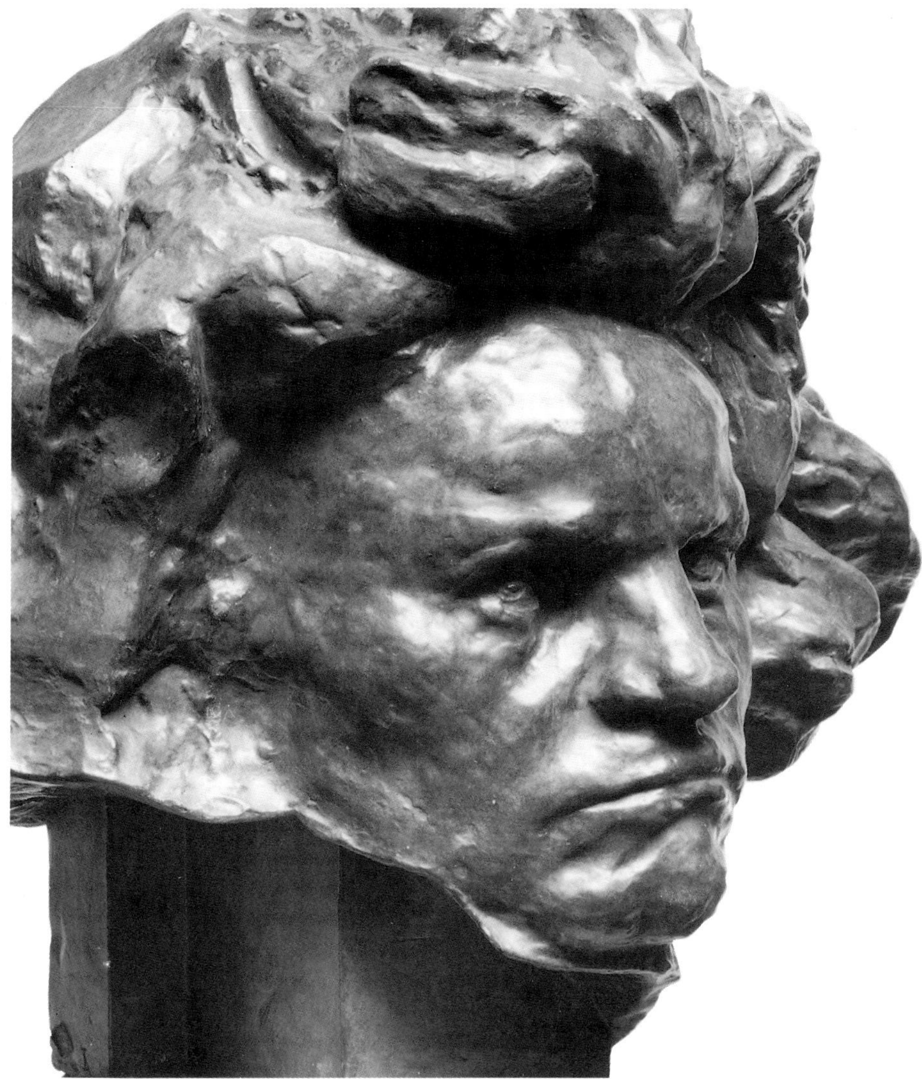

Beethoven aux Grands Cheveux
Beethoven with Long Hair
1889-1890
0.47m x 0.45m x 0.30m

Beethoven "Métropolitain"
Beethoven "Métropolitain"
1902
1.04m x 0.53m x 0.50m

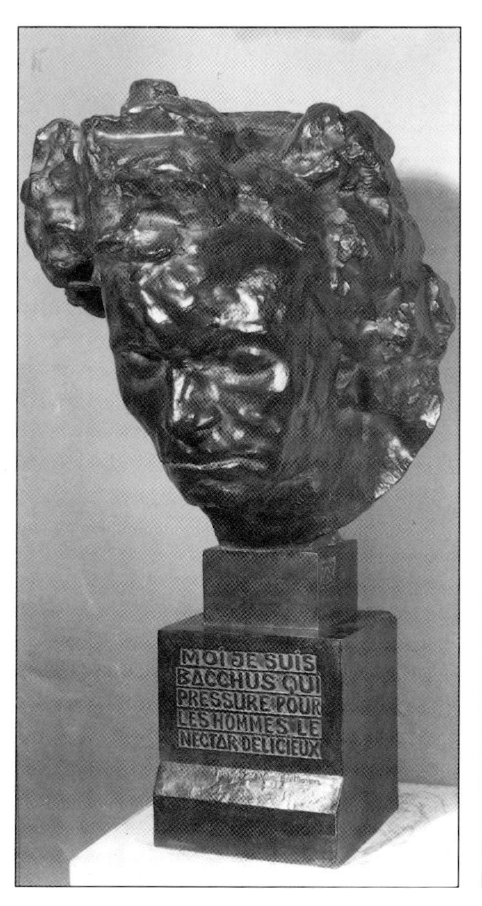

Beethoven's music. While Rembrant's or Van Gogh's self-portraits have left a personal record of their physical and some-times emotional development Bourdelle felt compelled to create many images based upon the head of Beethoven. It is tempting to accept Peter Cannon-Brookes' assertion that *"...the cathartic function of the Beethoven theme is quite clear"* as the series does reflect different moods; employing a visual language ranging from carefully modelled to frenzied statements where the shapes and masses appear to burst forth from the inner core of the sculpture.

In 1893 Bourdelle took a decisive step. Although his reputation was growing he joined Rodin as an assistant. Rodin (1840-1917) was at the height of his success and the regular work that the great master could give provided the young Bourdelle with a source of income enabling him to support his family and continue his career as an independent artist. Much has been written about the working relationship which developed between the two artists. Ionel Jianou commenting on this said,

"Bourdelle was for many years the one who did the roughing out, the friend and companion of Rodin. He came under his influence and shared his struggle for the revival of sculpture. But after learning from Rodin he went his own way and followed his own destiny".

It was while working for Rodin that Bourdelle tackled his first major monumental commission: the Monument to the Defenders of 1870-71 (*Montauban Monument*). The commission, originally intended for the centre of his home town of Montauban, was not only to test his skill as a sculptor but his tenacity and determination to produce monumental commemorative sculpture without compromising his integrity. The great French writer and philosopher Anatole France said,

"...Bourdelle is the greatest artist of our time. Has there been in the history of arts a creative genius with a more fertile and powerful mind? He has only one drawback, that I can see, he carries his conception beyond the limit of possibility. A noble defect".

It took nine years of struggle, argument, controversy and hard work before the sculpture was finally unveiled in 1902. The explosive rhythm of the sculpture, the passion and sculptural invention go well beyond the academic theme. This powerfully unconventional approach, not normally associated with public memorial sculpture, is what provoked an outcry. Without the support of Rodin, who thought very highly of the sculpture, it is unlikely that the commission would have been accepted.

Grand Jeune Sculpteur au Travail
Young Sculptor at Work
(Large Version)
1918
1.26m x 0.40m x 0.40m

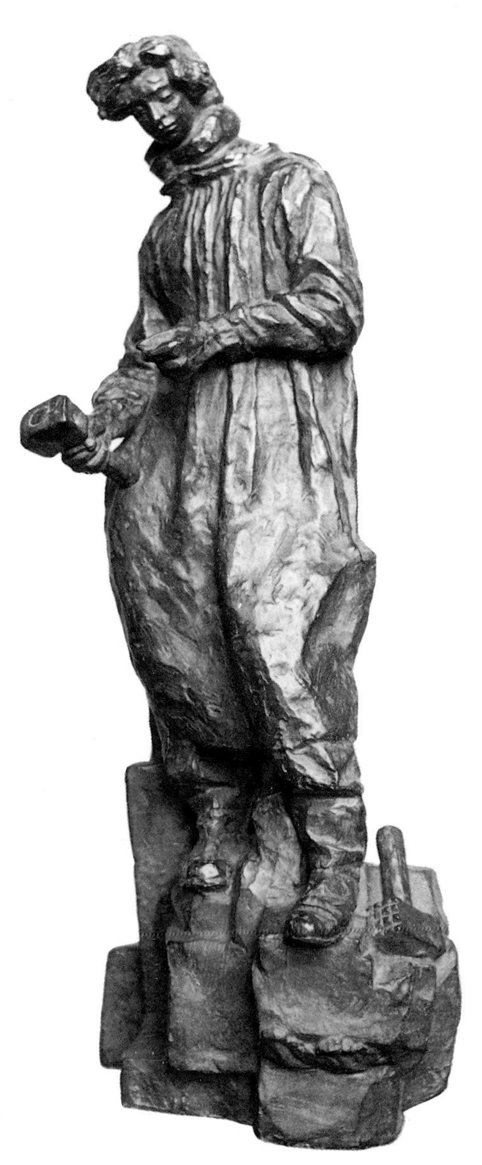

Bourdelle started work on the *Montauban Monument* with strong influences and overtones of Rodin's expressionism and ended with a statement which was uniquely his own. The sculptural success of the monument was a decisive turning point in his development as an artist and he went on to produce the magnificent *Head of Apollo*. A synthesis of balance and harmony, with its well defined planes pre-empting Cubism, it provides a striking contrast to the impressionistic work of Rodin, who perhaps also recognised the significance of the work when he said, *"...Bourdelle you are leaving me".*

From the early part of the century onwards Bourdelle taught regularly and with great conviction until the end of his life. He was by all accounts an inspired teacher who encouraged his students to *"Sing your own song: listen to and know your own self".*

Bourdelle was by this time well established as an important sculptor producing authoritative work with an emphasis on order, the spirit of geometry, construction and sculptural invention. Although his work was now almost the antithesis of Rodin's his respect and admiration for his old master was still strong,

"...there has never been and will never be a master able to convey the outlines of human feelings into clay, marble or bronze with the profound feeling and intensity of Rodin".

He said to his students,

"...I am sorry for those sculptors who have not known him. You may discover Rodin's faults, but you will only know what sculpture really means when you have discovered Rodin's qualities".

In 1909 he completed three sculptures dedicated to Rodin. These were followed by the important *Hercules the Archer*, full of

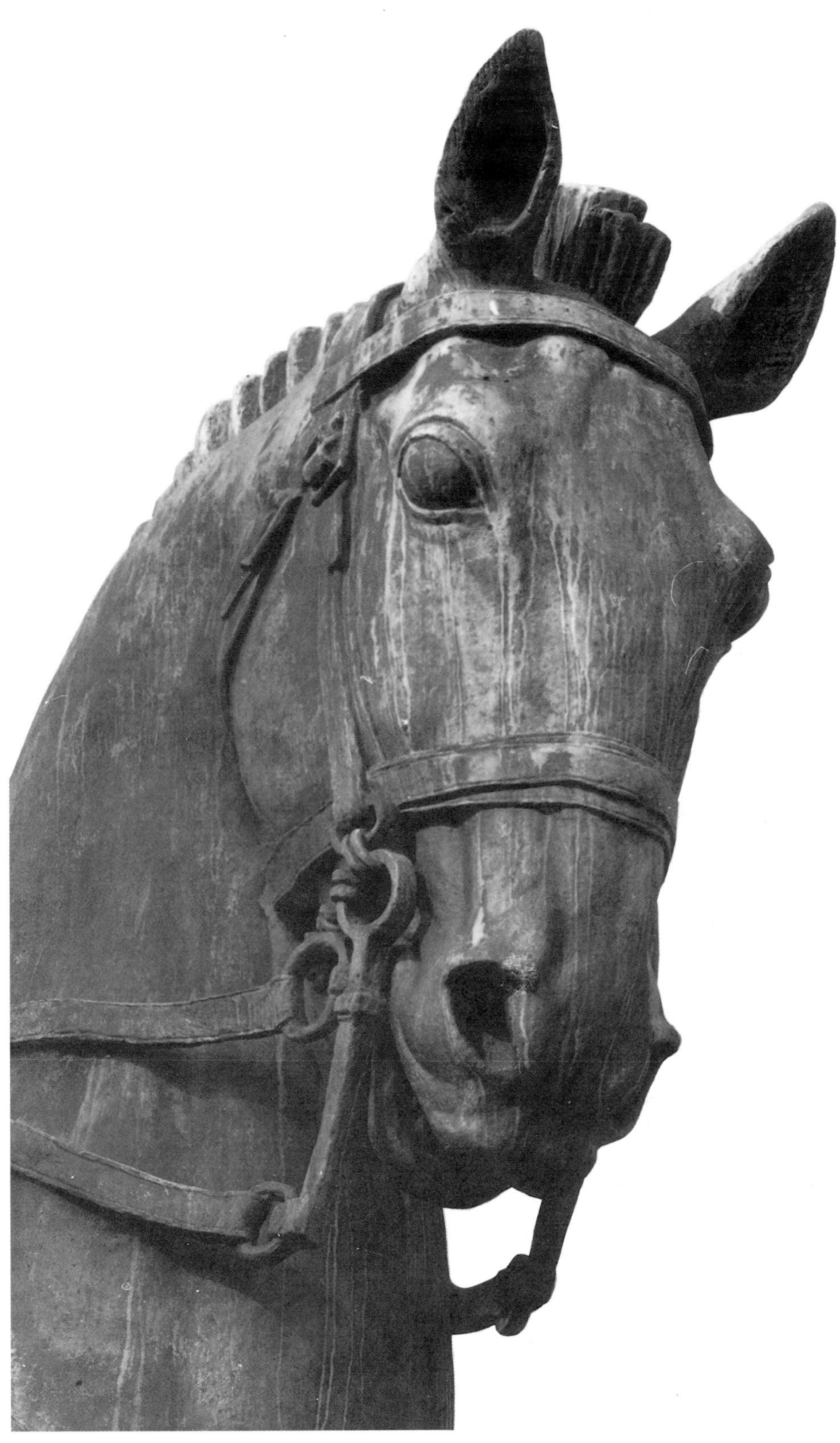

Grand Cheval sans Cavalier
Monumental Horse without Rider
(detail)
1914-1917
4.60m x 4.30m x 2.25m

dynamism, rhythmic outlines and an inventive use of space. Another masterpiece, the *Dying Centaur* (1914), again emphasises Bourdelle's concern with the language of sculpture. The theme is compressed into a composition which allows the exploration of space, volume and contours all enclosed within a rectangle or block.

Depite disappointments Bourdelle's appetite for memorial and monumental sculpture never abated nor did the controversy and set backs surrounding each proposal. Plans for the *Mickiewicz Monument* started in 1908. It was finally sited in Paris in 1929, just

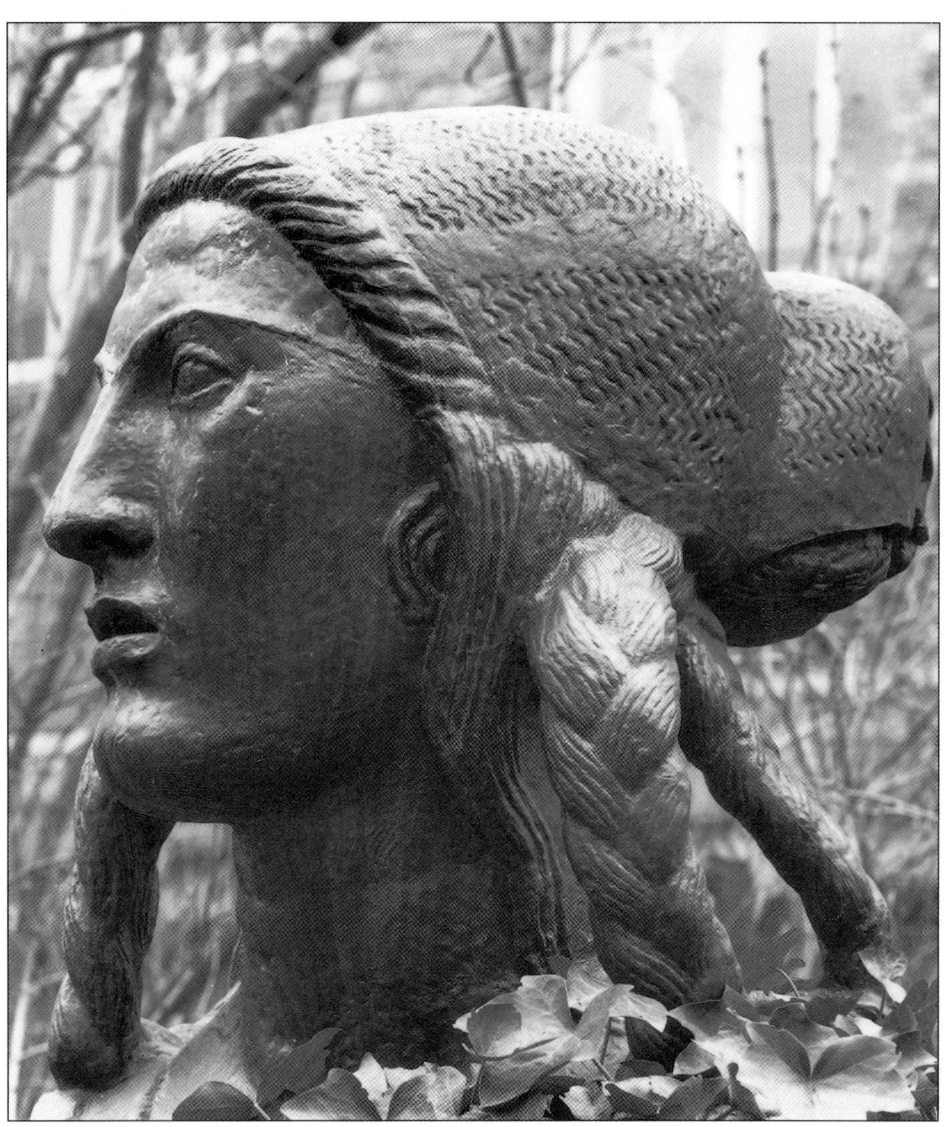

Grande Tête de la Victoire
Monumental Head of Victory
1914-1917
0.90m x 0.85m x 0.65m

before Bourdelle's death, only to be moved again in 1965.

The circumstances surrounding the commissioning of his work for the facade and interior reliefs for the Théâtre des Champs-Elysées (1910-1913) were much less controversial. Other major monumental sculptures included *La France,* which Bourdelle thought to be one of his greatest masterpieces and the *Virgin of the Offering* sited in Niederbruck, Alsace in 1922.

In 1912 he accepted the largest public commission of his career. This was a monument to General Alvear, the liberator of Argentina, to be sited in Buenos Aires. Although many thousands of miles away from his home Bourdelle saw this as the most important commission of his life. Larger than any previous work, the magnitude of its dimensions taxed him to his technical limits.

Here in the Yorkshire landscape the magnificent Alvear Horse and the four corner figures of *Strength, Eloquence, Liberty and Victory,* are all sited independently. These sculptures demonstrate that they have the power to assert themselves and to take on an autonomous existence in a new environment.

In 1913 Bourdelle participated in the Armory Show in New York and towards the end of his life he began to attract the recognition and prestige he deserved. This led to important

Grande Isadora Duncan
Isadora Duncan (Large Version)
1911
1.00m x 0.36m x 0.36m

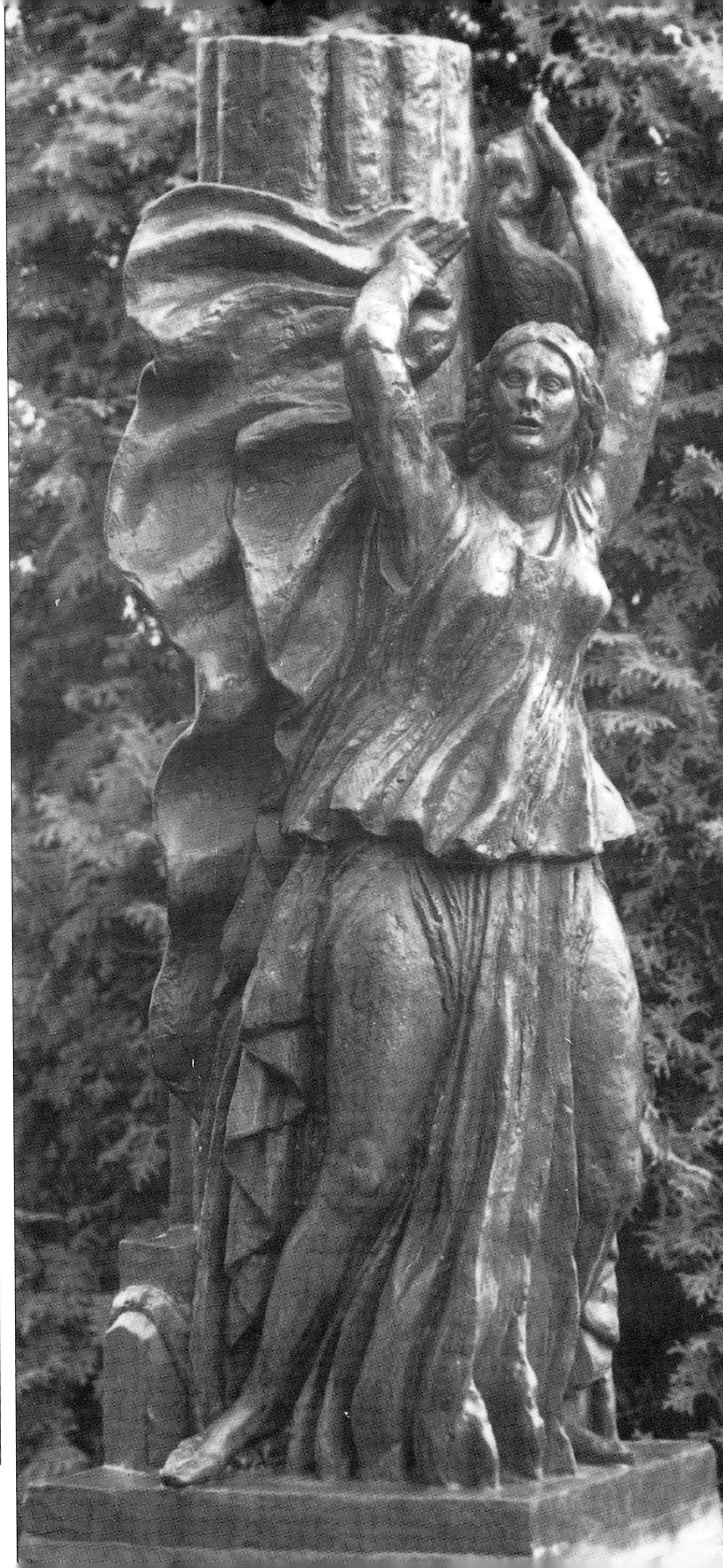

exhibitions in America and the triumphant retrospective in 1928 at the Palais des Beaux-Arts in Brussels. It is nevertheless a tragedy that he was not provided with an opportunity to execute and site a major commission in Paris. Bourdelle believed implicitly in commemorative sculpture. His ideas and proposals are all there in the Musée Bourdelle in Paris, including tributes to Carpeaux, Beethoven, Debussy, Isadora Duncan,Daumier, Rodin, Anatole France and many others. However, none of these were realised as public sculpture. André Suarès wrote, *"...All men and women made by Bourdelle are a hundred times more themselves in bronze or in stone than they are in the flesh"*. Bourdelle is one of the few artists who, with his passion and verve could have produced memorials without losing sight of the integrity of the sculpture.

His empathy with the natural forces and rhythm of life, his feeling for the universal and his understanding of the structure of natural forms developed within him a mistrust for the elaborate and a concern for the essentials of form determined by inner strength. When sitting for his portrait Anatole France said,

"...What effort Bourdelle, what attention to the form of the skeleton, to calculations of space and to interior architecture. I understand more and more your hatred for the superficial. Thanks to you I am entering into sculpture...".

Bourdelle's classical themes and concern for the heroic in art cannot mask his modernity and sculptural innovation. His sculpture was above all a synthesis of diverse concerns and interests.

Bourdelle died in 1929. In a funeral oration the French painter, Maurice Denis, paid this fitting tribute to his friend Bourdelle,

"...We can ask ourselves where did Bourdelle's power of attraction come from? What was his genius? Rodin would say Bourdelle's characteristic was his impetuosity. But Bourdelle would say it was lyrical poetry. He could not conceive matter without spirit nor beauty without thought. Imagination should play an essential part in art. Whether a symbolist or an idealist Bourdelle created expressive geometrical shapes and he told stories; he was a dramatist; a lyric, epic poet. Somehow he used stone, earth and bronze as the outlet of his thought; he moulded matter into whatever he wanted the world to hear, be it grief or joy, anguish or truth, war or peace".

Today Bourdelle's sculpture can be seen in many major collections throughout the world and his presence can be felt in the fine Musée Bourdelle which has been lovingly developed by his daughter, Rhodia Dufet Bourdelle, and her late husband, Michel Dufet, for the City of Paris. The exhibition at the Yorkshire Sculpture Park is as much a tribute to their work as to the greatness of Bourdelle, the builder, who made sculpture *"...in harmony with the earth, the sky and the light"*.

Monument à Debussy
Monument to Debussy
1908-1909
1.18m x 0.87m x 0.72m

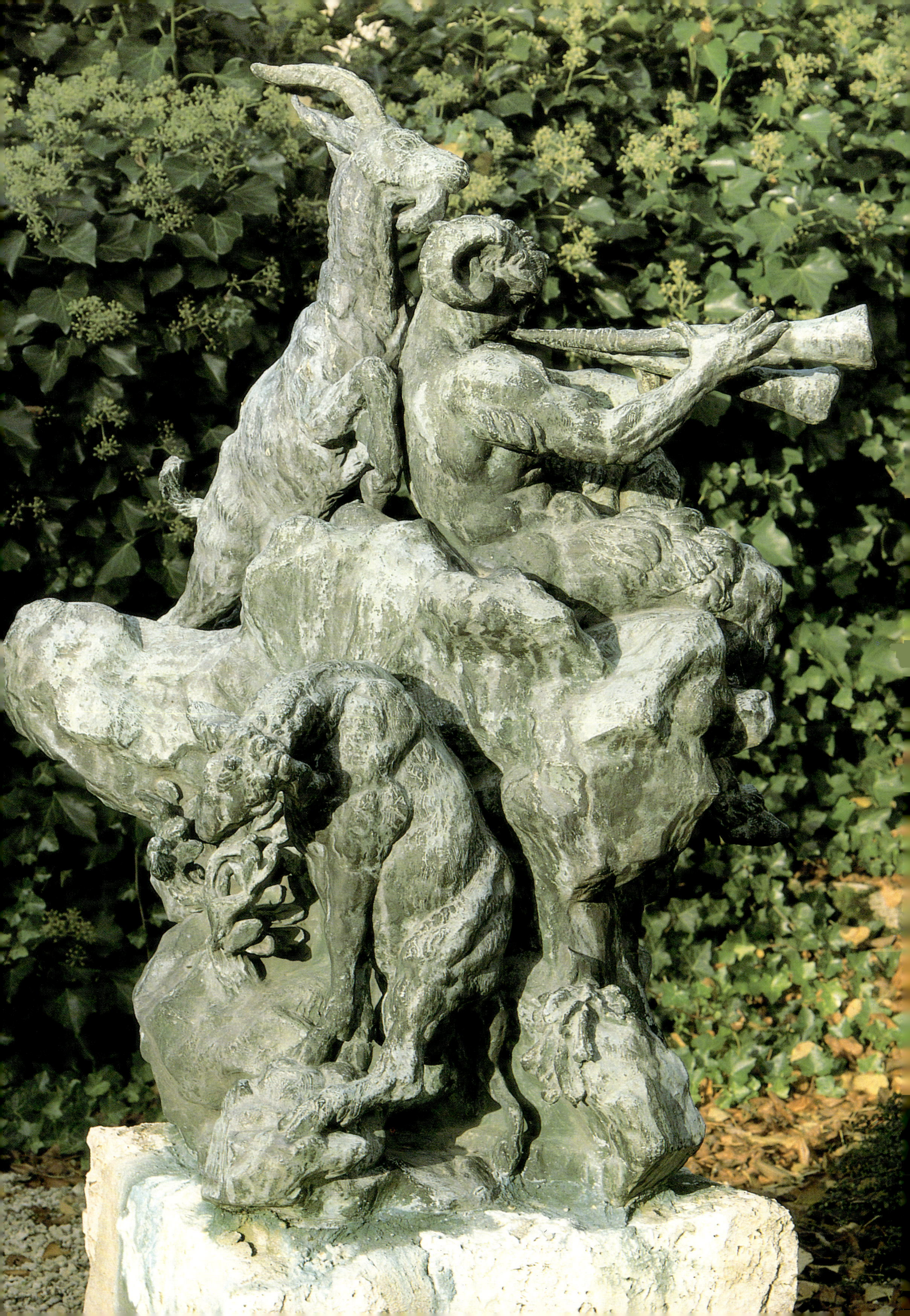

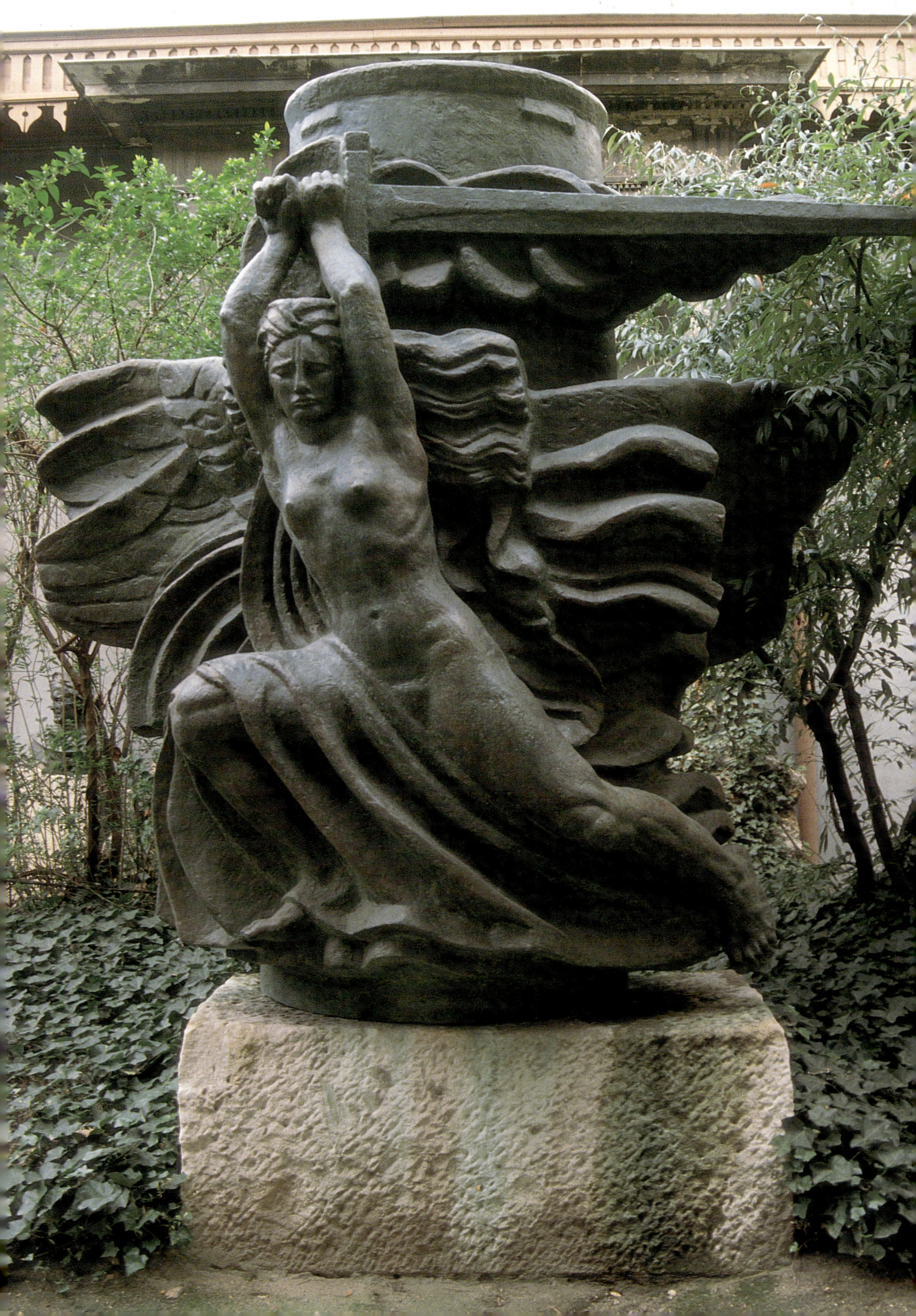

DOUGLAS HALL

EMILE ANTOINE BOURDELLE HEROIC POST-MODERNIST

Grande Epopée avec Dos
Monumental Epic Figure with Back
1917
3.35m x 2.60m x 1.70m

Monument à Adam Mickiewicz
Monument to Adam Mickiewicz
1909-1910
1.41m x 0.45m x 0.43m

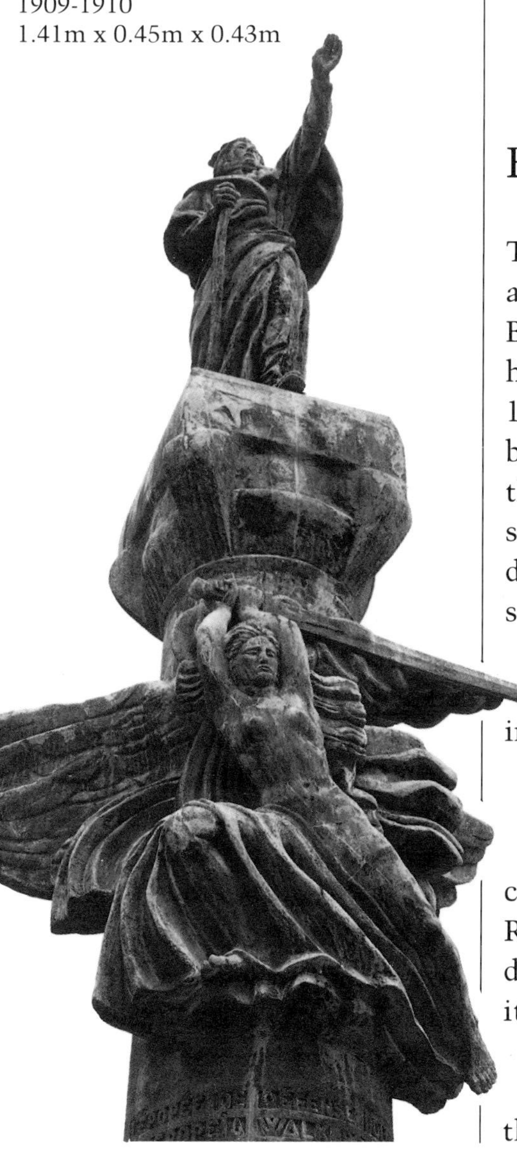

BOURDELLE AND RODIN

The influence of Rodin gave rise to conflicting trends in sculpture, and among them, initiated by his assistant Emile Antoine Bourdelle, was the development of a modern monumental and heroic sculpture. Bourdelle was assistant to Rodin from 1893 to 1906. Like Rodin he was of artisan origin, but while Rodin was born a Parisian Bourdelle was from Montauban, the birthplace of the renowned painter, Ingres, and a region rich in architecture and sculpture. From these promising roots Bourdelle went to the Ecole des Beaux-Arts in Toulouse in 1876 and in 1884 proceeded with a scholarship to Paris. Already mature he soon rebelled against the jejune teaching of the sculptor, Falguière (1831-1900), and gravitated first to Dalou (1838-1902) and then almost inevitably into the orbit of Rodin (1840-1917).

In 1893 Bourdelle received a commission from his native town of Montauban for a monument to the French defenders in the war of 1870-71. It was perhaps the demands of this commission that led to Bourdelle's professional relationship with Rodin. Some of the preparatory studies for the monument are derived from aspects of Rodin's *Gates of Hell*. In the monument itself the composition of the several parts is both more complex and more open, linked together in a freer association of sculptural forms than Rodin ever achieved. More important in considering the heroic in Bourdelle's work is the appearance in the monument

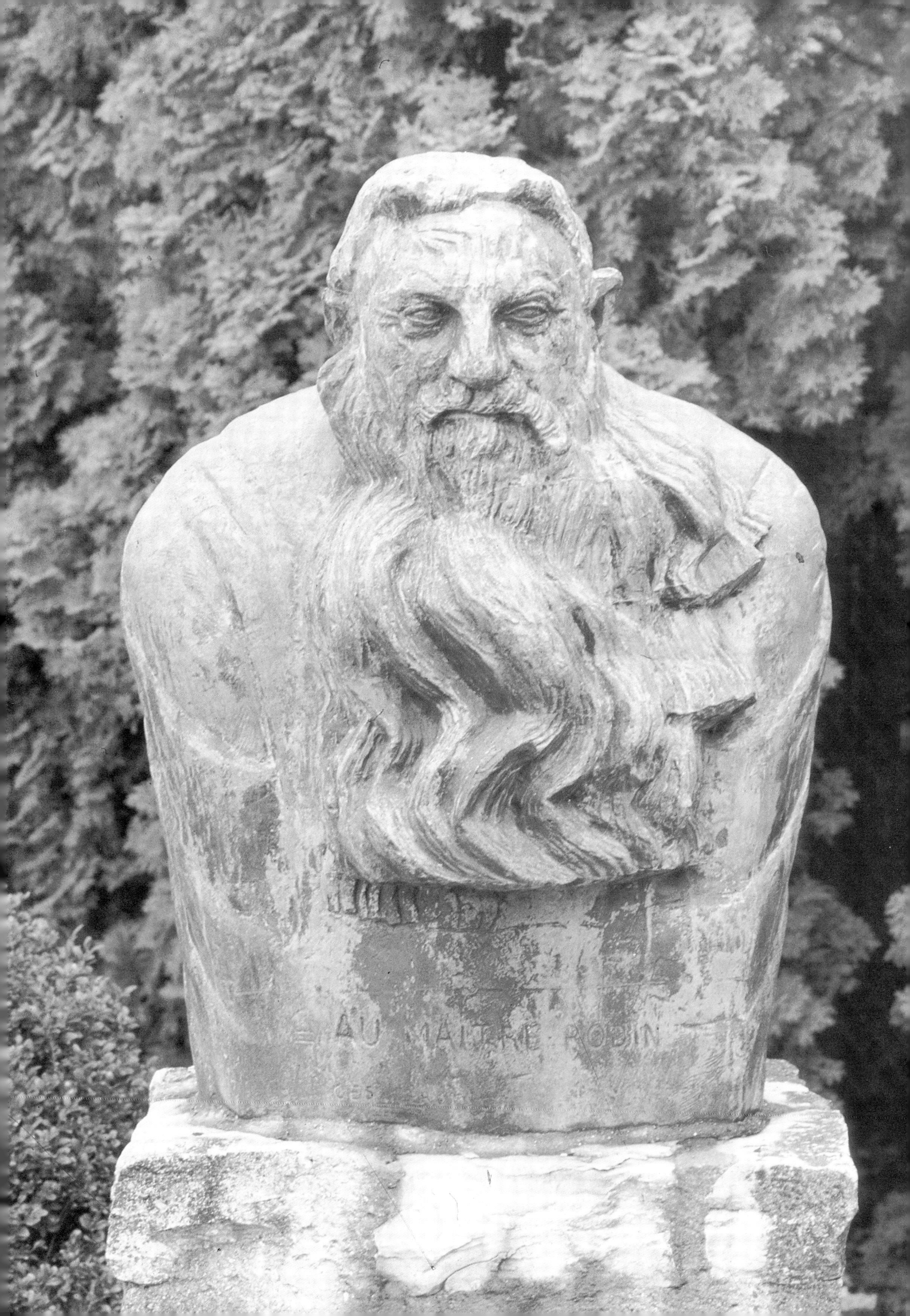
AU MAITRE

Rodin Penché en Arrière
Rodin Leaning Back
1909
0.67m x 0.75m x 0.50m

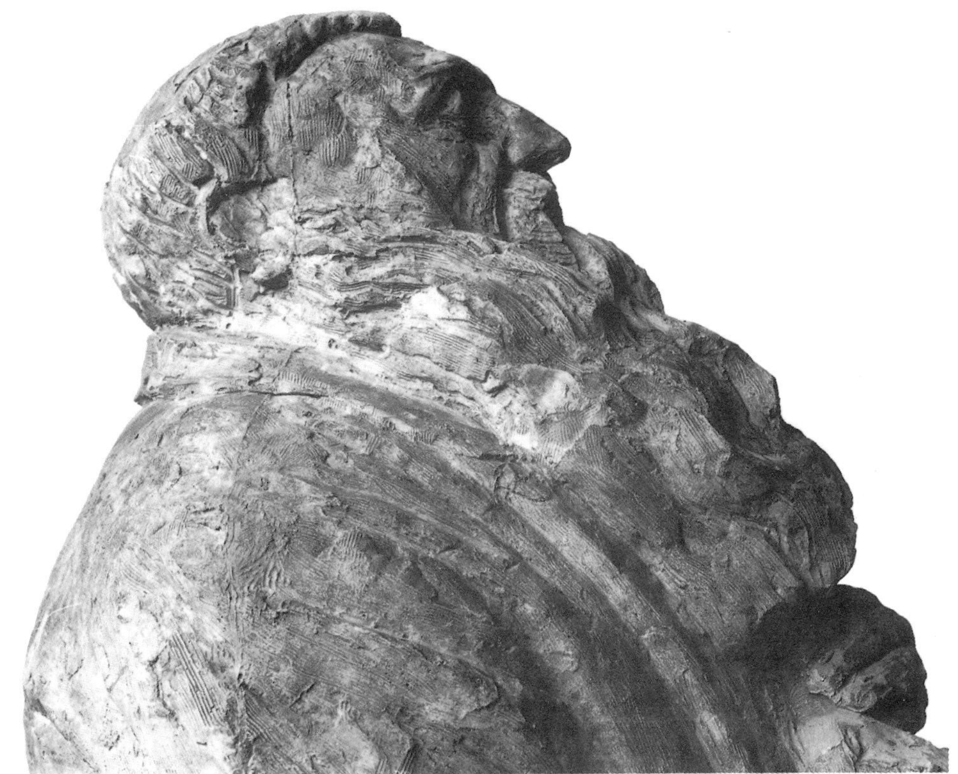

of a Cyclopean figure, a male nude in which the undulating flow of Rodin's modelling has been both arrested and swollen to grotesque proportions. This immense warrior is the predecessor of Bourdelle's most celebrated and, at the time, most successful work, *Hercules the Archer* (1908-09).

HERCULES THE ARCHER

Since the *Hercules* is a single figure it invites comparison with Rodin and especially with a number of the works of Rodin in which he uses a torso in a similar very open pose. Rodin's interest in the most extreme movements of the body finds its most dramatic expression in *Iris, Messenger of the Gods* (1890-91) and in several more or less fragmentary figures of a later date. *Hercules the Archer* is far from fragmentary. A man of stupendous physique kneels with his right knee on the ground and raises his left leg to waist height, straining with the foot against a rock as he draws his bow of superhuman size. The rock and bow, which have necessarily to be included in the sculpture, become stage props in a physically exciting *tableau vivant*. It is an effective symbol of human force, appealing at the most universal human level to the empathetic faculty and arousing a primitive admiration for size and strength. Unlike Rodin in most of his sculptures, Bourdelle put this exaggerated muscular stress to an obvious use. The figure is all there, it has a clear locus and identity, and is engaged in a precise act. Moreover it is provided with the necessary checks and balances so that the vast energy generated by the parallelogram of

Buste Rodin
Bust of Rodin
1910
0.90m x 0.70m x 0.60m

limbs is visibly contained within it. The rock will not yield to the pressure of the leg and if the arrow were to be discharged it could be at the moment of your own choosing. All this is quite opposite to Rodin, even though Bourdelle had not yet broken away decisively and publicly from Rodin's influence.

Recent criticism has been inclined to dismiss Bourdelle's *Hercules* as demonstrative, anecdotal and eclectic, a false dawn of modern sculpture. It is nevertheless a work of great interest. Only a slightly ingenuous sculptor could have made such a blatant appeal to the contemporary worship of power. As we have seen, a Rodin-like torso lies at the heart of the image. It is the sort of tribute that an older artist might well fear from a younger one. Bourdelle had no sympathy with the ambiguity that was the very basis of Rodin's art. But the *Hercules* shows clearly an ambiguity in Bourdelle himself between the turbulent shapeless romanticism evident in his writings and his ideal of a modern art of balance and generalised truth. If the figure of *Hercules* is blatantly romantic, the composition of the piece is carefully balanced, even contrived.

"The unbelievably audacious movement of this archer balancing himself in mid-air, supported against the ridge of a rock, that human form that even appears to leap in its immobility, that summary, precise, full and vibrant modelling is one of the most prodigious endeavours of living art. Here realism borders on idealism. A model may have sat for this anatomy but none could have given it this countenance or this movement. Bourdelle's art marks the transition from the long period of enslavement by reality, which we have experienced, to the new, necessary phase in which the artist will review in his heart all the secrets of nature and reflect them in a creation more faithful to general truth and at the same time revealing his own personal, intimate truth".

Charles Morice

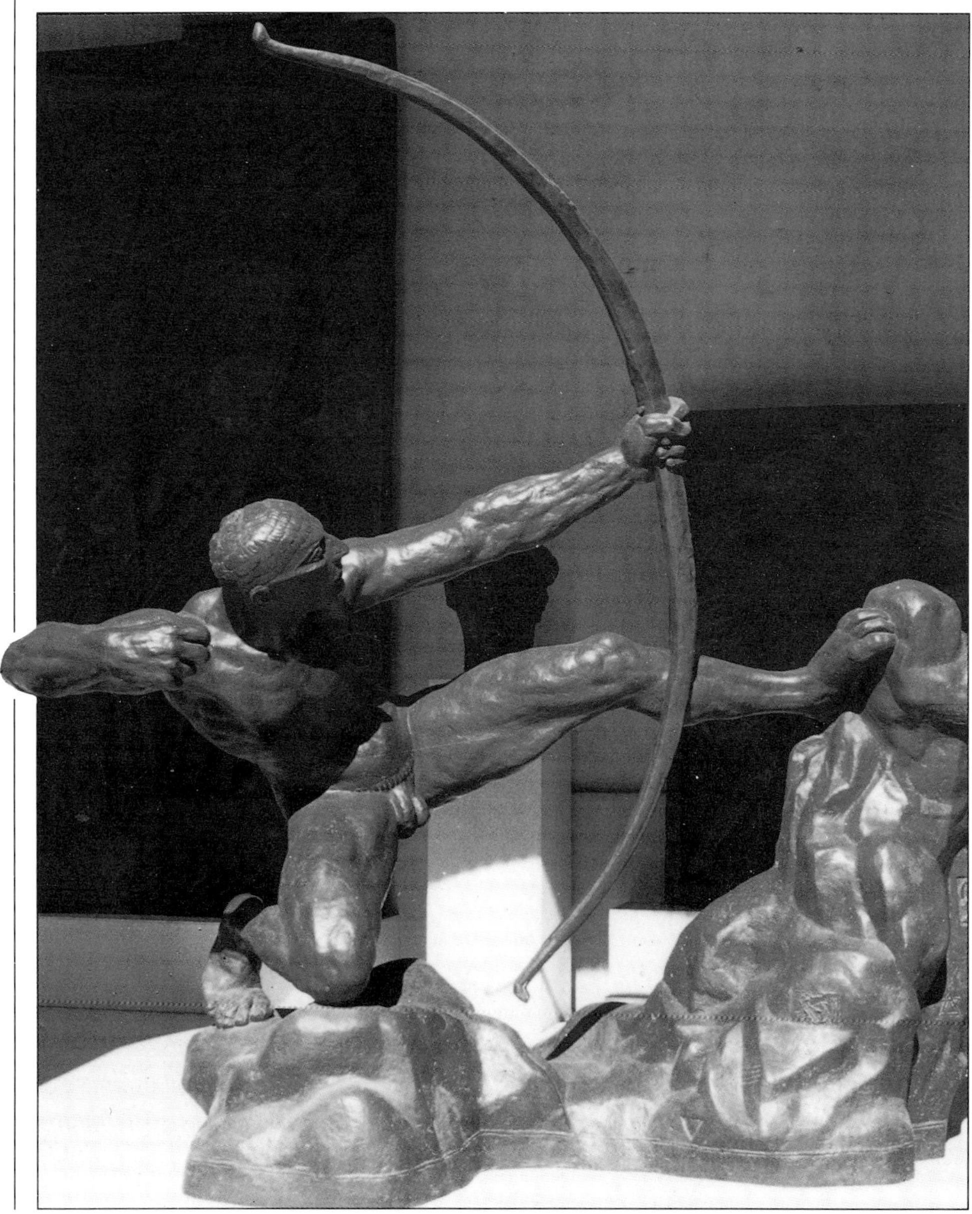

Grand Héraclès l'Archer
Hercules the Archer (Monumental)
1909
2.48m x 2.40m x 1.10m

Beethoven Grand Masque Tragique
Beethoven Tragic Mask
(Large Version)
1901
0.77m x 0.47m x 0.45m

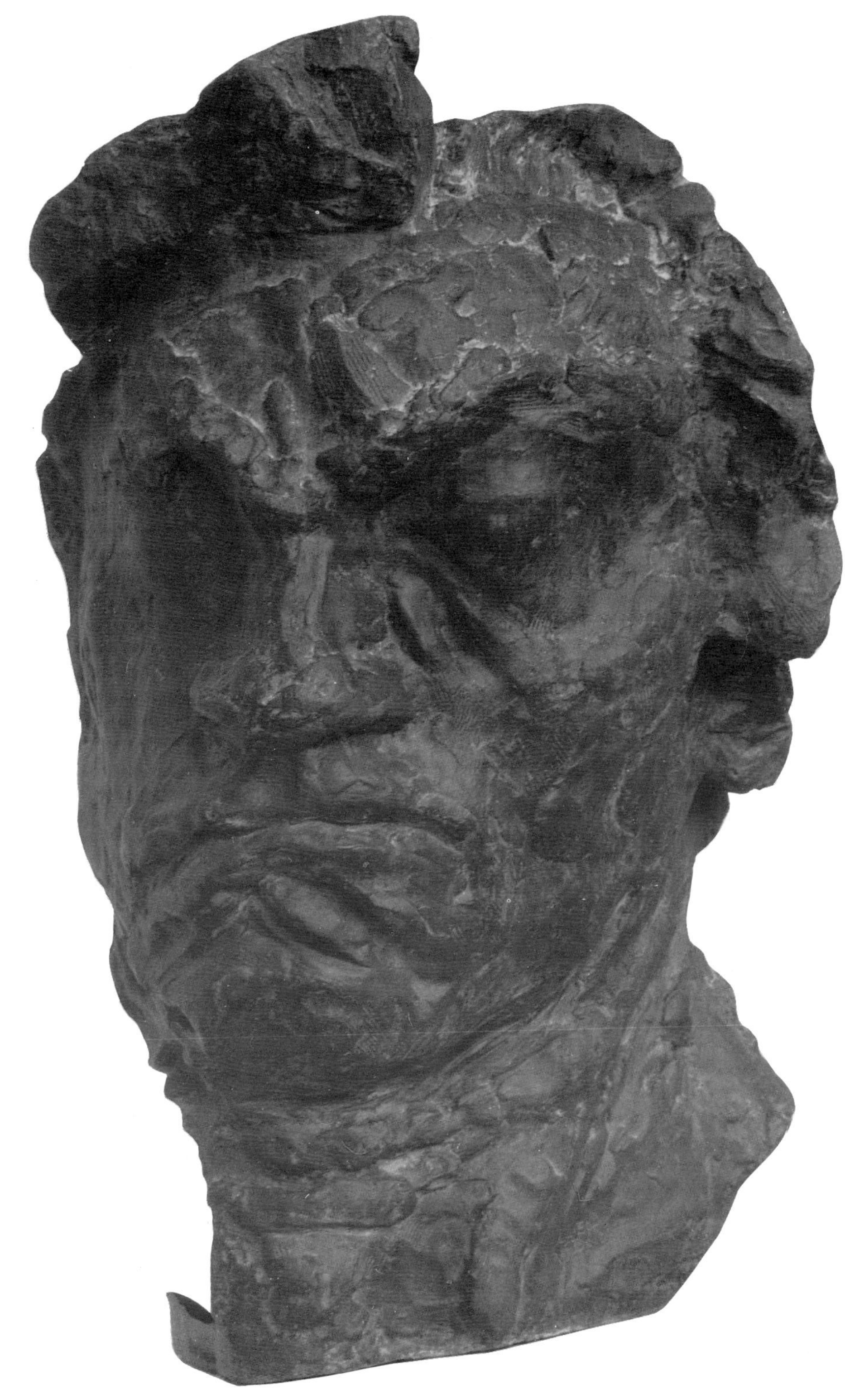

In few other works by Bourdelle is the conflict resolved in this way. Bourdelle was divided about Rodin's art. It is not surprising that Rodinesque work alternated with Bourdelle's own new synthesis which was opposed to Rodin. Rodinesque echoes predominate in some of the heads of Beethoven where the composer stands for the modern intellectual hero and victim, doomed to perpetual pain because the fire that burns him is self-fuelled. The most extreme example is the over life-size expressionist *Beethoven Grand Masque Tragique* (1901). This contorted face might have been paralleled by Rodin in one of the little heads ranged above the tympanum of the *Gates of Hell*, but

Buste Grand Guerrier au Glaive
Monumental Bust of Warrior with Sword
1894
0.61m x 0.75m x 0.39m

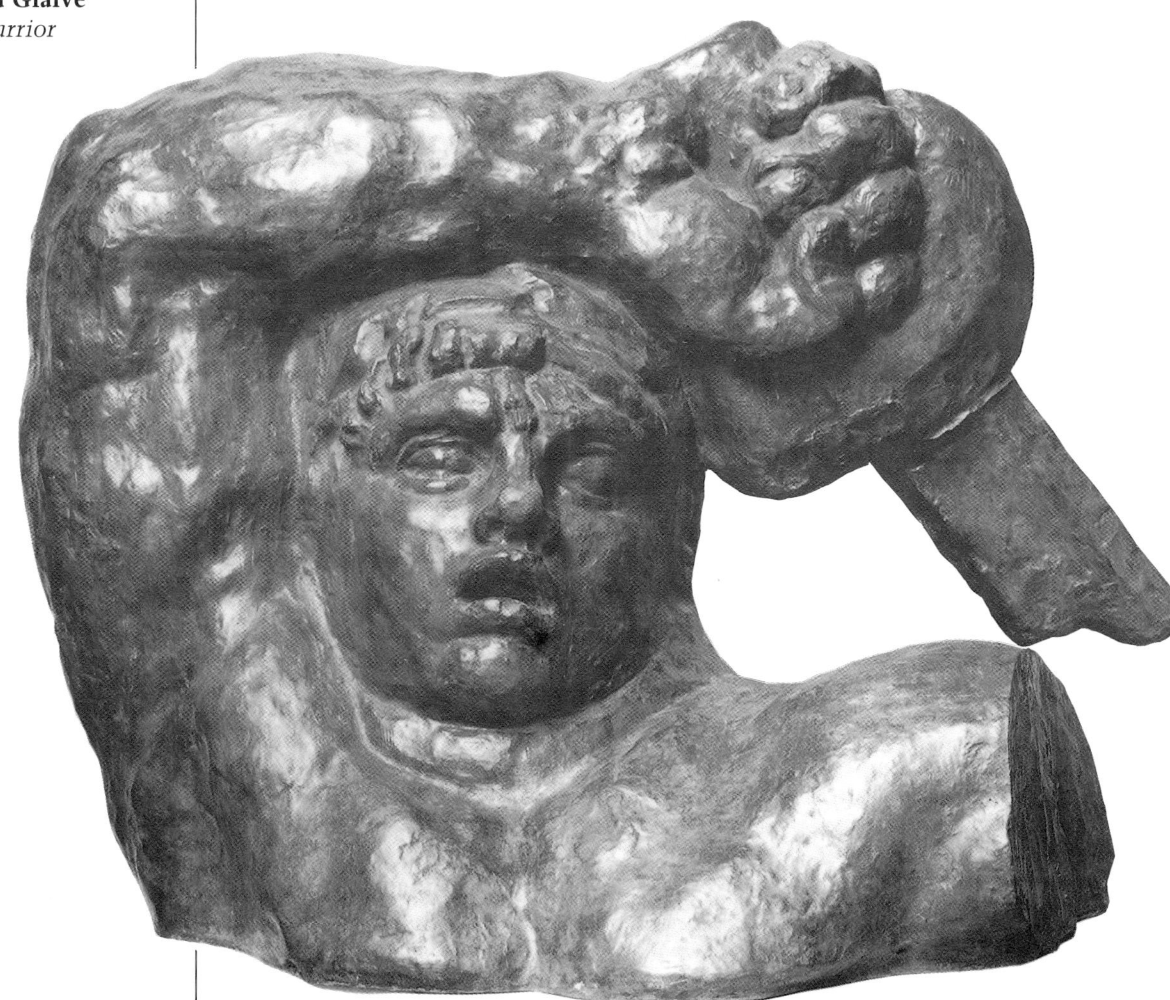

he would not have permitted himself this licence on a scale larger than life.

Bourdelle's break with Rodin was not sudden, immediate or ever final. Perhaps as early as 1900, while he was working for Rodin, the latter was impressed and disturbed by Bourdelle's *Head of Apollo*. It was the head of a fierce and handsome young man with high cheekbones, prominently bridged nose and stern mouth, all of which are rendered in sharply defined, smoothly modelled surfaces. In later years Bourdelle was quite clear that this piece marked the decisive break with Rodin's way of modelling (which however he continued to use in his sculptural sketches) in holes and bosses. This head is the predecessor of the head of *Hercules the Archer*, the most un-Rodinesque feature of the complex piece. Rodin's heads, when not omitted as part of his process of fragmentation, generally function as the outflow of the psychic current generated by the body. Their modelling is usually extremely marked by Rodin's characteristic exaggeration of the cavities and their expressions are hooded, anguished or enigmatic. But the head of Hercules is small, pointed, chiselled and without expression other than malign concentration on the action. One notes the almost protuberant eyes, the flat planes of the cheeks ending in a ridge below the eye socket, the slit mouth and the tight curls of the hair.

BOURDELLE THE PIONEER

What was the source of this important change? It would be underrating Bourdelle to take him for no more than an eclectic sculptor casting around for a new example to follow and finding it in some form of archaic classicism. The *Head of Apollo* is the first and clear projection of a new ideal humanity, and it is impossible to distinguish Bourdelle's rejection of Rodin's furrowed modelling from his desire to project this ideal. Whereas Rodin followed a romantic realist literary tradition which saw human frailty, misery and fallibility as absorbingly interesting and in some sense sacred, Bourdelle was beginning to express a contemporary yearning for a race of supermen. For Bourdelle this does not seem to have been a matter of present politics. He sprang from an ancient part of rural France and far more than Rodin, the Parisian, he had preserved something of what he called his *"adolescent pride"* in a past which he idealised. His writings are full of nostalgia for what he conceived to be the ancient order based on the family, the soil and the virtues of the French race. This ideal transcended in his mind, and to some extent merged with, the ideal of classical antiquity of which he had little direct knowledge having never been to Greece and seldom to Italy. By contrast he had a thorough knowledge of French Romanesque and Gothic architecture and sculpture. His conception of classicism was founded on French ideals of measure, restraint, simplicity and nobility.

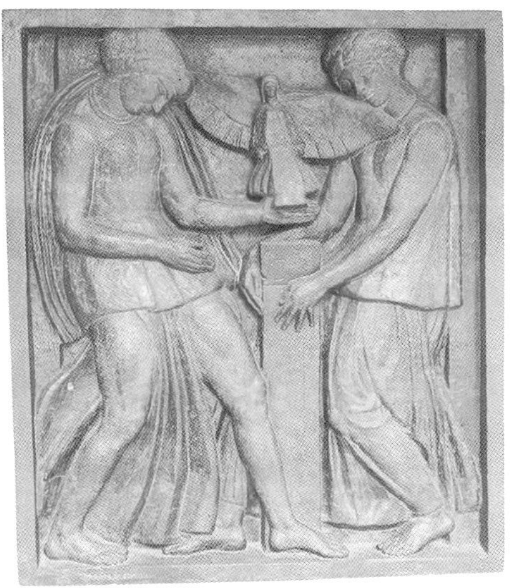

Architecture et Sculpture
Architecture and Sculpture
1912
1.77m x 1.50m x 0.18m

RELIEFS FOR THE THEATRE DES CHAMPS-ELYSEES

The reliefs Bourdelle designed for the Théâtre des Champs-Elysées in 1911 (he also designed, on a plan by August Perret, the facade to accommodate them) were probably his most influential work. Clearly Bourdelle was drawing on several sources in these reliefs. The convention of the flying draperies expressed in stylised folds comes from fifth century Greek sculpture, such as the *Running Maiden from Eleusis*, while the figure of Apollo in the central panel with his bulging shoulders and sharply simplified head provides another obvious point of contact with archaic Greek sculpture. But the primary source for the nine Muses who run towards Apollo from either side was the dancing of Isadora Duncan which had similarly fired Rodin in 1901. Bourdelle was present when she danced for Rodin's friends in 1903, and he saw her again at the Théâtre du Châtelet in 1911, when he made many drawings and afterwards revised his ideas for the relief panels. One Muse has entered the central panel and has halted her headlong rush before Apollo with a dramatic reversal of thrust, an intensely

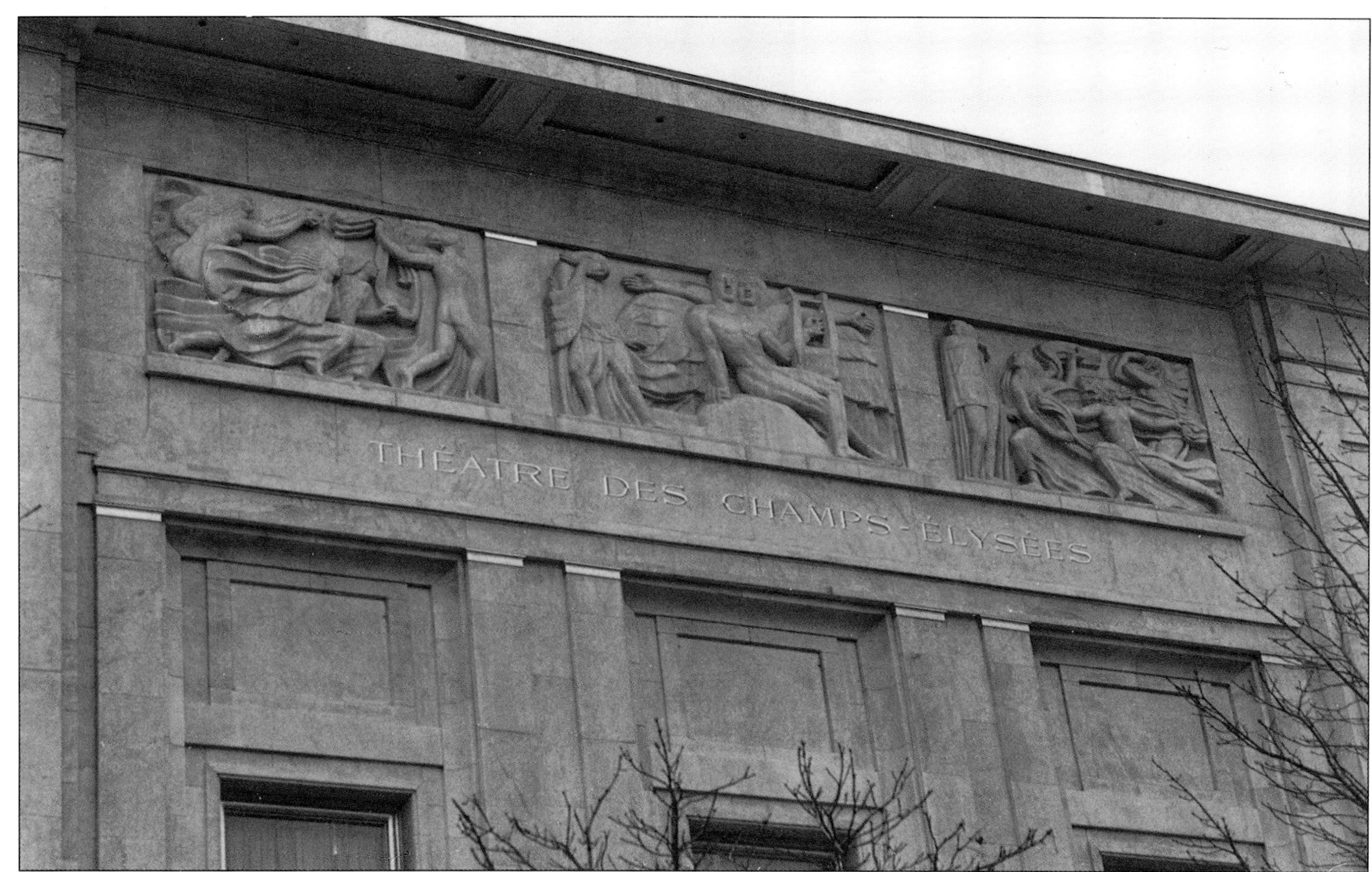

"I shall have to carve twenty-one figures in marble, and the lonely effort in forming a unity of these sculptures with the whole of the building will be overwhelming. The physical effort is small, but the spiritual work is enormous. All these sculptures must take into account and depend upon the proportions of the entire architecture. To my mind, it is the wall itself which must, at certain points selected with discretion, appear to be excited into acquiring human form, while at the same time keeping its own surface, its own light... Sculpture must graft itself to architecture like fruit grafts itself to the tree".

Emile Antoine Bourdelle

Grand Adam
Adam (Monumental)
1889
2.32m x 1.10m x 0.95m

theatrical conception closely derived from a drawing of Isadora Duncan by Bourdelle. But the theatre that is so evident in the reliefs cannot be only the theatre of Isadora Duncan. One must suppose that Bourdelle was also familiar with the Russian Ballet under Diaghilev who had just established himself in Paris.

While Isadora Duncan may have inspired individual poses, and Greek sculpture provided a certain convention, the actual visual metaphor by which Bourdelle represented her movements and draperies must also owe something to the stylisations that had already occurred in painting. When Bourdelle made these designs, the essential first steps towards an abstraction of forms had not only been taken by Picasso between three and four years before, but had already filtered down to less controversial painters such as La Fresnaye, Gleizes and Henri Hayden. Although silent about these developments Bourdelle must have been aware of them. So, most certainly, were the designers of Diaghilev's company, Bakst, Gontcharova and others, and advanced Parisian art of the period was only one of the sources of their rich decorative style. The drawing together of painting and sculpture in these reliefs is not confined to the figures of the Muses. In the figure of Apollo there is a twisting of the body in such a way that a torso parallel to the plane of the wall is reconciled with a leg in profile. This is a device familiar in pre-classical art but it is also one that Picasso had used extensively during his blue and rose periods of 1905-07, for example in the picture *La Fillette à la Boule* now in the Pushkin Museum in Moscow.

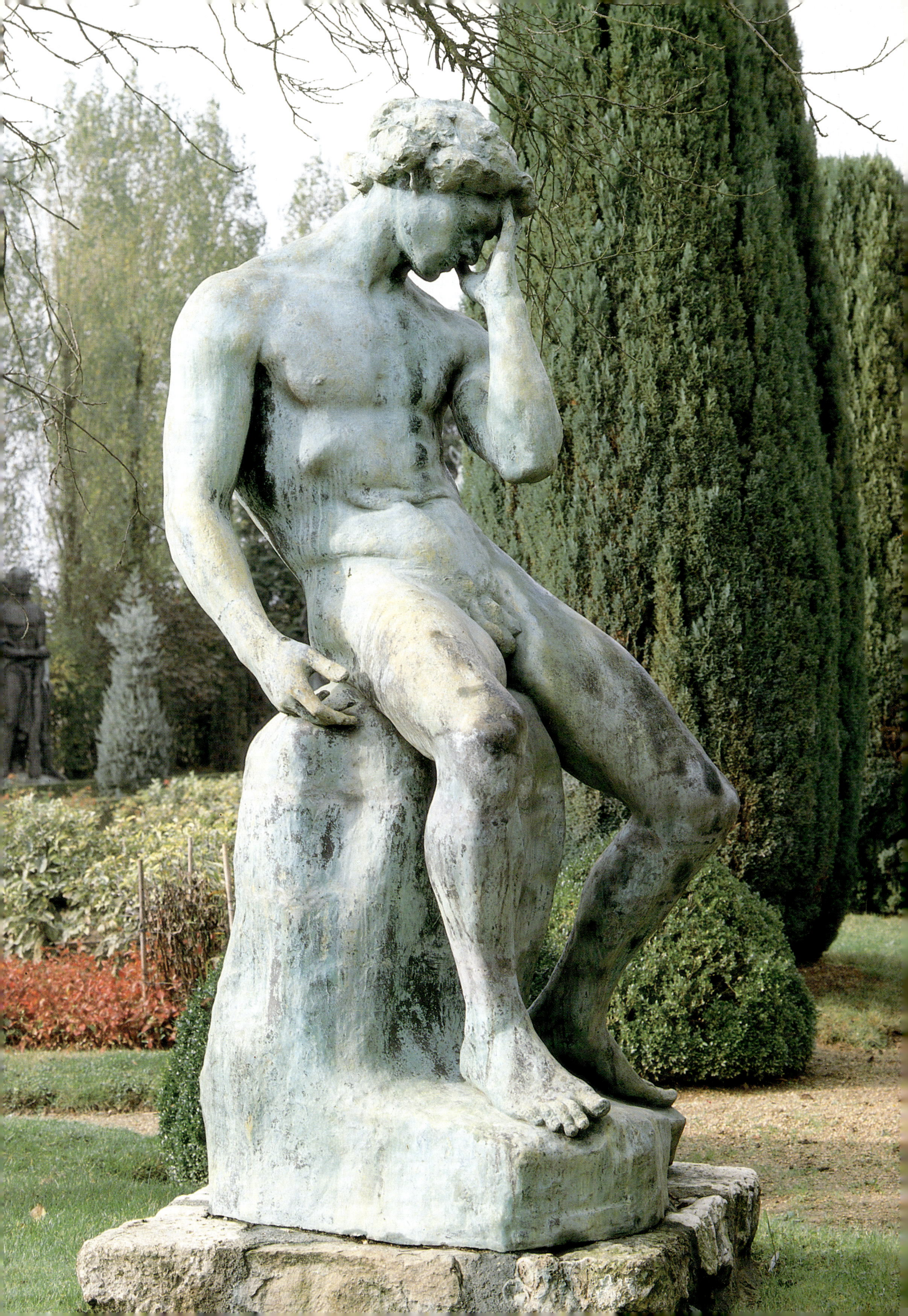

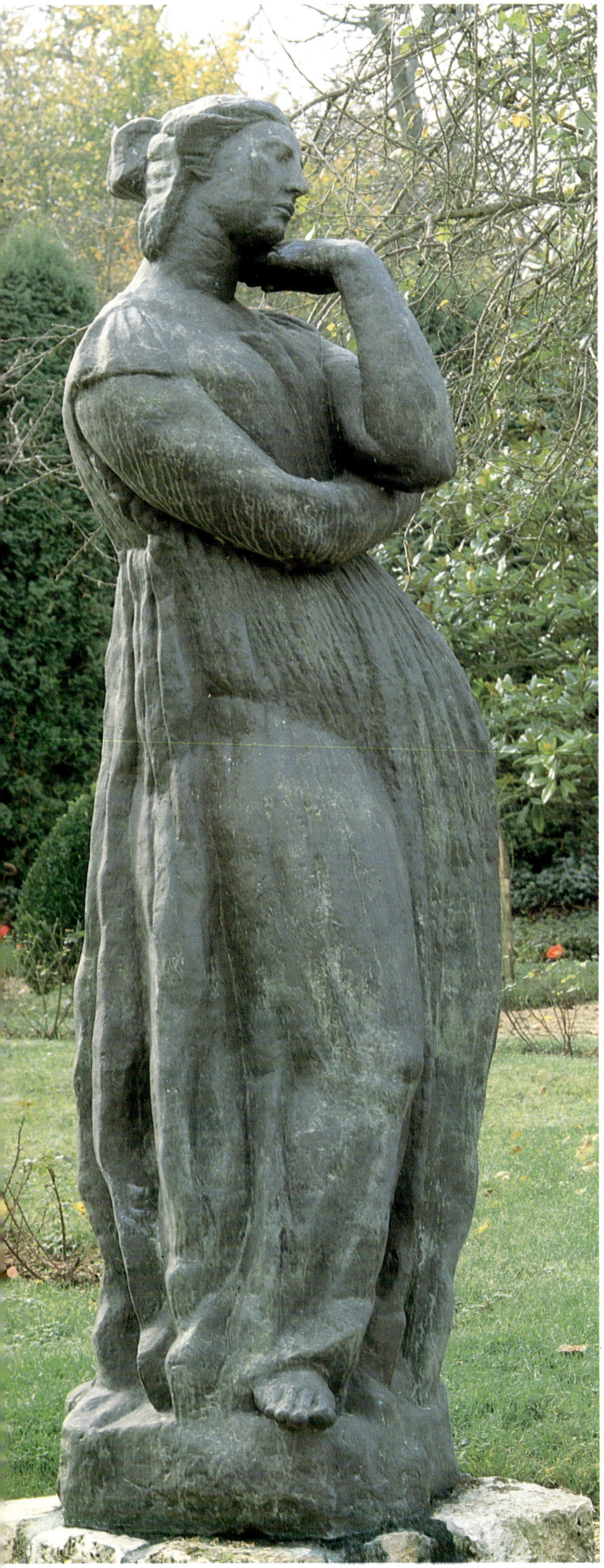

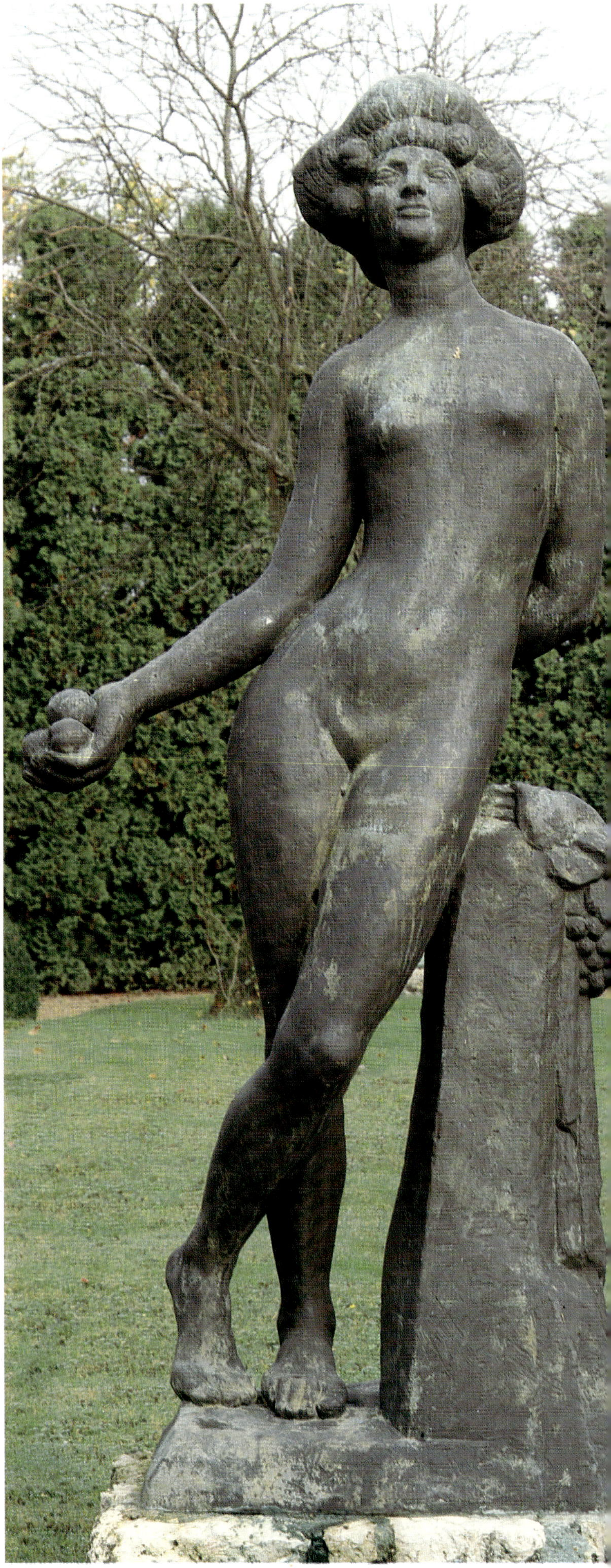

"Penelope has the fullness of fine architecture, of calm and majestic rhythm. The fluting of the drapery is similar to that of a Doric column, but the slight flexion of the figure lends a kind of dreamy grace to this monumental statue which has been composed on profound planes".

Ionel Jianou

CONTEMPORARY INFLUENCES

The reliefs of the Théâtre des Champs-Elysées were the first prominent sculptures that met the symbolist/synthetist point of view propagated by Gauguin, even though they occupied a moment of time when symbolism was about to give way to the newer kind of synthesis initiated by Cubism and already introduced into sculpture by Archipenko and Duchamp-Villon. Gauguin's ideas were fully capable of a more thorough sculptural interpretation than his own carving could bring to them, and it is a mark of the much more conservative pace of sculpture that Gauguin's succession included so little sculpture of importance.

The birth of a new modern classicism was already well recognised by the time Bourdelle executed the reliefs of the Théâtre des Champs-Elysées. The work of Bourdelle would not fit into that background but earned instead the epithet *archaic.* Bourdelle did not try to rebut the description but characteristically put his own interpretation on it,

"They think that the archaic belongs to the dead art of the distant past, but it is for all time. All that is a synthesis is archaic... the archaic is the enemy of deceit, of the foolish, hateful art of trompe-l'oeil, which turns a piece of marble into a corpse".

In words like these Bourdelle allied himself with the ideas inspired by Gauguin and formulated by Maurice Denis, Paul Sérusier and other artist writers. Bourdelle may come closest to Gauguin in one or two standing figures which could be reasonably described in the words that Gauguin once applied to his own vision, as having *"...a statuesque rigidity; ...august and religious in the rhythm of their gesture".* One such figure is *Les Nobles Fardeaux* of 1912. This is an immensely statuesque woman carrying on her head a great basket of fruit. She is pregnant and also supporting a child in front of her with the other arm. The subject is a kind of hymn of praise to fecundity. The style is a synthesis of late Gothic and classical art and, as such, fits in with Rodin's ideas, while the broad, simplified features of the head are typical of Bourdelle's archaism. In this fine work Bourdelle gave expression to an ingenious grandeur, attributing to it something worshipful that Gauguin too knew how to convey. The child enthroned on the woman's arm and carried before her like the image of a God, or like a protective amulet, helps to give the group a religious dignity. Picasso was to obtain a similar effect of a ruder, more animist kind in his *Man with Sheep* of 1944. Braque came very close to the actual forms of *Les Nobles Fardeaux* in a number of paintings of the Canephori type painted in the 1920's.

La Vierge à l'Offrande, also known as *La Vierge d'Alsace* or the *Madonna of the Vosges* (1922), is one of Bourdelle's monumental works in which the monumentality comes from interior necessity and not only from the demands of the commission. More stylised and conventionally Gothic than *Les*

Grande Pénélope
Penelope (Large Version)
1912
2.41m x 0.75m x 0.65m

Grand Fruit
Fruit (Large Version)
1902-1911
2.26m x 1.10m x 0.70m

Grande Sapho
Sappho (Large Version)
1887-1925
2.08m x 1.40m x 1.00m

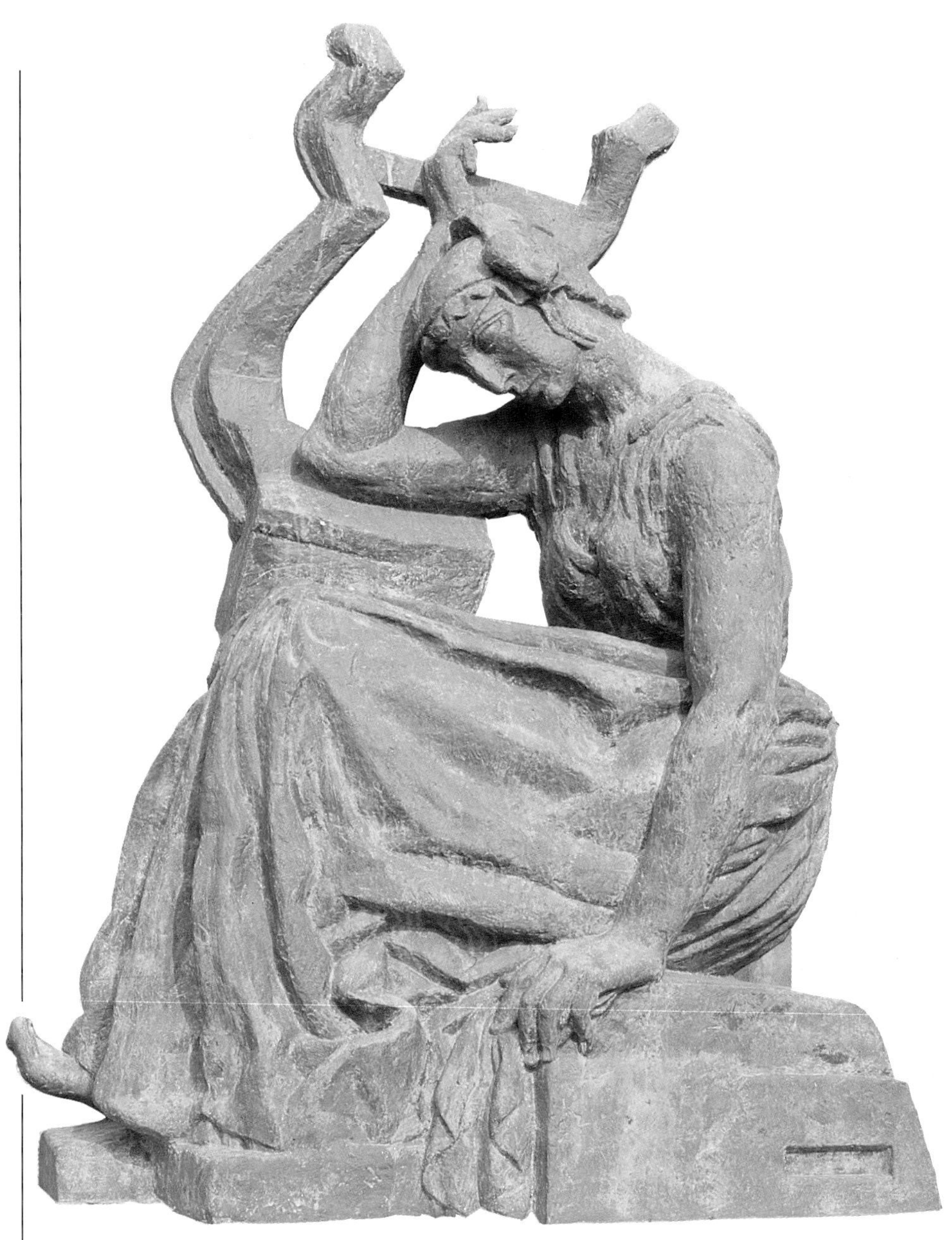

Nobles Fardeaux, it is still the product of Bourdelle's own synthesis of what was important to him in the sculpture of the past, with his feeling for the requirements of a splendid commission, and with his admiration for the formal embodiments that spring from deep down in the consciousness of the race. Mother, goddess, tree and sculpture; statuesque, august, religious and rhythmical - *La Vierge d'Alsace* is all of these. One of Bourdelle's last works is an elaborately pictorial bas-relief which he executed in the space of two months in 1924 to surmount the curtain of the Opera House in Marseilles and in it the seeds of what is now called Art Deco are plain to see.

Parallel to the production of his large monuments Bourdelle also produced an immense number of minor works in which the stylisation of the monuments had little part. Some of them were the studies for specific projects, some were ideas to which he hoped later to give a monumental form and some were done for their own sake. All his life Bourdelle tended to use a Rodinesque type of modelling for small works. The effect of the sculptural impressionism, especially of *Medardo Rosso,* is occasionally seen in Bourdelle before 1910, as in *Maternity* (1893). *Street Dancers on Bastille Day* (1906) offers the same quick characterisation of posture as *Rosso*, and so does *Madame Roussel with Hat* (1895-1900), a deft, pictorial image of great charm. In contrast to these the *Torso of Pallas Athene* (1905) has a smooth, columnar form, which challenges Maillol on his own ground.

LE FRUIT AND PENELOPE

The *Torso of Pallas Athene* is related to one of those few works by which Bourdelle's reputation was kept alive during the decades of anti-rhetorical sentiment: namely the standing nude known as *Le Fruit* (1911). The personality of this strange figure seems quite different from Bourdelle's usual intentions. The sinuous line of its long torso, its high small breasts, enigmatic smile and elaborate head-dress suggest a thoroughly mannerist prototype, at a time when mannerist art had very little following. At about the same period, Bourdelle was producing a series of works around the theme of a standing woman dressed in a long pleated smock. The grandest of these is the *Pénélope* (1912) which like *Le Fruit* is based on a curve but a curve in two dimensions. *Pénélope* and *Le Fruit* have a strong complementary relationship. They might also form counterparts in an allegorical confrontation representing, say, Agapé and Eros respectively. *Pénélope,* a massive woman with bare powerful arms, cannot easily be attributed to one of Bourdelle's eclectic sources. The pose of the woman with tilted pelvis, the left leg carrying the weight while the right is bent and slightly extended; the head inclined in the contrary direction while the right shoulder is advanced in counterpoise to the left hip; all this is based on the well-known High Renaissance ideal of deportment. The naked right foot emerging from the drapery recalls the many hundreds of such feet in the nineteenth century religious art in the manner of Raphael. In spite of all this, and in spite of the studied carriage of the head and arms, it is impossible to pin a style conscious label on this sculpture. It is imbued with an impressive bodily presence and the head and arms are modelled unaffectedly without stylistic mannerisms. In *Pénélope,* perhaps more than in any other work, Bourdelle approaches the realistic ideal, the natural dignified by art. This work is also one of the most successful resolutions of Bourdelle's inward conflict, and its idealism is expressed without rhetoric. Because of this, the heroic aspect of *Pénélope* appears more convincing than in any of the figures, real or allegorical, of the public monuments.

Grand Guerrier de Montauban avec Jambe
Monumental Montauban Warrior with Leg
1898-1900
2.11m x 1.60m x 0.59m

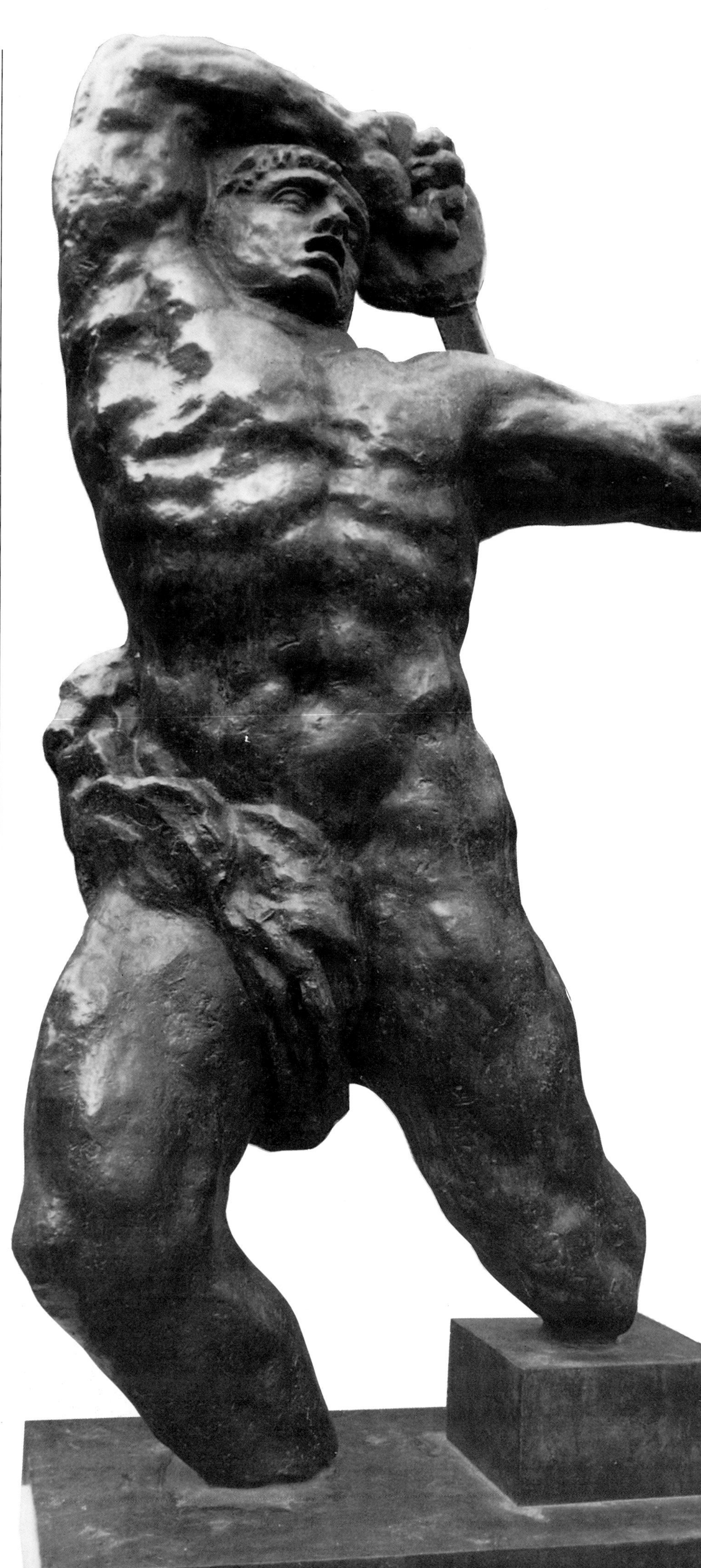

BOURDELLE'S LEGACY

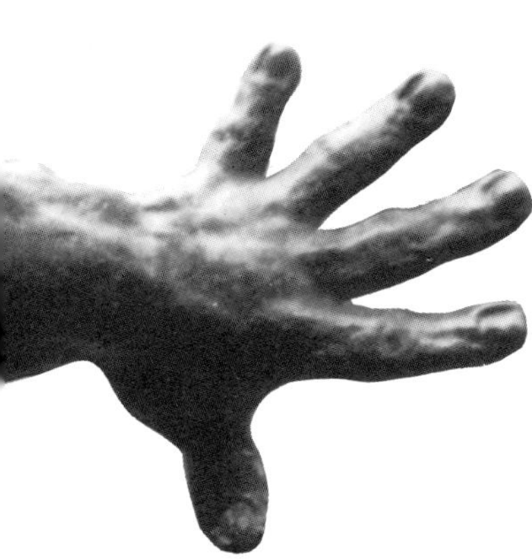

It is not too hard to see the premonitions of later sculpture in Bourdelle's work. One of the most obvious is the thin columnar figure of *Madeleine Charnaux* (1917), whose elongated shape, possibly inspired by an Etruscan statuette, anticipates Giacometti. But Bourdelle's importance to modern sculpture is not in a few unusual , individual works. It is in the attitude to form, that has already been described as synthetist, with a side reference to the theories of Gauguin and his followers. It could equally be described in more modern times as reductive. Unwilling to give up the heroic, wide-ranging aspect of what he conceived sculpture to be, and to confine sculpture to the limits that were being prepared for it, Bourdelle still imposed on it a radical simplification of its complexity. The result was called archaism in his own time but we can now see it as a series of oppositions important to modern art. The work was synthetist as opposed to analytical, reductive as opposed to additive, absolutist as opposed to relativist, and expressionist as opposed to impressionist.

TEXT ABRIDGED WITH THE AUTHOR'S PERMISSION FROM CHAPTER FIVE OF AN UNPUBLISHED WORK ENTITLED *SCULPTORS OF THE HEROIC*.

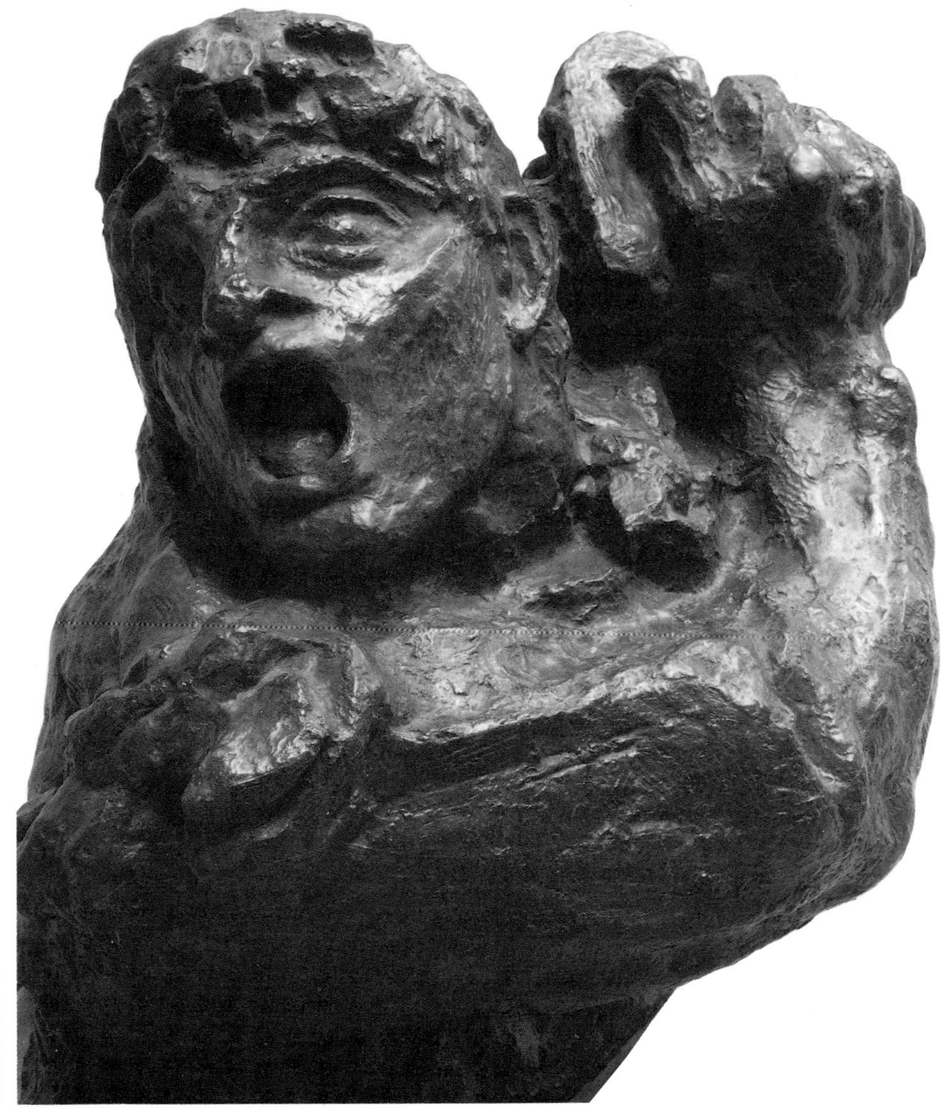

Guerrier à l'Epaulette
Warrior with Epaulette
1893-1900
0.65m x 0.75m x 0.45m

PETER CANNON-BROOKES

LA FRANCE

In the flurry of sculptural activity after the end of the First World War, the French Government conceived the idea of commemorating the intervention of the United States of America by a monument close to where the first American troops had landed. The site selected was the Pointe de Grave in Bordeaux and the monument was intended to face the sea from in front of a lighthouse 100 meters high. The sculptor selected, Bartholomé, was already old, but he proposed to construct a figure measuring, according to Bourdelle in a letter to Arnault (28 January 1923), twenty metres from the feet to the tip of the weapons. Bartholomé came to the conclusion that the commission for this gigantic figure was beyond his capabilities, and turned it over to Bourdelle who, out of patriotism, accepted it. However, as the tower consumed all the funds available, there were none left for the colossal statue: Bourdelle lost this commission. But in 1923 he had executed a version which was exhibited at the Salon that year in front of a model for the lighthouse. In 1925, for the Exposition des Arts Décoratifs, Paul Léon ordered the enlargement of the statue to its full size of nine metres: this was the only commission which Bourdelle received from the French State during his lifetime. After the exhibition the authorities took little interest in the sculpture, which was stored in a depot until the retrospective exhibition of Bourdelle's sculpture in 1931 at the Orangerie. Then Maurice Petsche, the Député for Briançon, requested the figure of *La France* for a position on Vauban's great fortress above Briançon. The

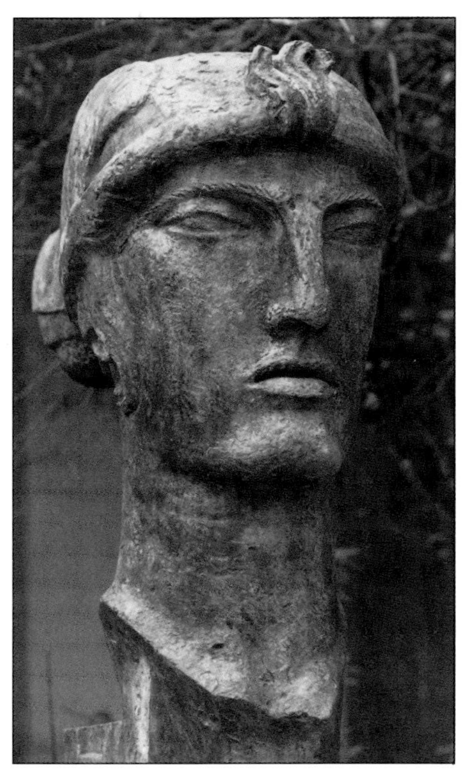

Grande Tête de la France
Monumental Head of France
1925
0.96m x 0.40m x 0.74m

sculpture was installed there in due course, where it remains and fights an unequal battle with a modern telecommunications mast nearby.

A second cast of the same size was commissioned by the town of Montauban as its 1914-18 War Memorial, and the sculpture was set up against a short screen of columns. The third cast of this size was commissioned as the *Monument aux Volontaires des Forces Françaises Libres Mort pour l'Honneur et la Liberté de la France, 18 juin 1940 - 8 mai 1945*. Erected on the terrace of the Palais de Tokyo in Paris (formerly the Musée Nationale d'Art Moderne) this is inscribed MERE/VOICI VOS FILS/QUI SE SONT/TANT BATTUS/PEGUY" (*"Mother! Here are your children who have fought so hard for you. Péguy"*). An *Apollo* was originally commissioned from Charles Despiau for the terrace but at his death in 1946 only the under-life-size maquette had been completed. A toned plaster *La France* by Bourdelle was placed in this position intended for *Apollo* in 1937, and this stayed in position throughout the Second World War until it was replaced by the bronze cast shortly after 1945.

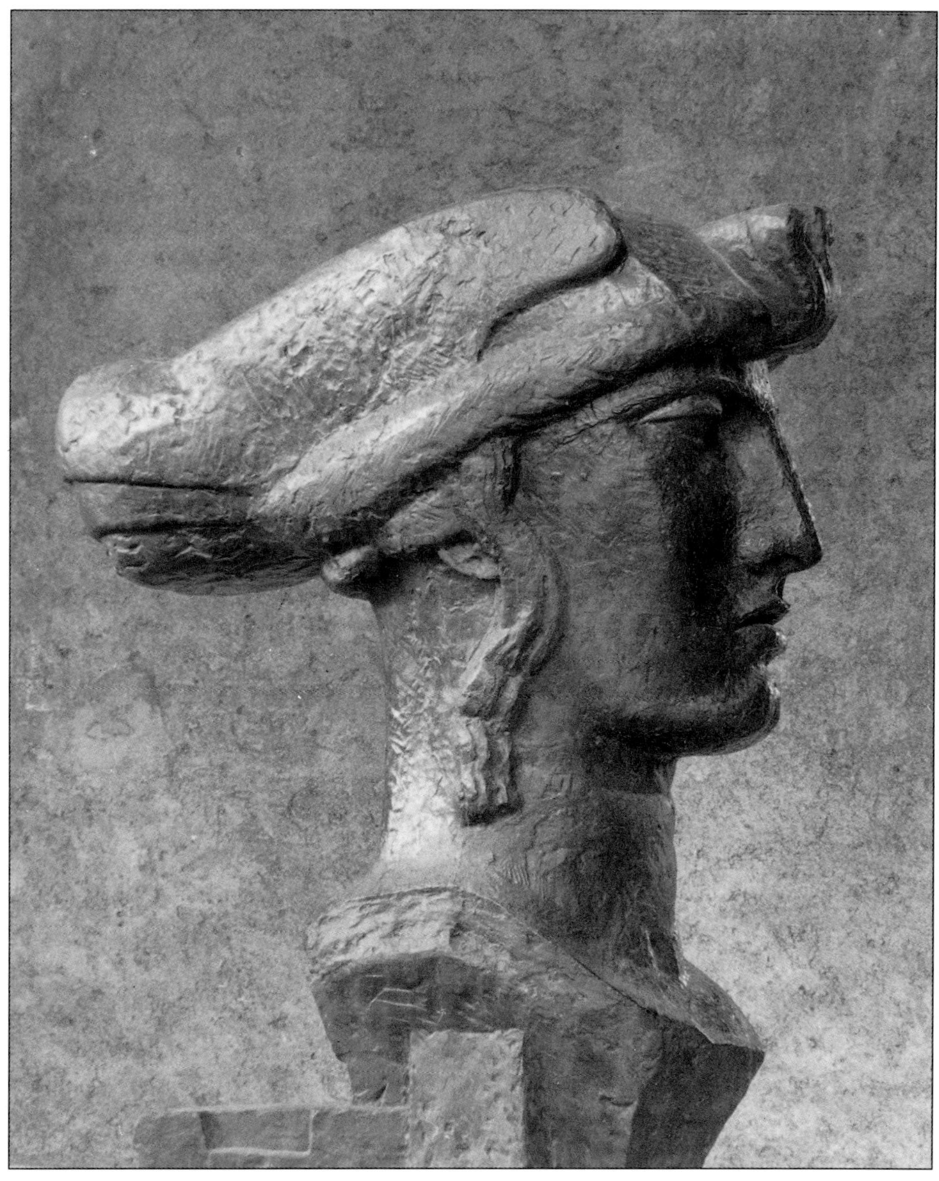

Grande France
Monumental France
1924
8.15m x 0.93m x 0.95m

The fourth cast formerly stood outside the Musée d'Alger, but it was dynamited by the OAS and, having suffered relatively little damage, it was repatriated to France and repaired. However, after a bureaucratic farce, it came to rest (without the serpent column) at the Ecole St-Cyr, Coëtquidan. Of the intermediate size (4.60m) which preceded the full-scale version, casts are in the Brooklyn Museum and three other collections..

Bourdelle himself believed *La France* to be his greatest masterpiece,

"...c'est ce que j'ai conçu de plus plénier dans l'harmonisation du Un au Tout. Une symbolisation, La France, une figure seule et nombreuse pourtant, nombreuse par l'appui des plans et les matériaux moraux, par les ordres précis dont elle se vêt et se pare et dont, avec l'acier intérieur, toute son âme de béton sera armée". ("...this is the most complete and harmonious of all my conceptions. La France is a symbol at once single and multiple: multiple because of the support of planning and ethical fact, because of the clear structure that clothes and decorates it ... With its core of steel, all her concrete soul is put on watch").

The extreme simplification of the forms, noted earlier in *Sappho*, is here again much in evidence, and the angular gesture of salute enhances the geometric effect of the figure. However, more than any other sculpture by Bourdelle, *La France* has the character of an icon, and its frankly nationalistic spirit has led it to be distrusted by many critics who would wish to see in it *"fascist tendencies"*. It cannot be denied that Bourdelle, above any other sculptor, forged the basic language for much figurative sculpture of the 1920's and 1930's, he can hardly be blamed for the nefarious uses to which that language was put subsequently. Bourdelle inherited his father's *communard* beliefs, but, as Anatole France once said of him,"si tout le monde vivait comme lui la révolution serait inutile" *(if everyone lived like him there would be no need for the revolution)*, and he expressed his beliefs through his sculpture and his way of life rather than by popular politics.

The model for the very stylised head of *La France* was Bourdelle's niece, Fanny, whilst Miss Florence B Colly posed for the arms. She lived a great deal with the Bourdelles, particularly during the First World War, at Montauban and in Marseilles, and *l'Americaine* displaced Fanny so that Bourdelle never completed his work on her head. Indeed, immediate members of the family and intimate friends of the family increasingly provided the models for much of his work: he claimed that *"je sculpte en patois" ("my sculpture is home-grown").*

REPRINTED, WITH PERMISSION, FROM *EMILE ANTOINE BOURDELLE* BY PETER CANNON-BROOKES PUBLISHED FOR THE NATIONAL MUSEUM OF WALES BY TREFOIL BOOKS.

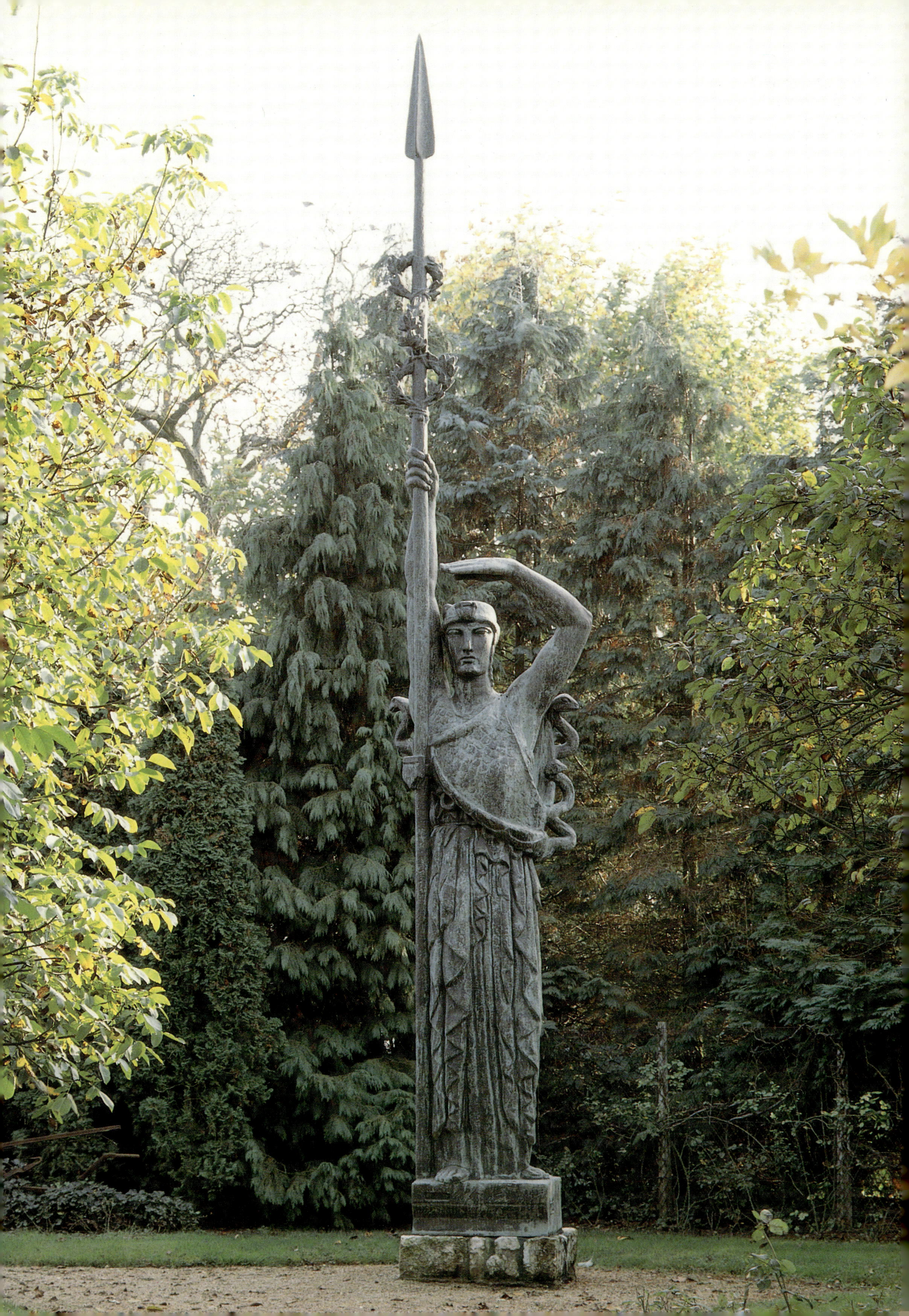

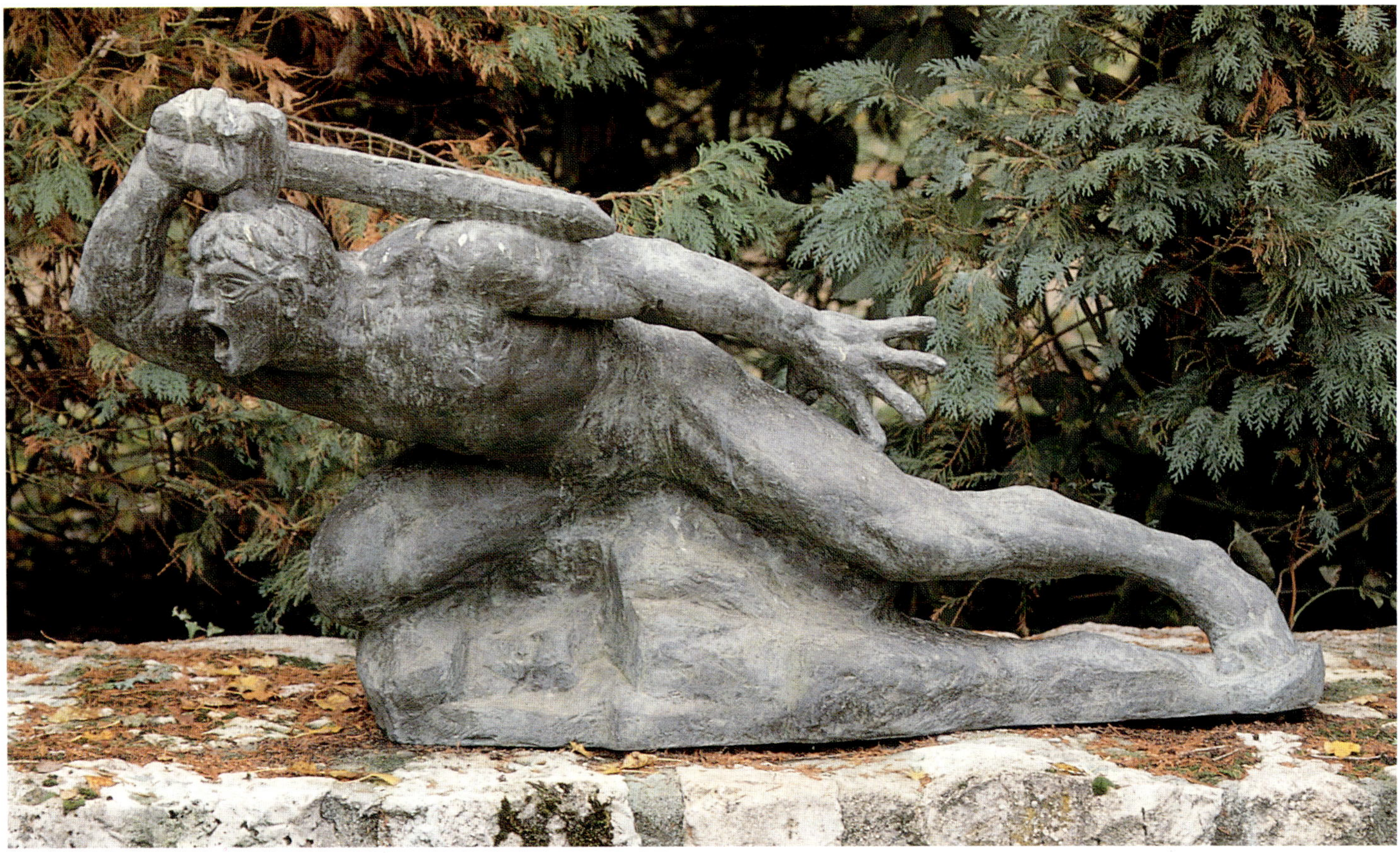

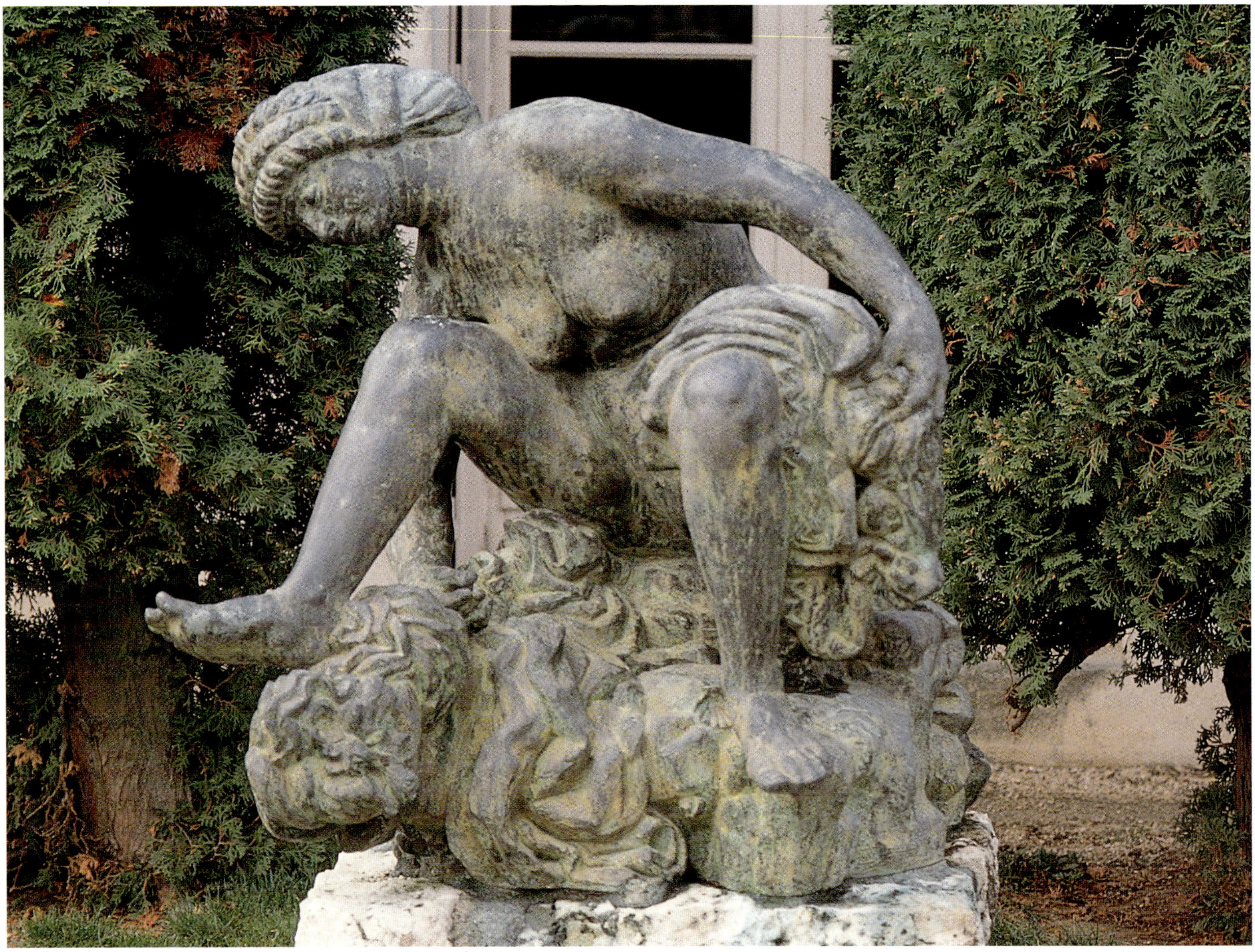

Grand Guerrier Couché au Glaive
Monumental Warrior Lunging with Sword
1898
0.83m x 1.48m x 0.56m

Grande Baigneuse Accroupie
Crouching Bather (Large Version)
1906-1907
1.02m x 0.90m x 1.04m

CHRONOLOGY

1861 Emile Antoine Bourdelle born on 30 October at Montauban in Périgord, France.

1874 Left school to work as a wood-carver in his father's joinery business.

1876 Obtained a scholarship to the Ecole des Beaux-Arts in Toulouse. Completed his first known work which was a wooden statuette made as an ornament for a sideboard.

1878-80 First signed and dated sculptures.

1881-83 Made numerous portraits in Toulouse and Montauban where he spent his holidays.

1884 Went from Ecole des Beaux-Arts in Toulouse to Falguière's studio in the Ecole des Beaux-Arts in Paris with scholarships from Montauban and Toulouse. First exhibited in the Salon des Aritistes Français. Hired a studio at 16 impasse du Maine where he lived and worked until his death.

1885 Received an honourable mention for *The First Victory of Hannibal* at the Salon des Artistes Français. Admitted into Necker Hospital with a sickness that endangered his life. Spent his convalescence in Toulouse and Montauban where he carved several portraits.

1887 His mother died. Made the first version of *Sappho*. Began the great series of portraits of Beethoven which he did not finish until 1929.

1890 Exhibited at La Closerie des Lilas where his sculptures were noticed by Félicien Champsaur.

1891 Sent his first exhibits to the Salon de la Société Nationale des Beaux-Arts and the Salon du Champ de Mars in Paris.

1893 Completed first studies for the competition for the *War Memorial of Montauban* for the victims of the Franco Prussian War of 1870-71. Rodin engaged him as an assistant.

1897 Obtained the final commission for the *War Memorial of Montauban*. Exhibited for the first time in the USA in Tennessee Centennial Exhibition in Nashville.

1900 Modelled the *Head of Apollo* which marked an important stage in his artistic evolution. Decorated the Théâtre of the Musée Grévin. Founded a short lived school of sculpture with Rodin and Desbois.

1905 First one-man exhibition at the Galerie Hébrard in Paris, where he showed 38 sculptures, 18 paintings and 21 drawings. The preface of the catalogue was signed by Elie Faure.

1906 Completed the first version of *Fruit*. His father died.

1907 Travelled to Geneva and Berlin.

1908 Travelled to Poland to take part in the judging for a monument to Chopin. Made the *Bust of Ingres*.

1909 Completed the first model for the *Mickiewicz Monument* and the first version of *Hercules the Archer*. Travelled to Prague to attend the opening of the exhibition of his work. Began to teach at La Grande Chaumière. He was made Knight of the Legion of Honour.

1910 Exhibited the *Bust of Rodin* and *Hercules the Archer* at the Salon de la Société Nationale des Beaux-Arts. Drew up his first projects for the facade of the Théâtre des Champs-Elysées. Exhibited the *Carpeaux* statue.

1911 Made the first version of *Dying Centaur*. Exhibited the large version of *Fruit*.

1912 Exhibited the large statue of *Penelope*. Commissioned to produce the *General Alvear Monument* for Buenos Aires.

1913 Finished his friezes and frescoes for the Théâtre des Champs-Elysées. Exhibited in the Armory Show in New York.

1914 Travelled to Italy. Enjoyed great success at Venice Biennale where he showed 30 sculptures. Made the *Bust of Dr Koeberlé* and a study for an *Equestrian Statue of Simon Bolivar*.

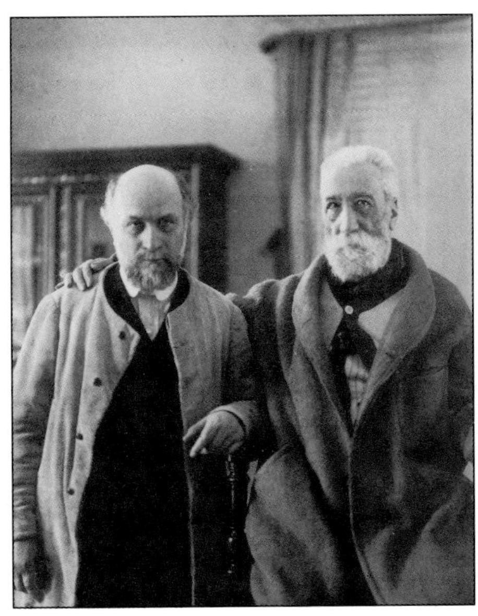

Antoine Bourdelle and Anatole France in early 1920's

1916 Participated in a competition for the interior of the Assemblé Nationale but did not get the commission.

1919 Completed the first version of *The Virgin of the Offering.* Made the busts of *Anatole France* and *Anastase Simu* as well as projects for the *Memorial of Montceau-les-Mines.* Made Officer of the Legion of Honour.

1921 Travelled to Italy with Auguste Perret whose bust he made.

1923 Founded the Salon des Tuileries with Albert Besnard and Auguste Perret.

1924 Designed the pediment for the stage of the Opera House at Marseilles and the *Victories* for the Crypt of Hartmannsweilerkopf. Made Commander of the Legion of Honour.

1925 Made the large statue of *La France*. Participated in the Book Pavilion at the International Exhibition of Decorative Arts in Paris showing *Sappho* and a self portrait. Exhibitions at Albright Art Gallery, Buffalo, the Carnegie Institute in Pittsburg and also in Cleveland, Chicago and New York. Participated in the exhibition of French art in Osaka, Japan. The *Monument of General Alvear* was unveiled in Buenos Aires.

1927 Completed projects for the *Daumier Monument,* the *Dr Soca Monument* and the reliefs to illustrate Georges Clemenceau's *Demonsthenes.*

1928 Retrospective exhibition held at the Palais des Beaux-Arts in Brussels showing 141 sculptures and 78 paintings and drawings.

1929 Unveiled the *Mickiewicz Monument* in Paris. Exhibitions in Basle and Paris. Bourdelle died at Le Vesinet on 1 October.

1931 Major retrospective exhibition of 199 sculptures and 128 paintings and drawings held at the Musée de l'Orangerie in Paris. Included in French Art Exhibition at Royal Academy of Art, London.

1949 The Musée Bourdelle in Paris was opened.

1961 Centenary of Bourdelle's birth. The Hall of Monuments was opened at the Musée Bourdelle and there were commemorative festivities at the Sorbonne University in Paris.

1968 Opening of three new galleries at the Musée Bourdelle.

1989 Plans approved by the City of Paris for the construction of a major new wing and sculpture garden for the Musée Bourdelle.

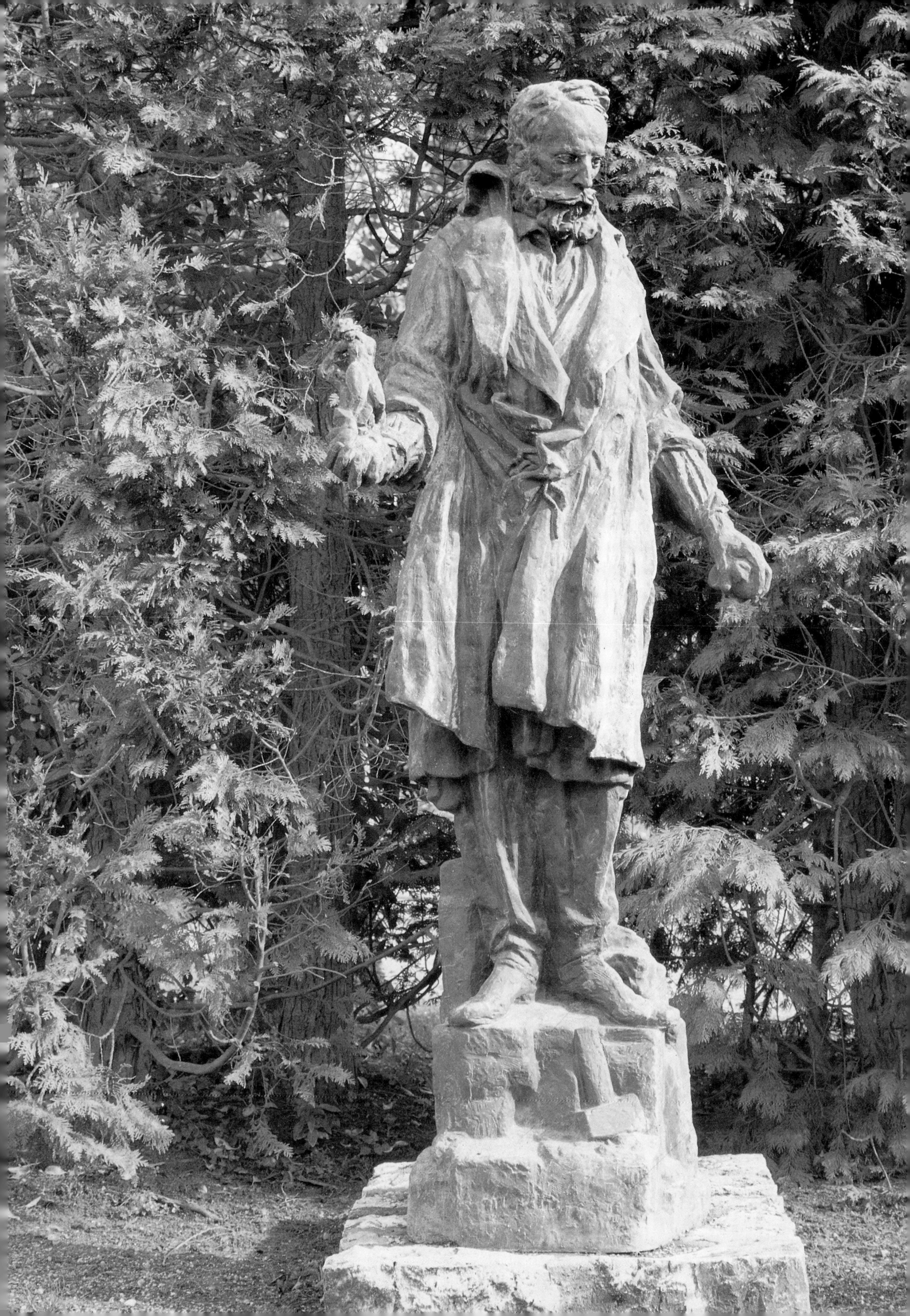

LIST OF WORKS

All Bourdelle's sculpture is cast in an edition limited to eight numbered bronzes and two artist's casts

Carpeaux au Travail
Carpeaux at Work
1908
2.46m x 1.08m x 1.00m

MONUMENT TO GENERAL ALVEAR

1. **Grand Cheval sans Cavalier**
   Monumental Horse without Rider
   1914-1917
   4.60m x 4.30m x 2.25m
2. **Cheval Intermédiaire sans Cavalier**
   Intermediate Horse without Rider
   1914-1917
   1.49m x 1.35m x 0.62m
3. **Cheval Intermédiaire avec Cavalier sans Epée**
   Intermediate Horse with Rider without Sword
   1914-1917
   1.85m x 0.75m x 1.36m
4. **Grande Eloquence**
   Monumental Eloquence
   1914-1917
   3.72m x 1.20m x 1.20m
5. **Grande Liberté**
   Monumental Liberty
   1914-1917
   3.72m x1.30m x 1.10m
6. **Grande Victoire**
   Monumental Victory
   1914-1917
   3.72m x 1.30m x 1.10m
7. **Grande Force**
   Monumental Strength
   1914-1917
   3.72m x 1.20m x 1.10m
8. **Tête Monumentale du Cheval Alvear**
   Monumental Head of Alvear Horse
   1914-1917
   1.60m x 0.72m x 1.60m
9. **Torse de la Force sans Tête**
   Torso of Strength without Head
   1914-1917
   1.15m x 1.00m x 0.77m
10. **Buste de la Liberté avec Tête**
    Bust of Liberty with Head
    1914-1917
    1.13m x 0.85m x 0.72m
11. **Grande Tête de la Victoire**
    Monumental Head of Victory
    1914-1917
    0.90m x 0.85m x 0.65m
12. **Grande Maquette du Monument Alvear**
    Large Maquette for Alvear Monument
    1914-1917
    1.73m x 0.58m x 0.63m
13. **Tête de Lion**
    Lion's Head
    1914-1917
    0.55m x 0.40m x 0.76m

MONUMENT TO THE DEAD OF 1870 MONTAUBAN

14. France avec Drapeau
France with Flag
1893-1896
1.24m x 1.00m x 0.41m

15. Figures Hurlantes
Howling Figures
1898-1900
0.93m x 0.75m x 0.63m

16. Grand Guerrier de Montauban avec Jambe
Monumental Montauban Warrior with Leg
1898-1900
2.11m x 1.60m x 0.59m

17. Colonne Roland
Column for Roland
1894-1900
1.55m x 0.49m x 0.46m

18. Grand Guerrier Couché au Glaive
Monumental Warrior Lunging with Sword
1898
0.83m x 1.48m x 0.56m

19. Grand Dragon sur Rocher
Monumental Dragoon on Rock
1897
1.81m x 1.10m x 0.70m

20. Guerrier à l'Epaulette
Warrior with Epaulette
1893-1900
0.65m x 0.75m x 0.45m

21. Buste Grand Guerrier au Glaive
Monumental Bust of Warrior with Sword
1894
0.61m x 0.75m x 0.39m

MONUMENT TO ADAM MICKIEWICZ

22. Grande Epopée avec Dos
Monumental Epic Figure with Back
1917
3.35m x 2.60m x 1.70m

23. Le Poète Adam Mickiewicz
The Poet Adam Mickiewicz
1924
2.62m x 1.70m x 1.10m

24. Grande Maquette Monument à Adam Mickiewicz
Large Maquette for Monument to Adam Mickiewicz
1909-1910
1.41m x 0.45m x 0.43m

25. Torse Epopée
Torso of Epic Figure
1917
1.25m x 0.63m x 0.40m

LA FRANCE

26. Grande France
Monumental France
1924
8.15m x 0.93m x 0.95m

27. Grand Serpent
Monumental Serpent
1924
3.03m x 2.10m x 0.80m

28. Grande Tête de la France
Monumental Head of France
1925
0.96m x 0.40m x 0.74m

THEATRE DES CHAMPS-ELYSEES

29. Ame Héroïque (Bas-relief)
Heroic Soul (Low Relief)
1912
2.60m x 0.80m x 0.10m

30. Ame Passionnée (Bas-relief)
Passionate Soul (Low Relief,
1912
2.60m x 0.80m x 0.10m

31. Léda (Haut-relief)
Leda (High Relief)
1912
1.68m x 1.02m x 1.16m

32. Architecture et Sculpture
Architecture and Sculpture
1912
1.77m x 1.50m x 0.18m

33. La Danse (Bas-relief)
Dance (Low Relief)
1912
1.77m x 1.49m x 0.22m

34. La Comédie (Bas-relief)
Comedy (Low Relief)
1912
1.77m x 1.49m x 0.22m

35. La Musique (Bas-relief)
Music (Low Relief)
1912
1.77m x 1.52m x 0.18m

36. La Tragédie (Bas-relief)
Tragedy (Low Relief)
1912
1.77m x 1.60m x 0.25m

37. Muses de Gauche (Bas-relief)
Muses (Left-hand Panel) (Low Relief)
1912
2.84m x 4.40m x 0.43m

38. La Méditation d'Apollon (Bas-relief)
Meditation of Apollo (Low Relief)
1912
2.84m x 5.20m x 0.43m

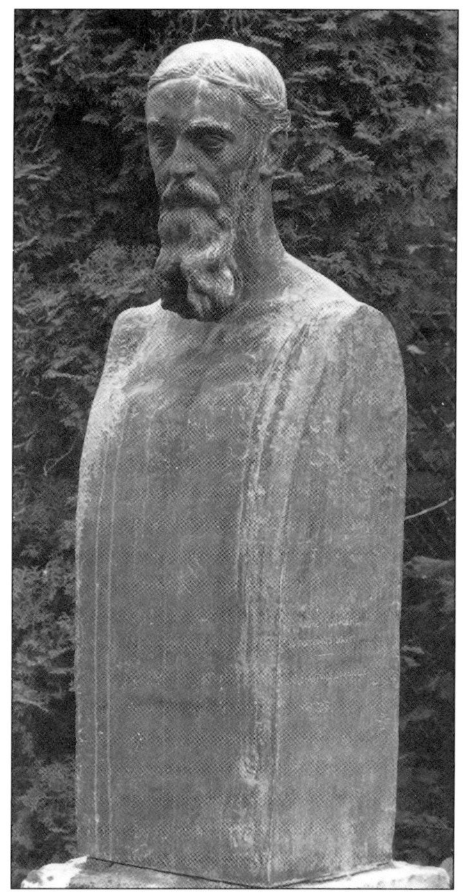

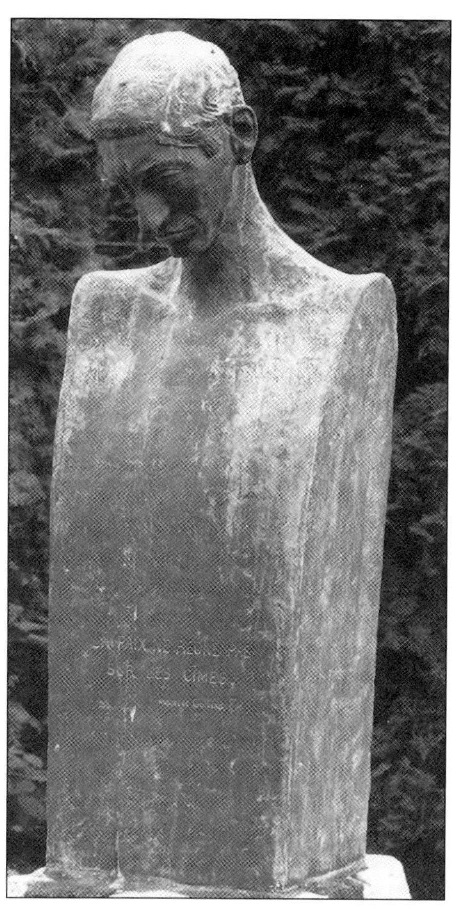

Stèle à André Rouveyre
Stele to Andre Rouveyre
1909
1.08m x 0.37m x 0.26m

Stèle à Mécislas Golberg
Stele to Mecislas Golberg
1898-1899
1.03m x 0.39m x 0.28m

39. Muses de Droite (Bas-relief)
Muses (Right-hand Panel) (Low Relief)
1912
2.84m x 4.40m x 0.43m

40. Génie Portant la Lyre
Genius Holding a Lyre
1911
1.46m x 0.47m x 0.15m

FEMALE FIGURES

41. Grande Baigneuse Accroupie
Crouching Bather (Large Version)
1906-1907
1.02m x 0.90m x 1.04m

42. Grand Fruit
Fruit (Large Version)
1902-1911
2.26m x 1.10m x 0.70m

43. Grande Pénélope
Penelope (Large Version)
1912
2.41m x 0.75m x 0.65m

44. Grande Victoire Aptère
Victory without Wings (Large Version)
1924-1925
2.35m x 1.46m x 0.90m

45. Grande Sapho
Sappho (Large Version)
1887-1925
2.08m x 1.40m x 1.00m

46. Grands Nobles Fardeaux
Noble Burdens (Large Version)
1910-1912
2.20m x 0.65m x 0.78m

47. Vierge à l'Enfant
Virgin and Child
1921
2.50m x 0.90m x 0.70m

48. Grande Jeanne d'Arc à l'Etendard
Joan of Arc Bearing Standard (Large Version)
1909
2.31m x 0.75m x 0.55m

49. Grande Isadora Duncan
Isadora Duncan (Large Version)
1911
1.00m x 0.36m x 0.36m

50. Torse de Pallas Guerrière
Torso of Pallas the Warrior
1911
0.98m x 0.42m x 0.35m

51. Vieille Bacchante
Old Bacchante
1903
0.87m x 0.53m x 0.40m

52. Bacchante et Petit Faune
Bacchante and Small Faun
1900-1904
0.68m x 0.52m x 0.45m

53. Femme et Roses
Woman and Roses
Circa 1898
0.72m x 1.00m x 0.40m

La Comédie (Bas-relief)
Comedy (Low Relief)
1912
1.77m x 1.49m x 0.22m

La Tragédie (Bas-relief)
Tragedy (Low Relief)
1912
1.77m x 1.60m x 0.25m

La Danse (Bas-relief)
Dance (Low Relief)
1912
1.77m x 1.49m x 0.22m

La Musique (Bas-relief)
Music (Low Relief)
1912
1.77m x 1.52m x 0.18m

MALE FIGURES

54. Grand Héraclès l'Archer
Hercules the Archer (Monumental)
1909
2.48m x 2.40m x 1.10m

55. Torse Héraclès
Torso of Hercules
1909
0.95m x 0.66m x 0.47m

56. Grand Adam
Adam (Monumental)
1889
2.32m x 1.10m x 0.95m

57. Carpeaux au Travail
Carpeaux at Work
1908
2.46m x 1.08m x 1.00m

58. Grand Centaure Mourant
Monumental Dying Centaur
1914
2.88m x 0.80m x 1.85m

59. Grand Jeune Sculpteur au Travail
Young Sculptor at Work
(Large Version)
1918
1.26m x 0.40m x 0.40m

60. Buste Cladel
Bust of Cladel
1894
1.23m x 0.68m x 0.59m

61. Buste Rodin
Bust of Rodin
1910
0.90m x 0.70m x 0.60m

62. Rodin Penché en Arrière
Rodin Leaning Back
1909
0.67m x 0.75m x 0.50m

VARIOUS MONUMENTS

63. Monument à Debussy
Monument to Debussy
1908-1909
1.18m x 0.87m x 0.72m

64. La Fontaine (Inachevée)
The Fountain (Unfinished)
Circa 1898
2.55m x 1.20m x 0.50m

65. Stèle à Mécislas Golberg
Stele to Mecislas Golberg
1898-1899
1.03m x 0.39m x 0.28m

66. Stèle à André Rouveyre
Stele to Andre Rouveyre
1909
1.08m x 0.37m x 0.26m

67. Stèle à Onésime Reclus
Stele to Onesime the Recluse
1919
1.68m x 0.52m x 0.32m

BEETHOVEN

68. Grand Beethoven Accoudé
Beethoven Resting on His Elbow
(Large Version)
1903
1.22m x 0.61m x 0.50m

69. Beethoven aux Grands Cheveux
Beethoven with Long Hair
1889-1890
0.47m x 0.45m x 0.30m

70. Beethoven Grand Masque Tragique
Beethoven Tragic Mask
(Large Version)
1901
0.77m x 0.47m x 0.45m

71. Beethoven "Métropolitain"
Beethoven "Métropolitain"
1902
1.04m x 0.53m x 0.50m

72. Grand Beethoven dans le Vent avec Draperie
Monumental Beethoven in the Wind with Drapery
1904-1908
1.26m x 0.55m x 0.68m

73. Grand "Pathétique" Beethoven
Beethoven "Pathétique"
(Large Version)
1929
0.73m x 0.45m x 0.44m

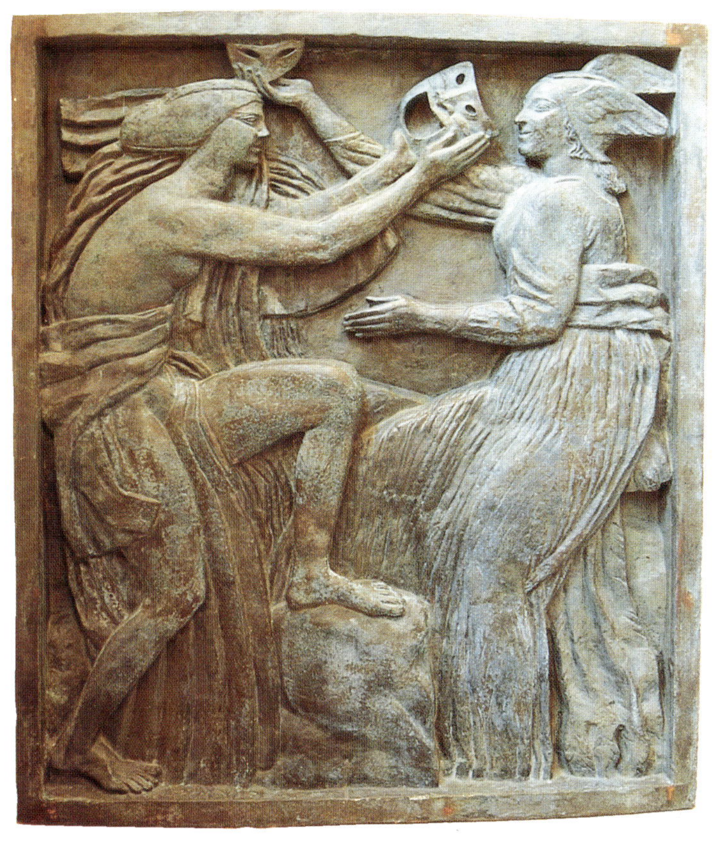
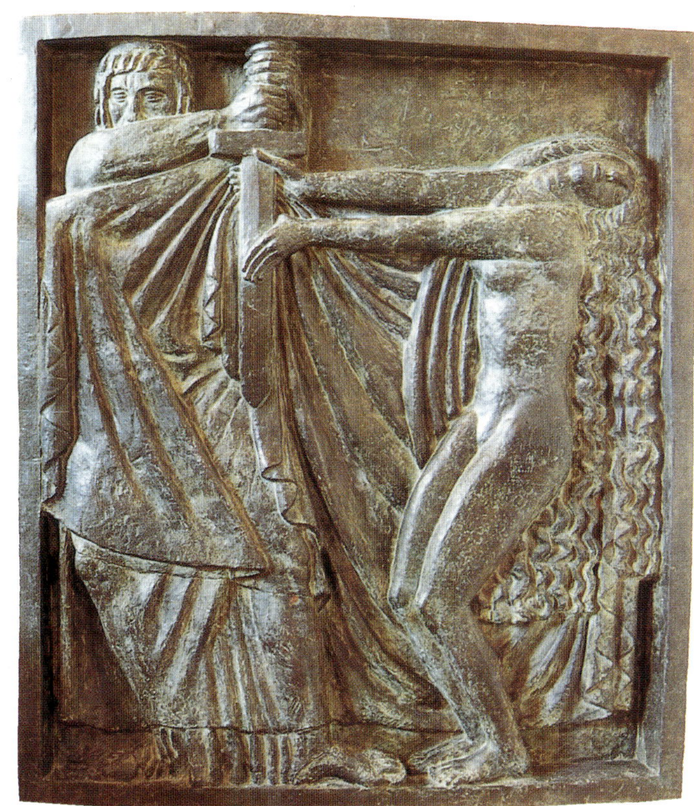
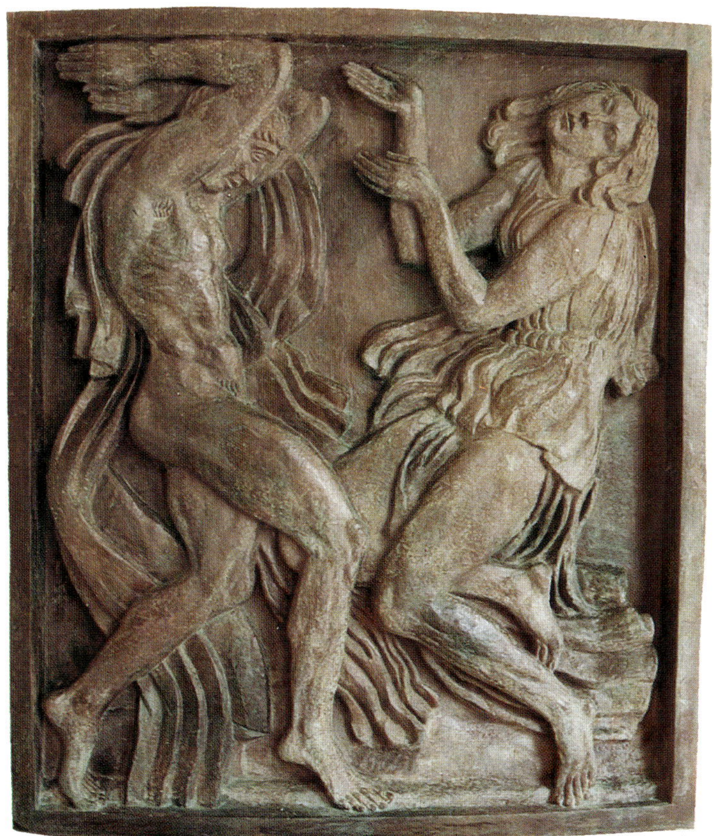
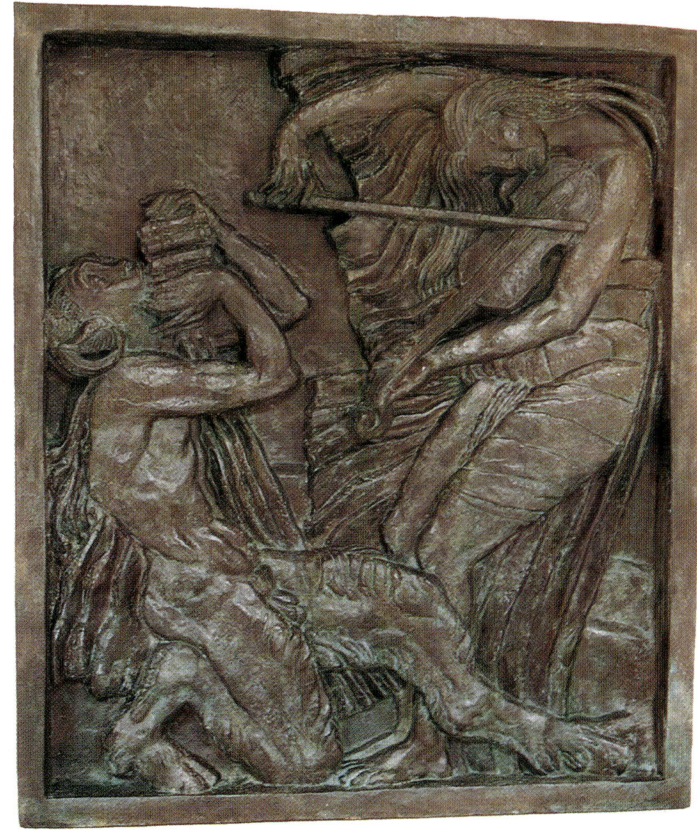

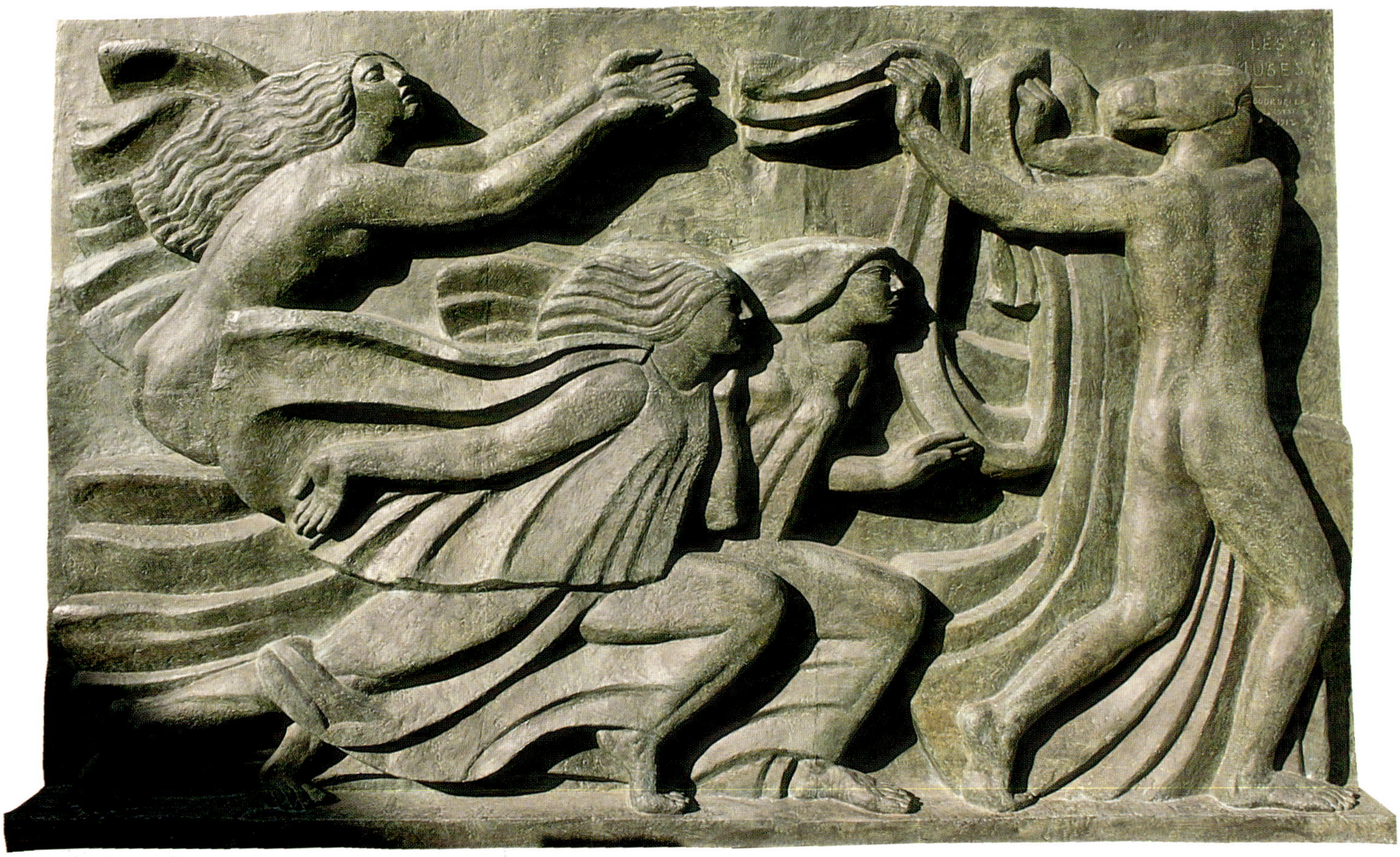

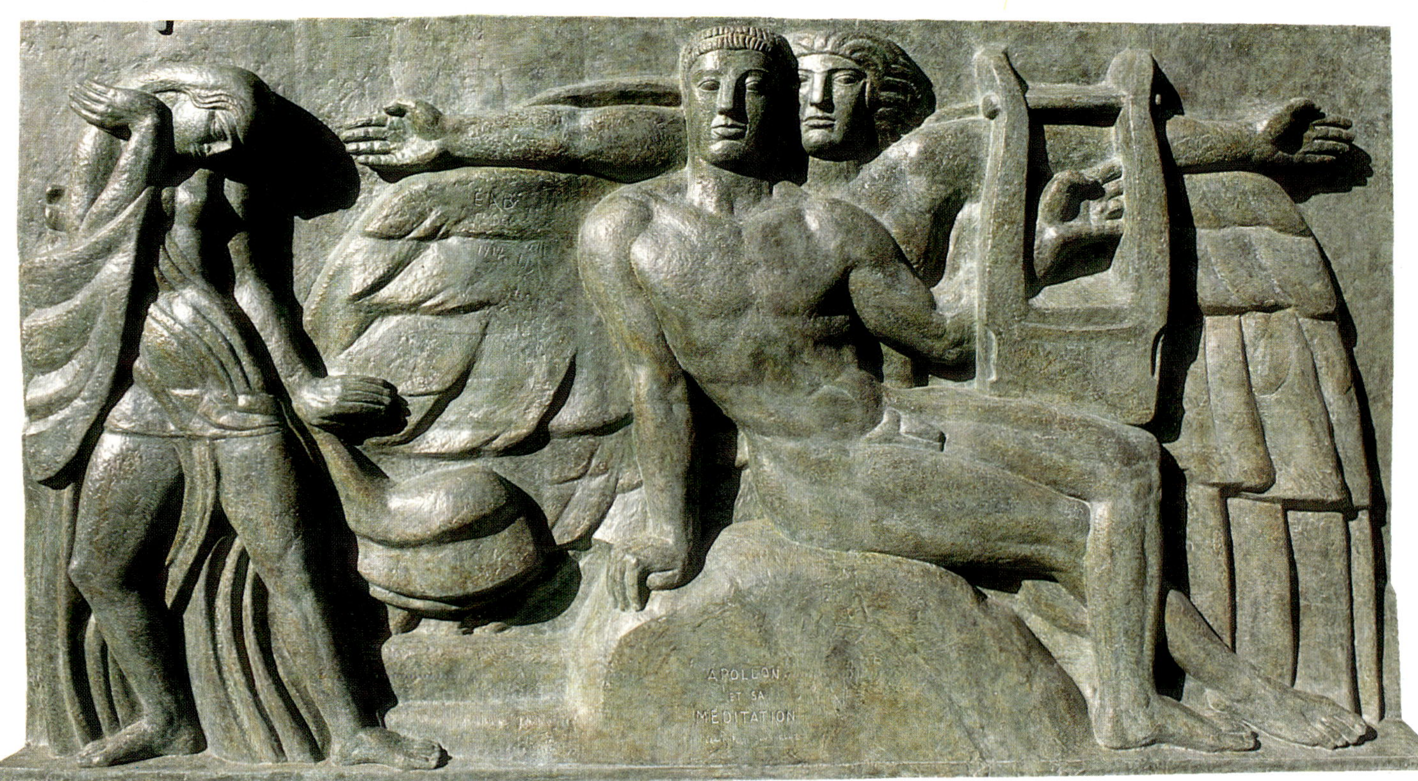
APOLLON
ET SA
MÉDITATION

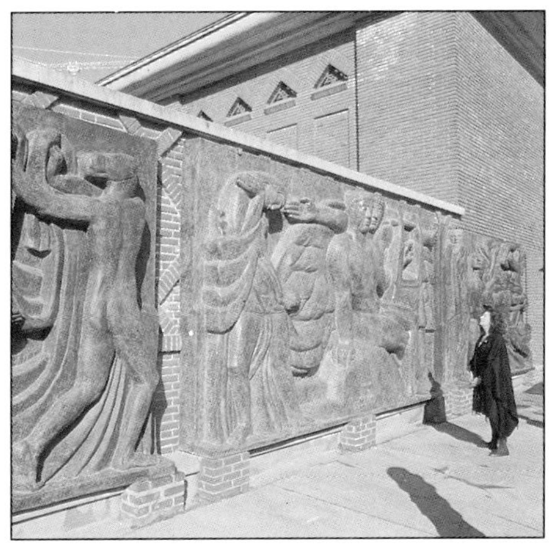

The Reliefs from the Théâtre des Champs-Elysées at the Musée Bourdelle, Paris

Muses de Gauche (Bas-relief)
Muses (Left-hand Panel)
(Low Relief)
1912
2.84m x 4.40m x 0.43m

La Méditation d'Apollon (Bas-relief)
Meditation of Apollo (Low Relief)
1912
2.84m x 5.20m x 0.43m

ACKNOWLEDGEMENTS

This exhibition is a cultural event bringing the work of one of France's most renowned artists to Britain on a scale never previously undertaken. Without the generous and enlightened sponsorship of the exhibition by Rhône-Poulenc Ltd it would not have been possible. We wish to express our gratitude to Keith Humphreys, Chairman and Managing Director, Allan Morgan, Personnel Director, and Ian Arnold, Communications and Public Relations Manager, for their support of the project. We are also most grateful to Anne van Tongerlooy for initially recognising the potential of this sponsorship and to Aisling Mullen for her tireless and patient efforts in helping to promote the project as a major event.

We have received invaluable support and advice from Monsieur Philippe Guillemin, the Cultural Counsellor, and Monsieur Patrick Vittet-Philippe, the Cultural Attaché, at the French Embassy in London and are greatly honoured that Monsieur Luc de La Barre De Nanteuil, the French Ambassador, is attending the Opening. We have also benefited greatly from the help and advice of Monsieur Philippe Bazin, the Commercial Attaché, at the French Trade Commission in Manchester.

We would also like to thank the Trustees of the Henry Moore Foundation for their substantial financial support, the Visiting Arts Unit of Great Britain and Northern Ireland for a grant towards the exhibition costs and Elite Contract Security Limited for their "in-kind" assistance on the practical side. We are grateful to the Museums and Galleries Commission for arranging Government Indemnity for the exhibition.

From the outset we have received guidance and commitment from Michael and Sandra Le Marchant and the staff at the Bruton Gallery in Somerset. Their generosity of spirit and confidence in the project has been much appreciated. It was through them that we were introduced to Rhodia Dufet Bourdelle who immediately recognised the value and importance of organising a major exhibition of her father's sculpture at the Yorkshire Sculpture Park. Her support has been crucial and we are delighted that she will attend the Opening. We are also indebted to the staff of the Musée Bourdelle for their help with the arrangements.

We are pleased that Terry Friedman and Daru Rooke have used the occasion of this exhibition to organise a conference on Bourdelle at the Henry Moore Centre for the Study of Sculpture in the City Art Gallery, Leeds. This will take place during the first week of the exhibition and is funded by the Henry Moore Sculpture Trust.

An exhibition of this scale requires a great deal of hard work and goodwill. We would like to thank Brian Fell and Gordon Young for their sterling efforts both in Paris and Yorkshire and all the others who have helped with the installation. We are particularly grateful for the support given by Bretton Hall. Robert Hopper, Chairman of the YSP Management Committee, has provided enthusiastic support and advice throughout. I would like to express my appreciation and admiration for the commitment given by the staff of the YSP. They have toiled endlessly to ensure the success of this project, in particular Griselda Bear, Angela de Courcy Bower and Jeremy Mawdsley.

PETER MURRAY

CREDITS

The Yorkshire Sculpture Park is supported by Wakefield Metropolitan District Council, Yorkshire Arts, West Yorkshire Grants, the Arts Council of Great Britain through the Incentive Funding Scheme and the Henry Moore Foundation. Additional funding for this exhibition has come from the Visiting Arts Office of Great Britain and Northern Ireland. The sponsorship of the exhibition by Rhône-Poulenc Ltd has been recognised by an award under the Government's Business Sponsorship Incentive Scheme which is administered by the Association for Business Sponsorship of the Arts.

The YSP has received permission to use passages from the following books some of which have been translated by Simone Wyn Griffith-Mester: *Emile Antoine Bourdelle* by Peter Cannon-Brookes published for the National Museum of Wales by Trefoil Books in 1983; *Bourdelle* by Ionel Jianou and Michel Dufet published by Arted, Editions d'art, Paris in 1978; *Bourdelle et la critique de son temps* by Carol Marc Lavrillier and Michel Dufet published by Musée Bourdelle, Paris in 1979. The following have provided photographs for this catalogue: Michael Le Marchant, Director, Bruton Gallery; Musée Bourdelle, Paris.

A CONCURRENT EXHIBITION (20 MAY - 16 SEPTEMBER) *BOURDELLE - EVOLUTION* IS BEING HELD AT BRUTON GALLERY, BRUTON IN SOMERSET.

Bruton Gallery represents Bourdelle's Estate.

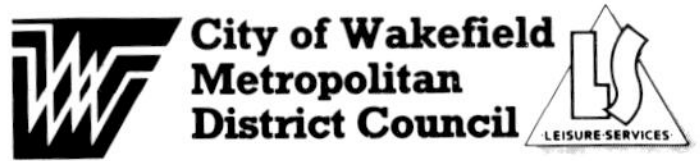

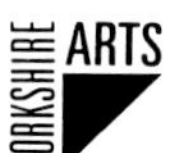

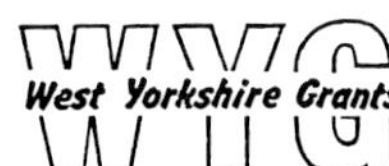

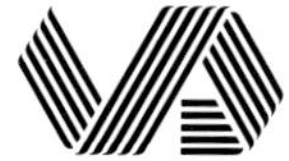

Designed by Jennings Design Consultants, Leeds

BOURDELLE AT THE YORKSHIRE SCULPTURE PARK

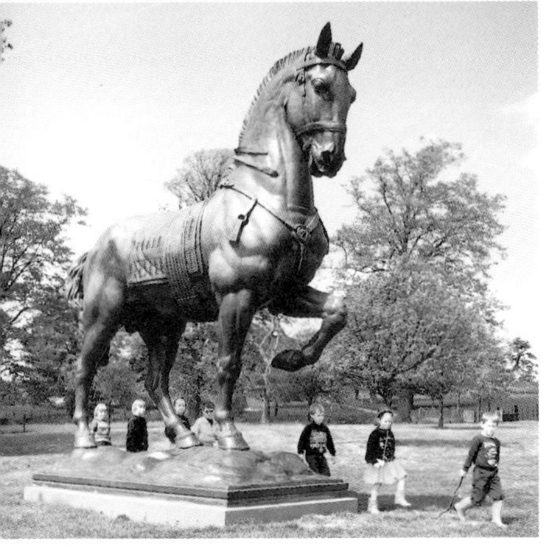

Organising the Bourdelle exhibition at the Yorkshire Sculpture Park was a major undertaking. This supplement is designed to celebrate the exhibition through colour illustrations of some of the sculpture sited in the landscape at the YSP. Not every work is included but this selection helps to provide a record of a memorable event.

The supplement also includes a statement from the Chairman and Managing Director of Rhône-Poulenc Ltd, the sponsors of the exhibition, outlining their reasons for becoming involved.

To complement the exhibition a conference on Bourdelle was organised by the Henry Moore Study Centre in Leeds. This took place in Leeds City Art Gallery and at the Sculpture Park. Contributors included Michael le Marchant, the artist's daughter Madame Rhodia Dufet-Bourdelle, Sir Alan Bowness, Penelope Curtis and Patrick Elliott.

To mark this occasion we are also publishing an article on Bourdelle by Penelope Curtis. She has recently completed a doctoral thesis on Bourdelle and contemporary monumental sculpture for the Courtauld Institute of Art in London.

Photographs for this supplement have been taken by Michael Le Marchant, Director, Bruton Gallery and Eric Spencer.

BOURDELLE

SPONSORED BY

RHÔNE-POULENC LTD

AT THE

YORKSHIRE SCULPTURE PARK

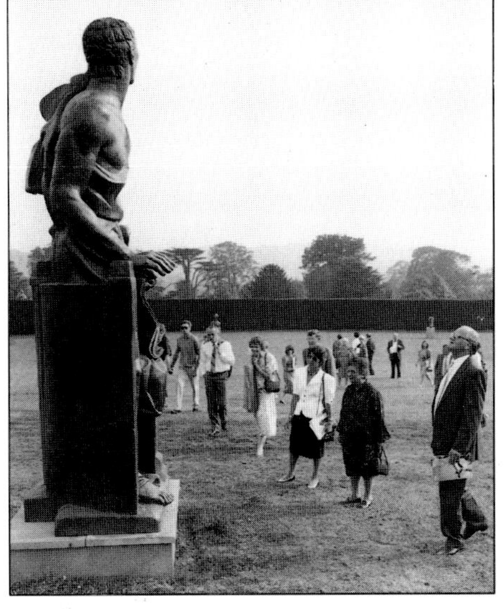

Opposite page

Grand Héraclès l'Archer
Hercules the Archer (Monumental)
1909
2.48m x 2.40m x 1.10m

The title of the exhibition 'Emile Antoine Bourdelle, Pioneer of the Future' includes a generous accolade from Bourdelle's one time mentor the great sculptor Auguste Rodin. It is a most fitting description of Bourdelle who was for many years at the forefront of French sculpture.

The sponsorship of this splendid exhibition is Rhône-Poulenc Ltd's first major venture in the arts. Rhône-Poulenc is an international chemical company, a world leader in health care, in agriculture, chemicals and fibres, considered in its own right to be a 'Pioneer of the Future'.

Bourdelle concerned himself with the relationship between art and nature. Similarly care for the environment is one of the company's highest priorities and this is reflected by deeds as well as words in all company activities. The sharing of ideas and opportunities between countries and cultures is part of our every day business: the group employs some 83,000 people and operates in 140 countries worldwide. By bringing Bourdelle's work from Paris to be enjoyed by so many people in the delightful setting of the Yorkshire Sculpture Park Rhône-Poulenc Ltd is further extending the group's internationalism.

I personally greatly enjoyed my visit to the exhibition and am pleased to contribute to this special supplement to the catalogue showing many of the sculptures in the YSP landscape.

Keith Humphreys
Chairman and Managing Director
Rhône-Poulenc Ltd

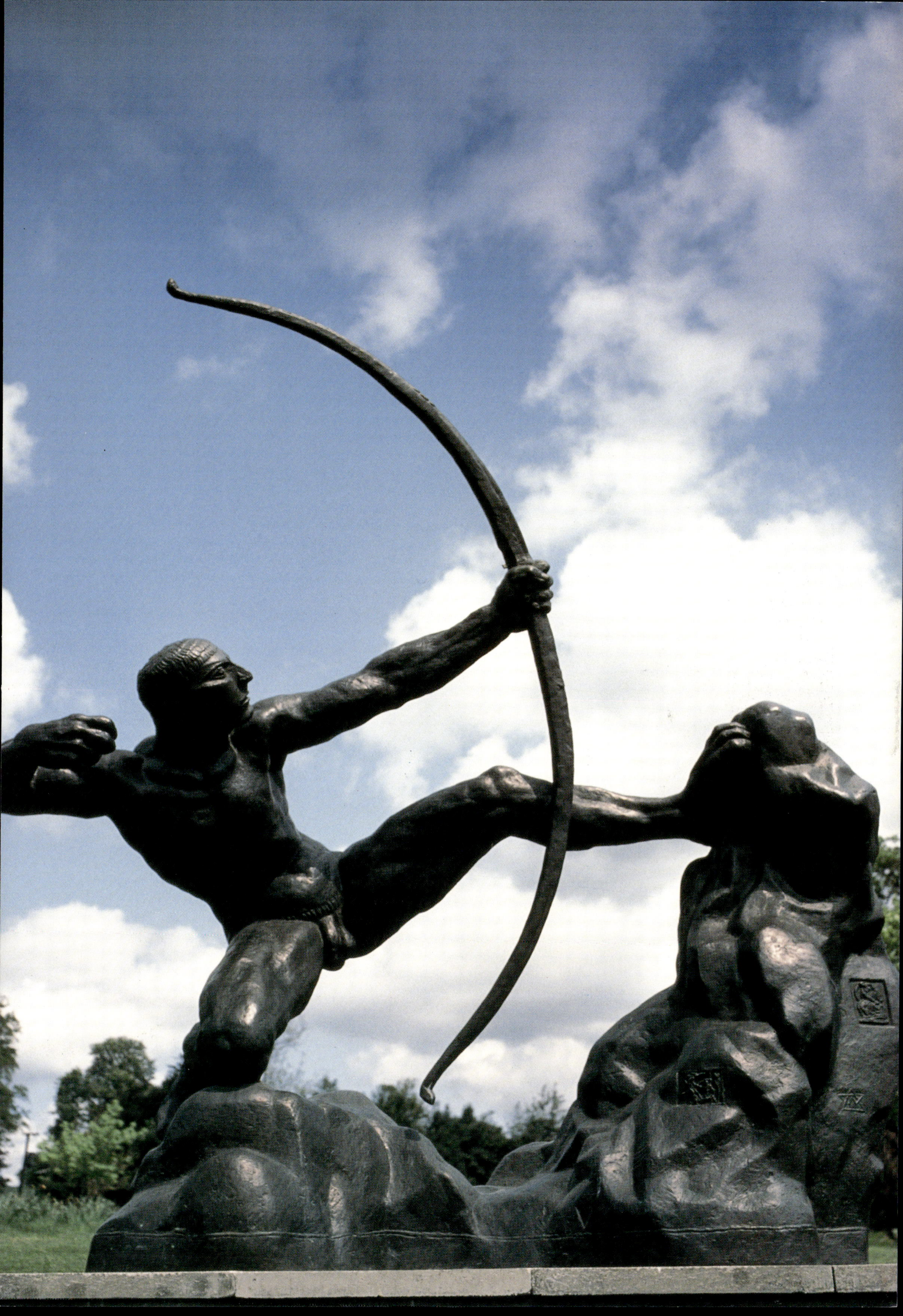

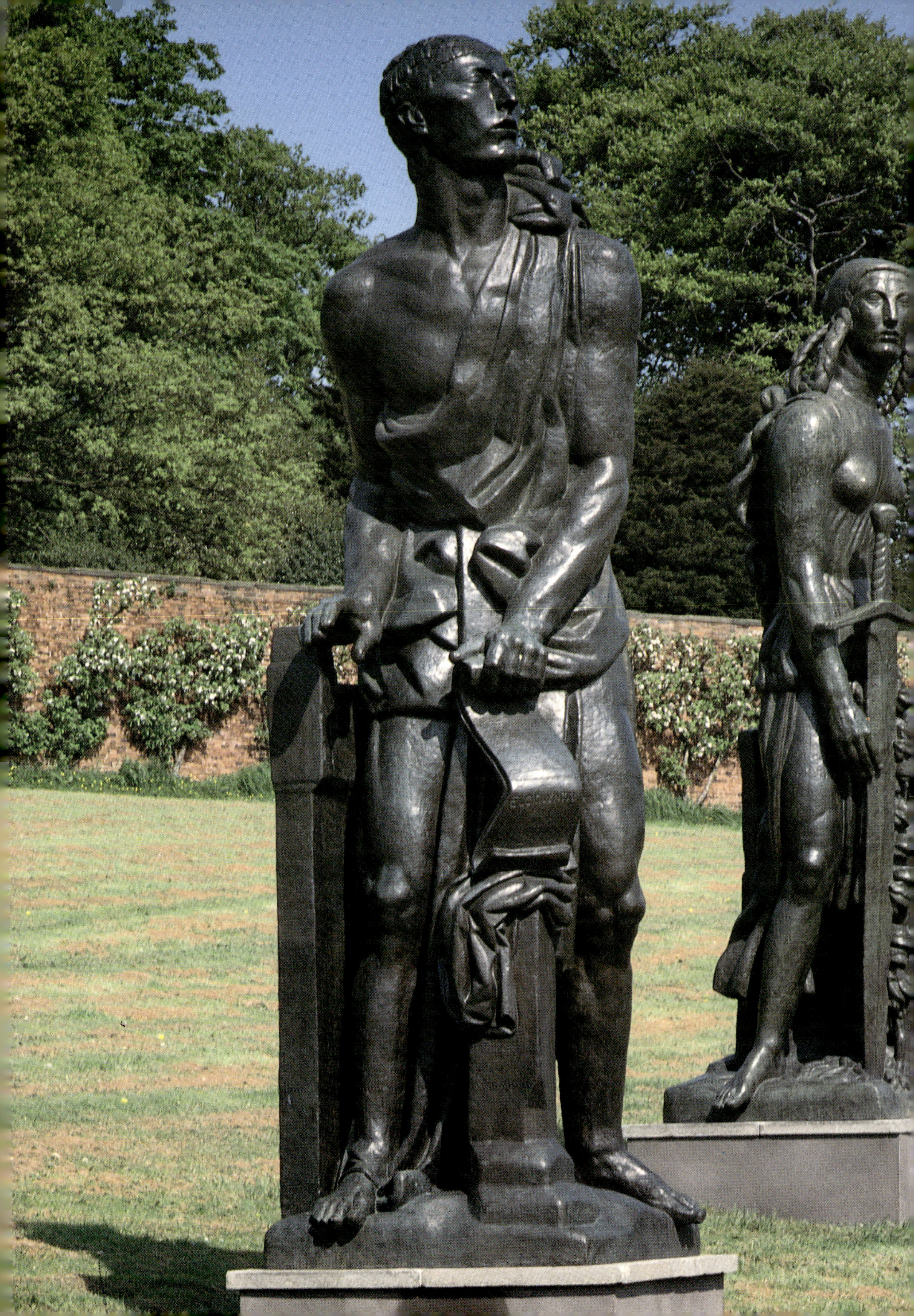

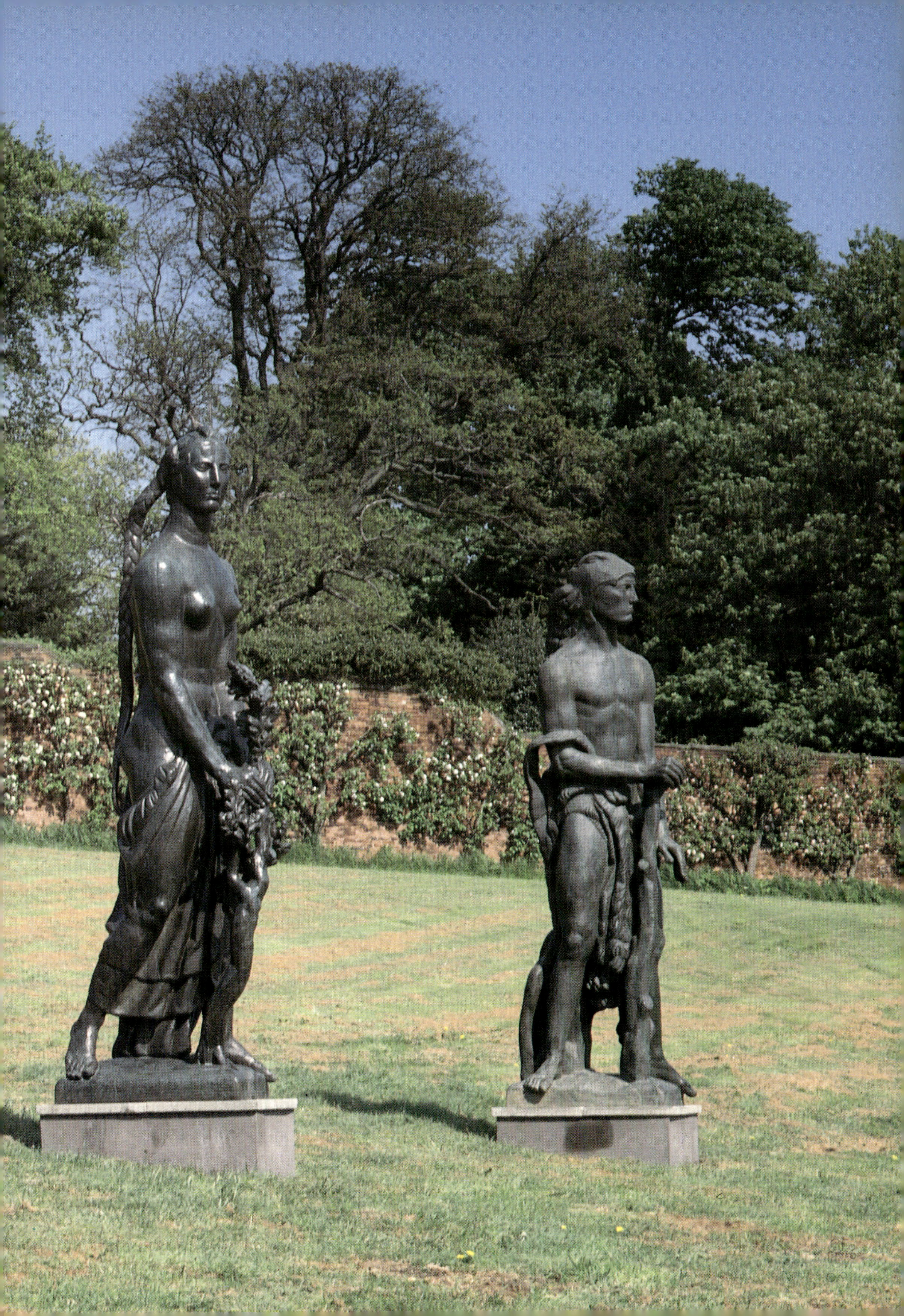

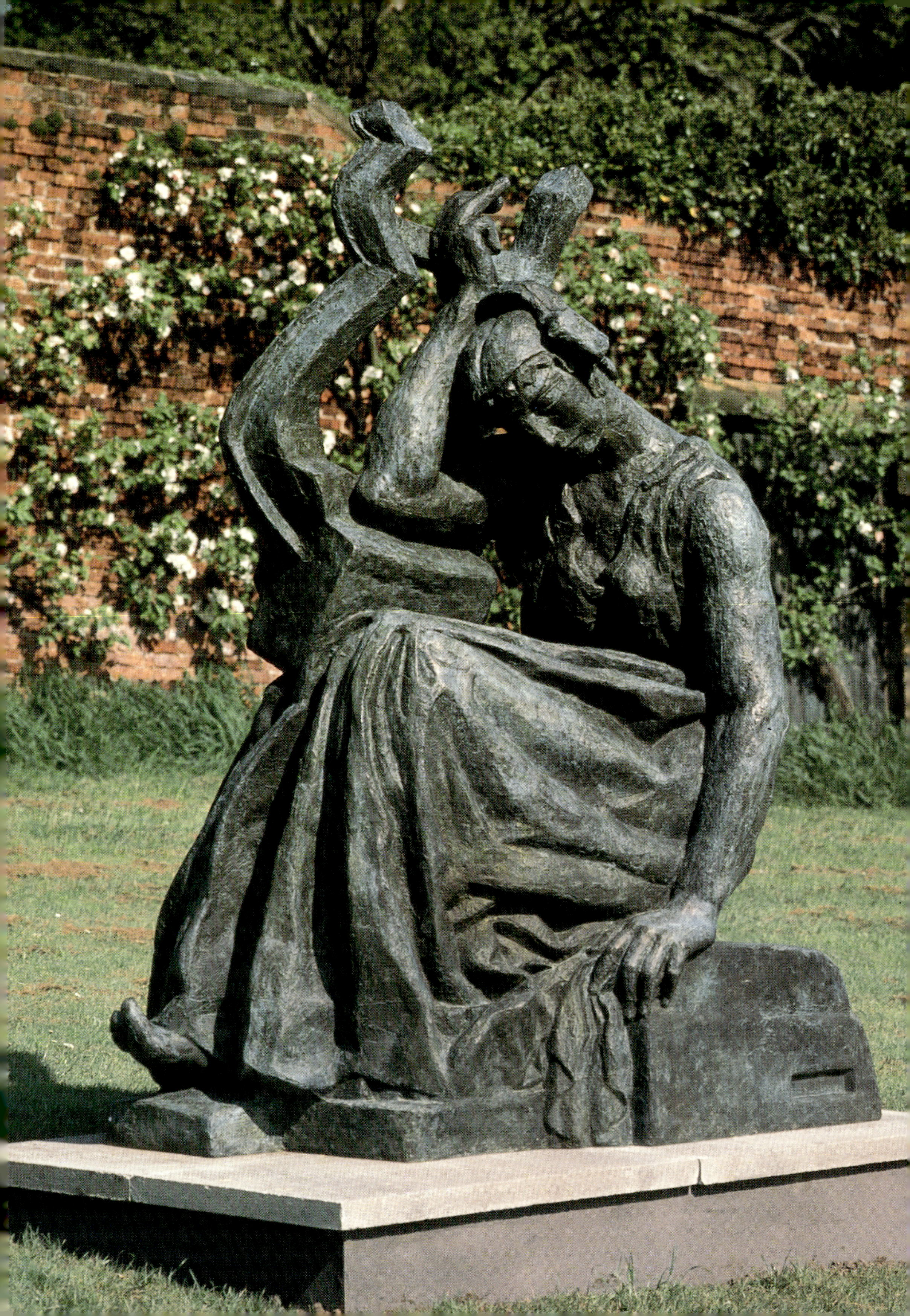

Previous pages

Grande Eloquence
Monumental Eloquence
1914-1917
3.72m x 1.20m x 1.20m

Grande Liberté
Monumental Liberty
1914-1917
3.72m x1.30m x 1.10m

Grande Victoire
Monumental Victory
1914-1917
3.72m x 1.30m x 1.10m

Grande Force
Monumental Strength
1914-1917
3.72m x 1.20m x 1.10m

These pages

Grande Sapho
Sappho (Large Version)
1887-1925
2.08m x 1.40m x 1.00m

Grande France
Monumental France
1924
8.15m x 0.93m x 0.95m
with
Grand Serpent
Monumental Serpent
1924
3.03m x 2.10m x 0.80m

Following pages

Grande Baigneuse Accroupie
Crouching Bather (Large Version)
1906-1907
1.02m x 0.90m x 1.04m

Grand Beethoven Accoudé
Beethoven Resting on His Elbow (Large Version)
1903
1.22m x 0.61m x 0.50m

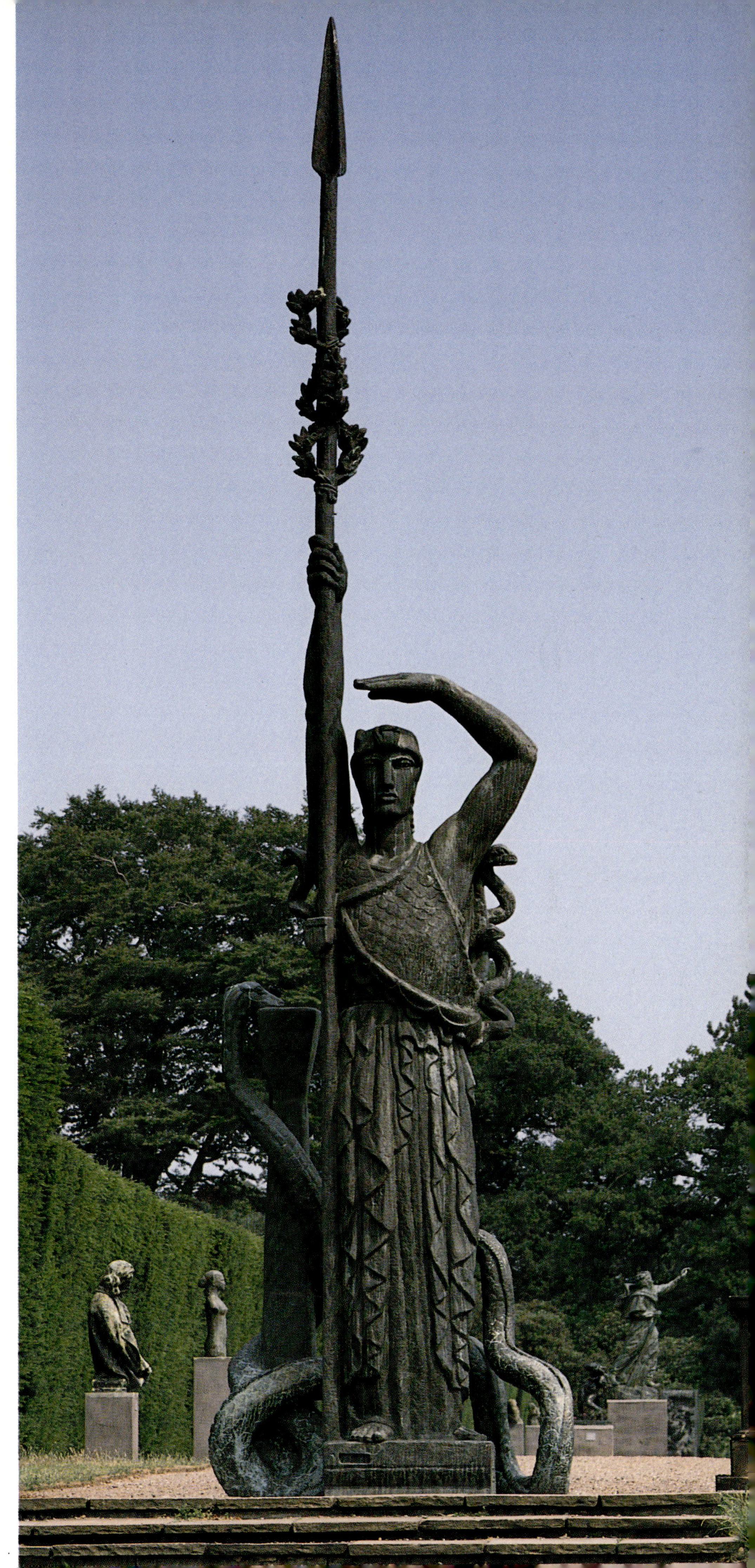

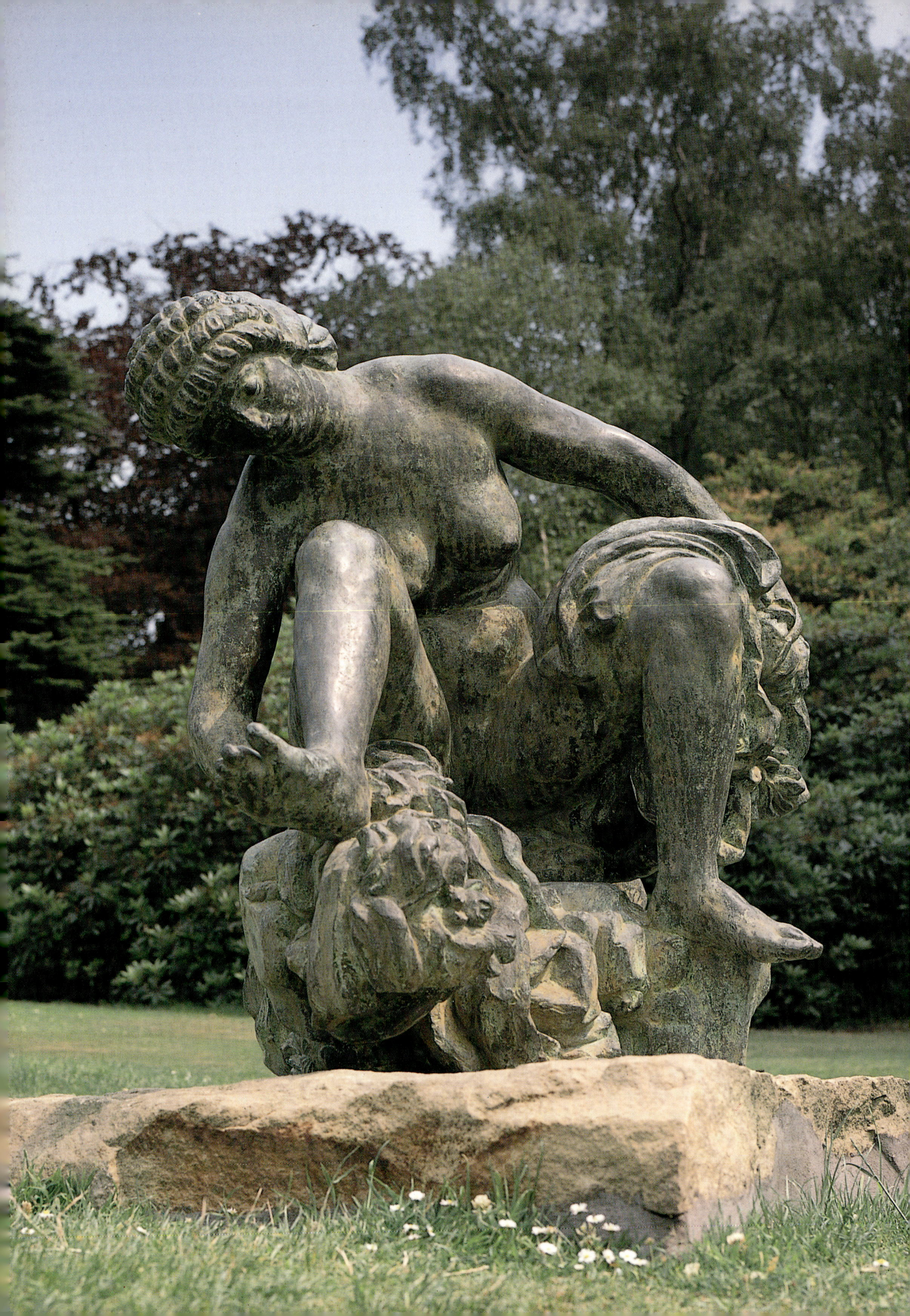

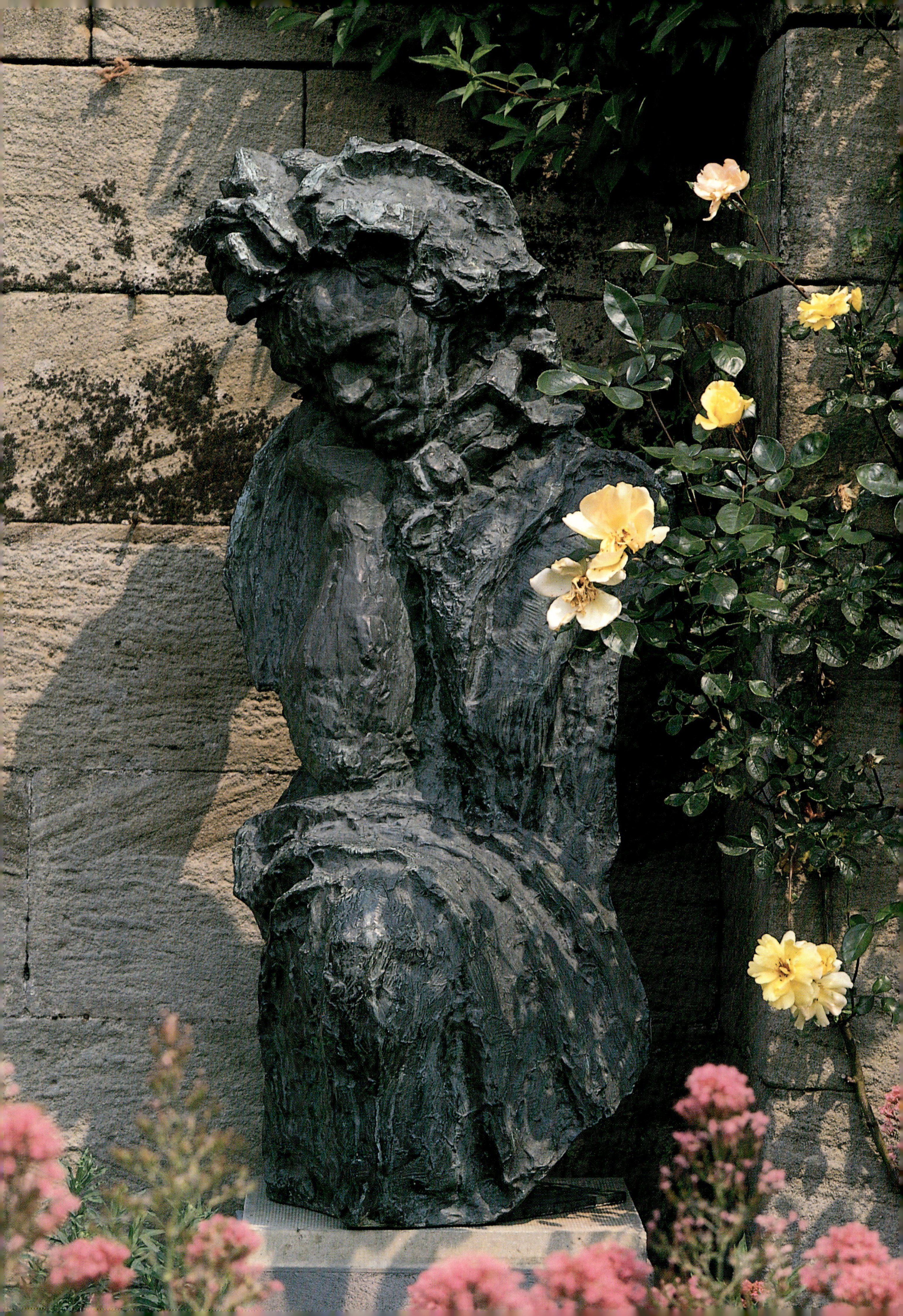

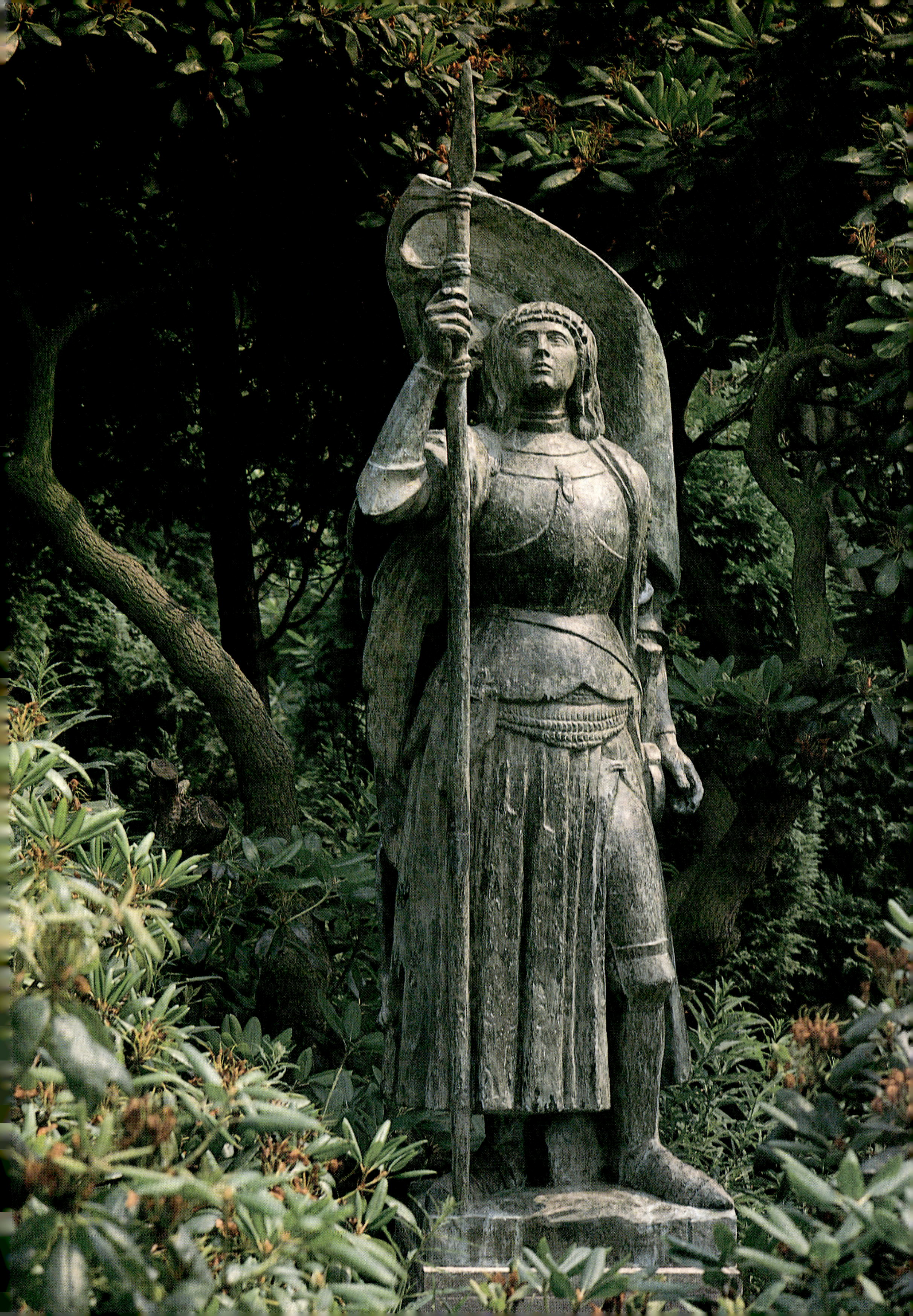

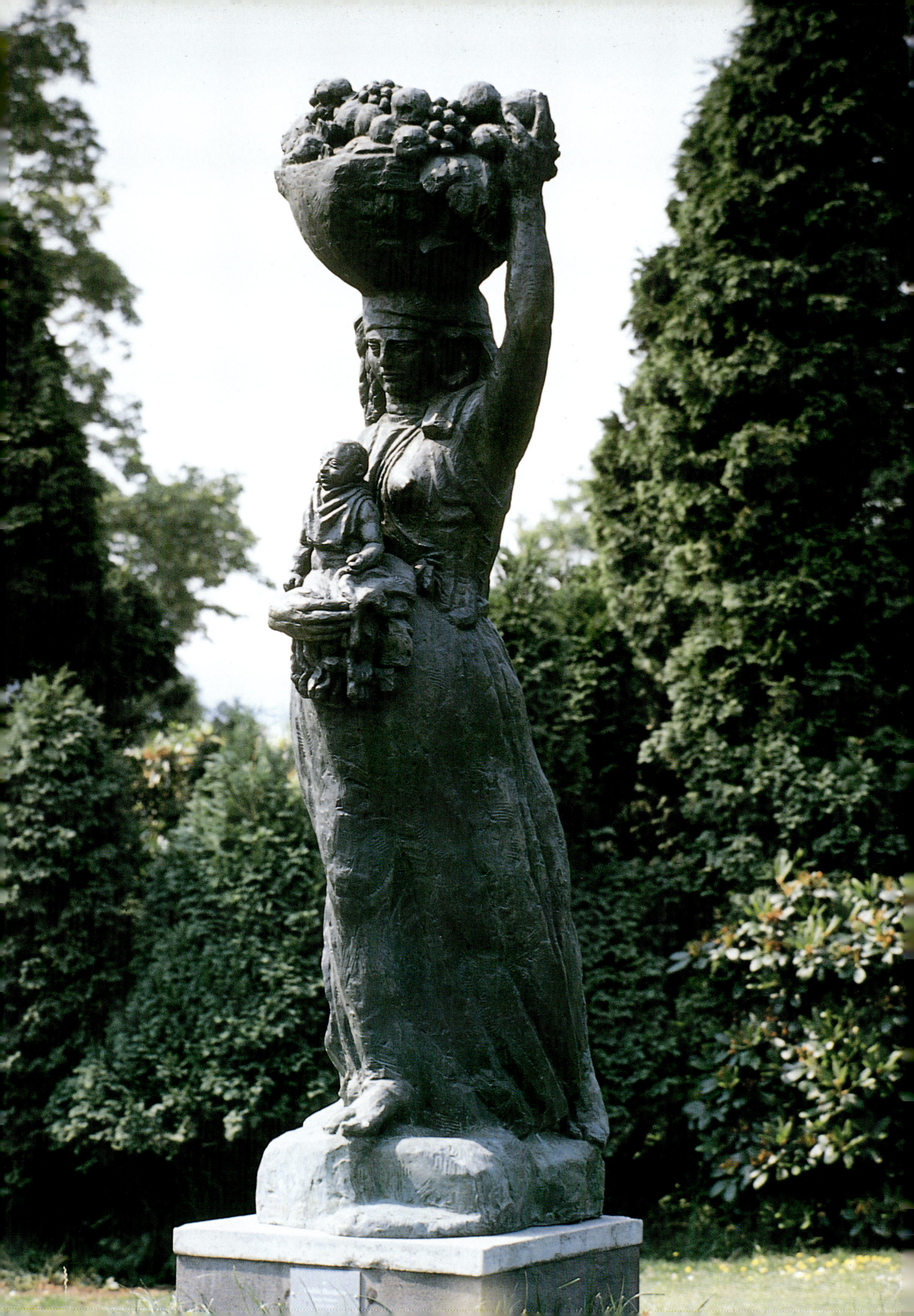

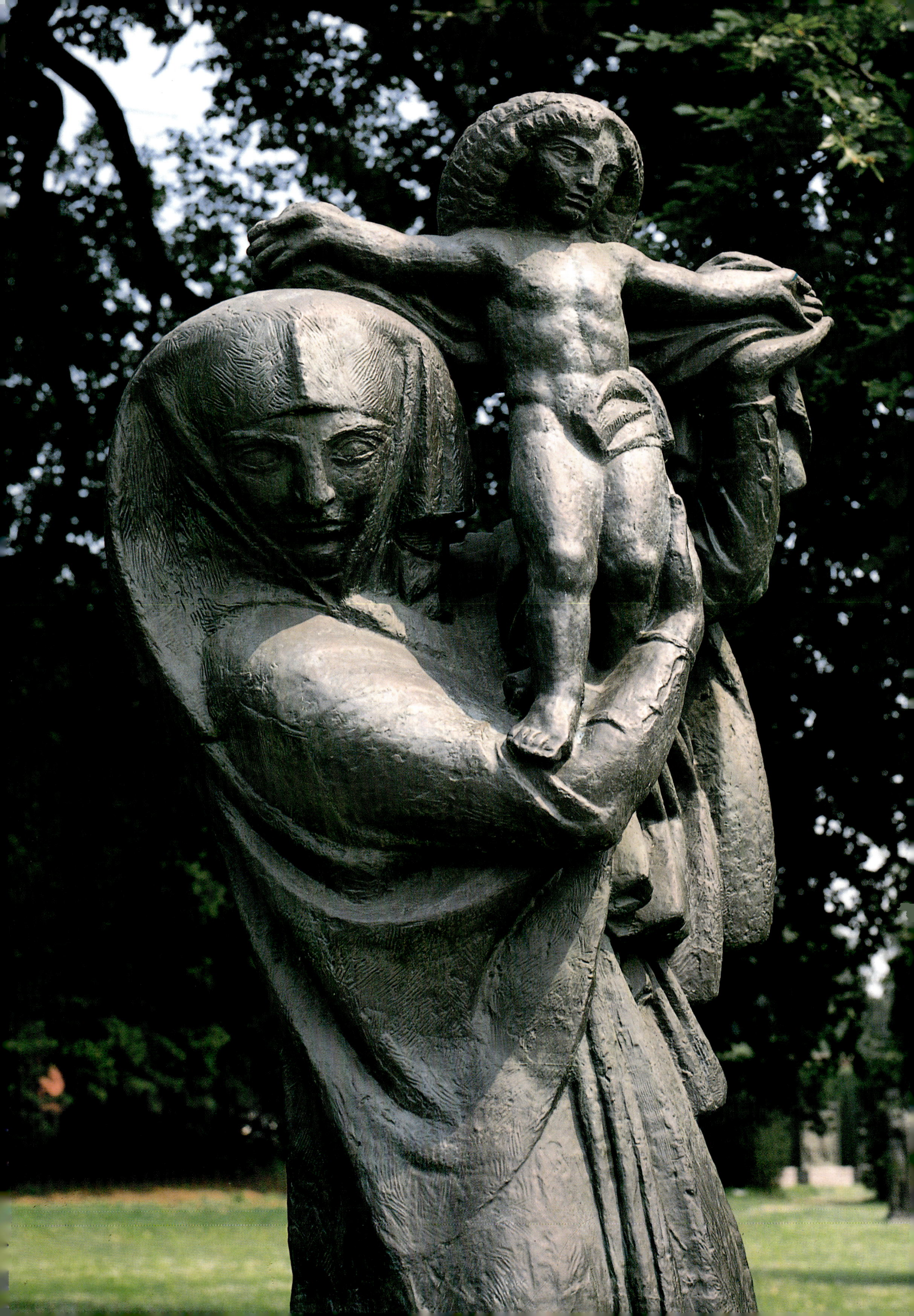

Previous pages

Grande Jeanne d'Arc à l'Etendard
Joan of Arc Bearing Standard (Large Version)
1909
2.31m x 0.75m x 0.55m

Grands Nobles Fardeaux
Noble Burdens (Large Version)
1910-1912
2.20m x 0.65m x 0.78m

These pages

Vierge a l'Enfant
Virgin and Child (detail)
1921
2.50m x 0.90m x 0.70m

Le Poète Adam Mickiewicz
The Poet Adam Mickiewicz
1924
2.62m x 1.70m x 1.10m

Following page

Grand Guerrier de Montauban avec Jambe
Monumental Montauban Warrior with Leg
1898-1900
2.11m x 1.60m x 0.59m

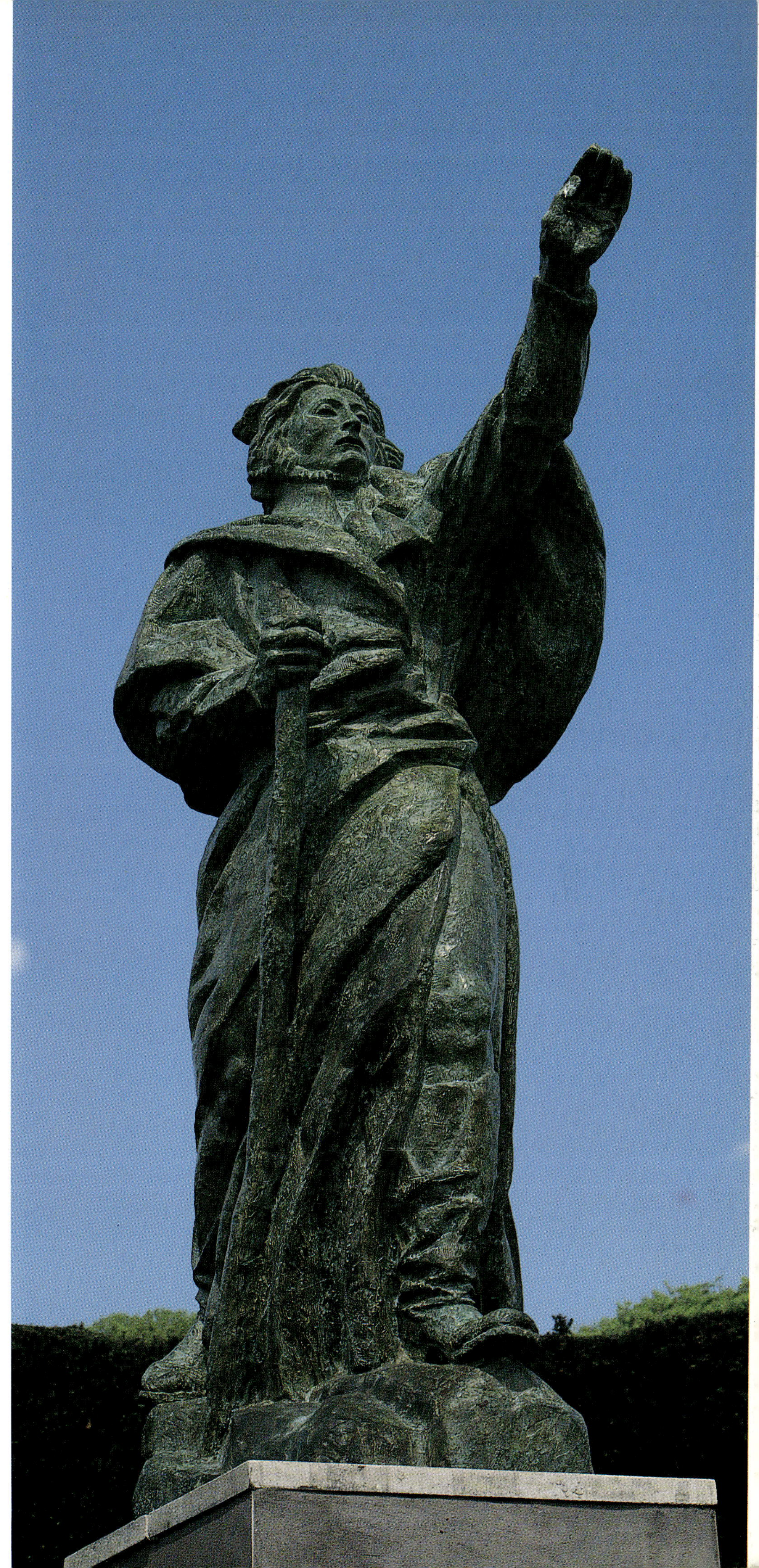

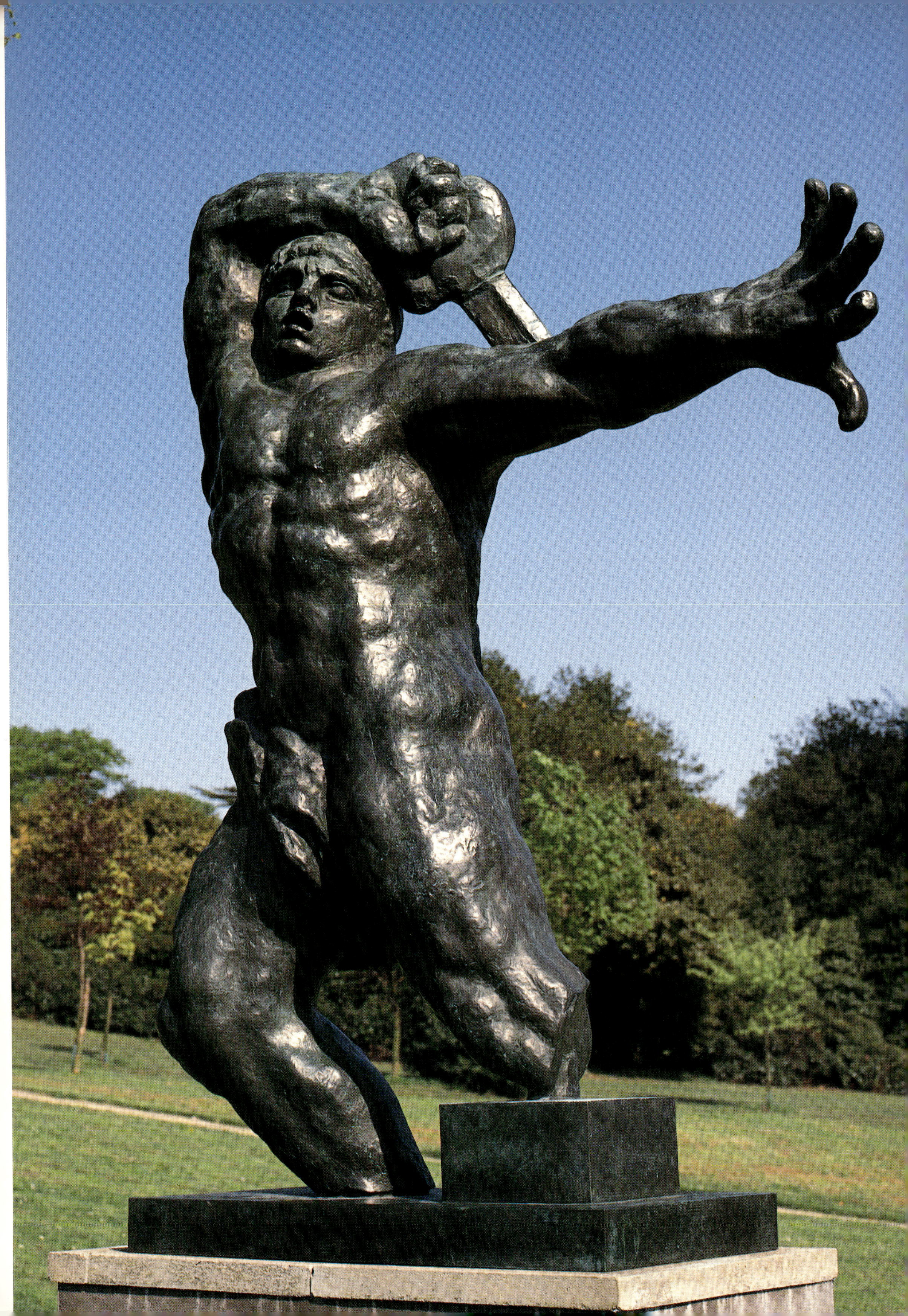

PENELOPE CURTIS

BOURDELLE MONUMENTAL SCULPTOR

The status of a monument-maker is a strange one. Bourdelle went down in history as a *statuaire* (maker of statues) rather than as a *sculpteur* (sculptor). He was considered to have had the nobility of mind and breadth of invention necessary to carry off great monuments. And yet, when we look only a little closer, we see that Bourdelle had few monuments erected. He worked on many more projects for monuments that were never erected.

Moreover his non-commemorative work (portrait and ideal) is much more extensive. Just as it is difficult for us to know to what extent Bourdelle should be seen as a monumental sculptor so it seems that he himself found it difficult to know where his priorities lay. He worked on some monuments for significantly long periods clinging tenaciously to their eventual erection. He cared enough about a few monumental projects to fight long and hard to win the commission enlisting whatever political help he could to support his case. He grieved over what he saw as a sad neglect of his abilities as a *statuaire* by the French state and clearly longed for a Parisian site for one of his creations. His reverence and passion for the outstanding individual, the cult hero, were very much in keeping with what was required of the man asked to commemorate such heroes. And yet, despite this, in Bourdelle's letters we often read of his despair over the lengthy and bureaucratic meanderings of the machinery which lay behind the erection of any public monument. Bourdelle did not get on notably well with the committees with which he had to deal. He described the commissions which he was obliged to fulfill as *"heavy burdens"*, as *"imperious, with their fixed deadlines"*, and himself as *"crushed by work, surrounded by furious committees"*. In 1929, the year of his death and the year of the erection of his first monuments in Paris to Adam Mickiewicz and Gustave Eiffel, Bourdelle wrote to a close friend, *"this year I will no longer allow myself to be the slave of great monuments regulated by committee"*. But though he may have described his non-commemorative work as *"works in liberty, the fruits of a few hours stolen from the great monuments"* he knew that it was only with the realisation of those monuments that he felt able to devote himself to more private work. *"...the immense bronze of Mickiewicz"*, he continued, *"gives me the right to behave more independently"*. Around the same time he wrote to his close friend Suares, *"The drama of Mickiewicz that I have carried with me for at least twenty-five years is finished....I may sleep"*. It is notable how long Bourdelle's most famous monumental projects took from inception to erection. His first large-scale commission (from his home town as was then customary), a monument to the dead of the 1870 Franco-Prussian War, and the monument to General Alvear both took ten years. The *Mickiewicz* project spanned twenty. It must have been significant in several ways that prewar works, conceived in an almost nineteenth century frame of mind, were erected only well after the First World War. When the fruits of Bourdelle's great monumental labours appeared in the public arena, when he finally had the opportunity to show himself as a *statuaire*, his work was perhaps already on the verge of appearing dated. Moreover his eventual coronation as a maker of great monuments occurred just as the age of *statuemania* was at last beginning to wane. Bourdelle had grown up with an unprecedented boom in public sculpture. This demand informed his own career as it informed that of his teachers and his peers. In the last years of the nineteenth century and the early years of this century Paris became home each year to yet more statues. The city, quite simply, could not take it. Concerned by both the overcrowding of the city's public spaces, and by the indifferent quality of work, the city councillors introduced measures in the years immediately preceding the War to regulate the flood of marble and bronze. As Bourdelle, already of mature years, emerged as a *statuaire* the rate at which statues were erected declined steeply. The decade from 1910 to 1920 saw less than a quarter of the monuments erected in Paris than in the previous decade and, while this was partly attributable to the War, the next decade followed suit. The provincial situation echoed Paris except in one important respect: the erection of First World War memorials in commune after commune provided *statuaires* with extensive job opportunities. Bourdelle engaged in this practice but what he really wanted was success in the capital and preferably with monuments to one man rather than to an anonymous army.

Nevertheless Bourdelle did not do badly. We can count a total of twenty-seven monuments which were erected. Figures can deceive, however, and in the field of monumental sculpture it is especially hard to make definitive tallies. When is a monument not a monument? One of the twenty-seven was erected after his death and this was a monument not conceived by the artist himself. One, the *Monument à Daumier,* was erected in a very much reduced and modified form using only the bust where Bourdelle had designed a whole monument. Others, such as the *Monument à Eiffel* in Paris, had originally been conceived as simple portrait busts. The use of such busts in commemorative fashion and the transition to *monument* came much later. The busts of Beethoven were private sculptural essays which have occasionally emerged into the public domain in the form of monuments. *Herakles l'Archer* was not executed with commemorative intent but over fifteen years after it was modelled it became the centrepiece of a monument in Toulouse honouring the footballer Maysonnié. The use of *La France* in a variety of locations, versions and commemorative functions during and after the artist's lifetime defies enumeration. (For some examples see pages 40 to 42 in the passage by Peter Cannon Brookes). This also highlights the particularly apposite note struck by Bourdelle in this figure which, in its formal dignity, lends itself to commemoration. Was Bourdelle coming to realise (some time after Maillol) that there was a trend towards an increasingly generic and abstract use of the monument? The popularity of *La France* would seem to confirm that such a trend was operative although for Bourdelle the figure is somewhat of an exception in his career as a *statuaire.*

This formal dignity is a note that is readily apparent in much of Bourdelle's work. It is this that tempts one to abandon a count of realised monuments and to appreciate instead a quality in the work that is indeed *monumental* whether or not it ever had a public and commemorative existence. Figures such as *Pénélope, Sapho* and *Le Grand Centaure mourant* immediately evoke the adjective monumental. They could have served, as did Malliol's sturdy classicised nudes, in a commemorative role. But Bourdelle did not define the monument in this way. He had been brought up in the latter half of the nineteenth century, educated by such great *statuaires* as Falguière, Dalou and Rodin, and for him the monument served to embody the likeness and the qualities of the individual. Moreover he believed in its function. Only when he moved away from the individual, as he did with *La France* which was originally designed to commemorate American intervention in the First World War, and with the *Victories of Hartmannswillerkopf* which ornamented a national ossuary, did his figures necessarily become generalised.

When we think of Bourdelle as a monumental sculptor we think of his huge works: the Montauban *Monument aux Combattants; Mickiewicz; Alvear; La France*. We are perhaps unthinkingly influenced by the common use of *monumental* as significantly large. These works clearly fit well with such a definition if indeed they have not helped to engender it. However, taking *monumental* in its strict sense of *commemorative*, we are bound to consider all Bourdelle's monumental work and we then come upon the surprising fact that a majority of it is not at all huge. Rather it is small-scale and unambitious with at least half the work adhering to the conventional formula of bust or portrait medallion on a pedestal, very occasionally embellished by a female muse figure, in itself another standard piece from the repertoire. It is against these rather obscure and provincial monuments that *Mickiewicz, Alvear* and *La France* stand out as exceptions. In the period in which Bourdelle was working *monumental* would be unquestionably taken first and foremost to mean *commemorative*. It is towards the end of his career that the shift towards a new meaning occurs and it is plausible that his own status and reputation played a part in this shift.

Grand Centaure Mourant
Monumental Dying Centaur
1914
2.88m x 0.80m x 1.85m

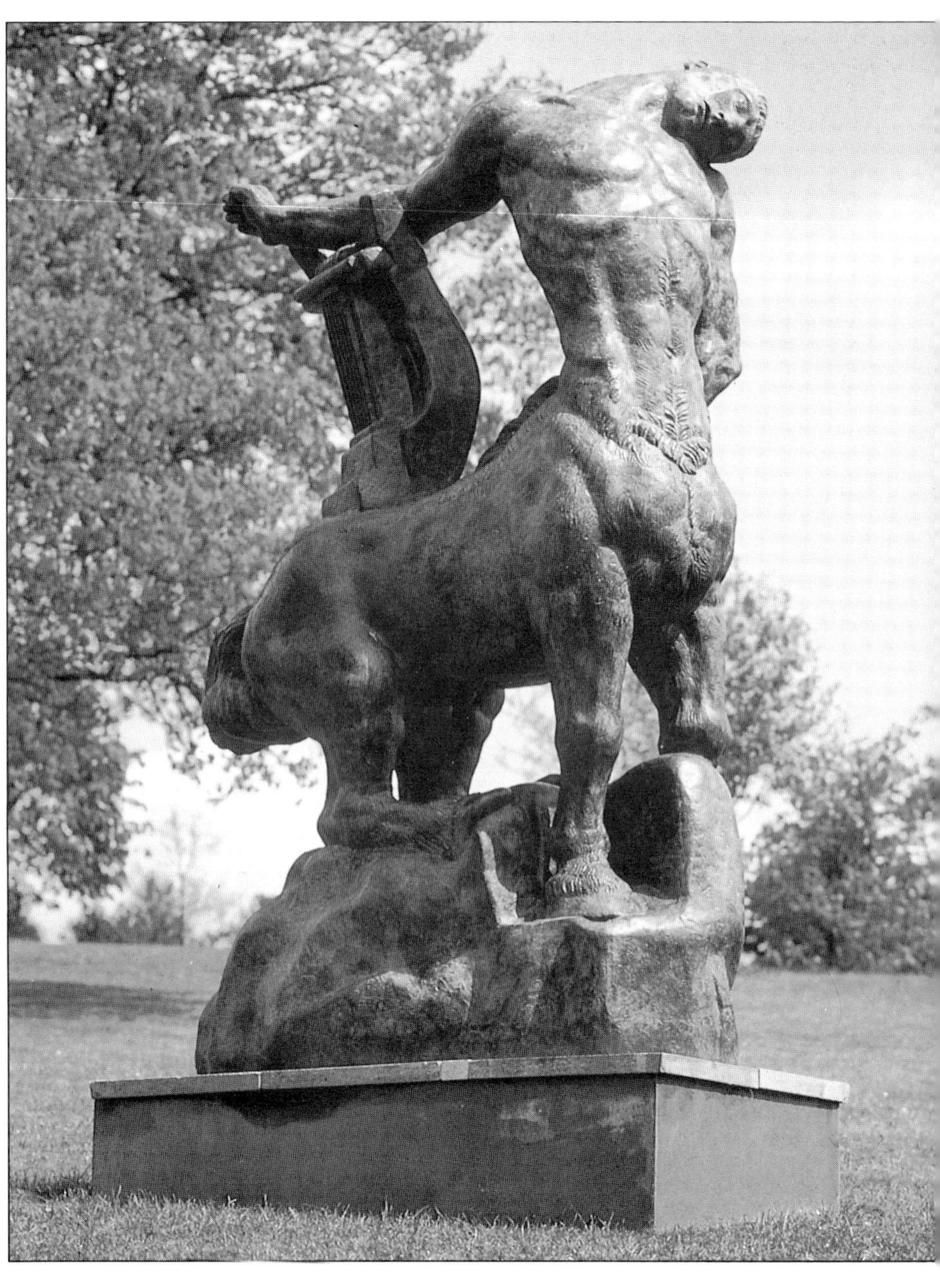

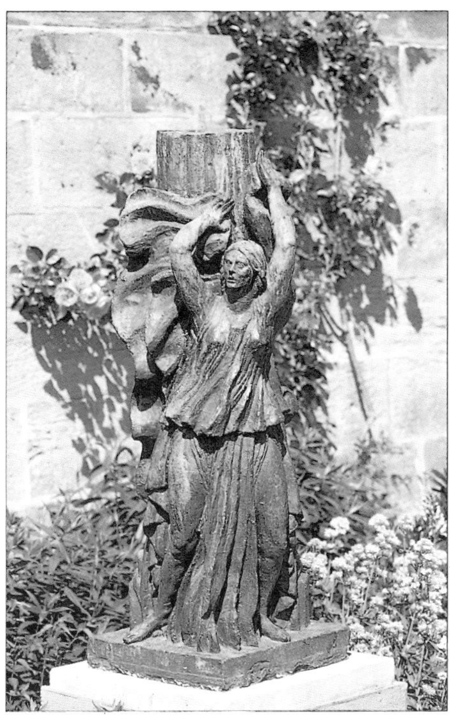

Grande Isadora Duncan
Isadora Duncan (Large Version)
1911
1.00m x 0.36m x 0.36m

To what extent does one judge the monument-maker by what he did not make, or rather by what was never erected? To do justice to the scale and scope of Bourdelle's conception of the monument we are bound to look at what was never realised. A particularly large proportion of the public artist's work is preserved only in the private domain. Preparatory work or documentation survives for nearly as many unrealised as realised monuments by Bourdelle. Some of these were sufficiently advanced for them to continue to enjoy a life of their own as independent art works. The model for the monument to the Députés, based on *Isadora Duncan*, is a notable example. Others, such as the projects to commemorate Baudelaire, Debussy, Moréas and Verhaeren, though less materially developed, were obviously cherished ideals. This becomes evident in Bourdelle's correspondence. The reasons for his works not being erected are various and not always transparent. Sometimes Bourdelle lost to a competitor, as with the monuments to the Députés, to Sarah Bernhardt, and to Debussy. Sometimes the project folded. Sometimes Bourdelle was accused of being unreasonably slow or expensive and the municipality withdrew the commission from him as was the case with the commission for a war memorial in Grenoble. With a surprising number of projects Bourdelle arrived on the field too late. With his death in 1929 it appears he lost the opportunity to commemorate Bolivar, Foch, Gallieni and the Marquis of Solages.

There is a sizeable number of recorded occasions on which Bourdelle chose not to take the opportunity to create a given monument. Whenever it was a case of the *statuaire* being chosen by competition Bourdelle declined to participate. He was vehemently against the choice of artist being made this way (as were most artists of any repute) and also opposed the use of the sketch model or maquette in this misleading and restrictive manner. He felt that it gave a false impression of security to the committee who was then loath to let the artist develop his idea. Nevertheless it seems likely that had Bourdelle been prepared to *"play the game"* he would have had further opportunities to erect his monuments just as, if once he had entered into a commission, he had been prepared to humour the committee, lower his prices, or keep to the deadlines. On the whole Bourdelle endeavoured to keep out of the fray stepping back as soon as it was clear that he was not the only *statuaire* being considered. Occasionally however the project meant, or came to mean, so much to him that he could not relinquish it. His desire to win the commissions for monuments to Bernhardt, Baudelaire, Debussy and most especially for the war memorials to the Députés and for the town of Toulouse brought him up against his colleagues and, in the latter two cases, involved him in lengthy behind the scenes manoeuvres.

Bourdelle's monumental sculpture has commonly been identified with his non-commemorative work: that is the decorative frieze for the facade of the Théâtre des Champs-Elysées in Paris. Its bold, chiselled, simplified lines, combined with the similarly bold architecture of Auguste Perret, caused a lot of critical enthusiasm both at the time of its erection in 1913 and throughout Bourdelle's career. Yet this is another work which stands out as exceptional in his oeuvre. There are other works which are perhaps more telling indicators of his formal developments as a monument-maker.

Bourdelle's career shows a subtle evolution in monumental form whereby he allows the pedestal or trunk of the monument to become monument itself. Moving from *Alvear* to *Mickiewicz*, Bourdelle has come to weld the two irrevocably. In the war memorial of Montceau-les-Mines pedestal and monument are indistinguishable. With his unrealised monuments to Rodin, Daumier and Brousse, and, those realised monuments of *La France*, *La Vierge d'Alsace* and *Pergaud*, the body is all monument and the monument all body. Although Bourdelle made formal inroads into the modernist conception of *monument as monument* he still adhered to its specifity, its connection to one man or one event. Moreover to see Bourdelle's monumentalism in terms of the Champs-Elysées project is much too restrictive depriving his career of its diversity and historical context. It would be to neglect Bourdelle's place in history, working as a *statuaire* in the aftermaths of two wars, in an era when there was both a need and a fashion to create monuments to victims or victors. Numerous sculptors were raising many monuments in this period. How those of Bourdelle stand up to being presented completely outside such a context (for what could provide a greater contrast for commemorative statues designed for town squares than a pastoral sculpture park?) is one consideration which we should have a fascinating opportunity to evaluate from this exhibition.

Penelope Curtis has recently completed a doctoral thesis on Bourdelle and contemporary monumental sculpture for the Courtauld Institute of Art in London.

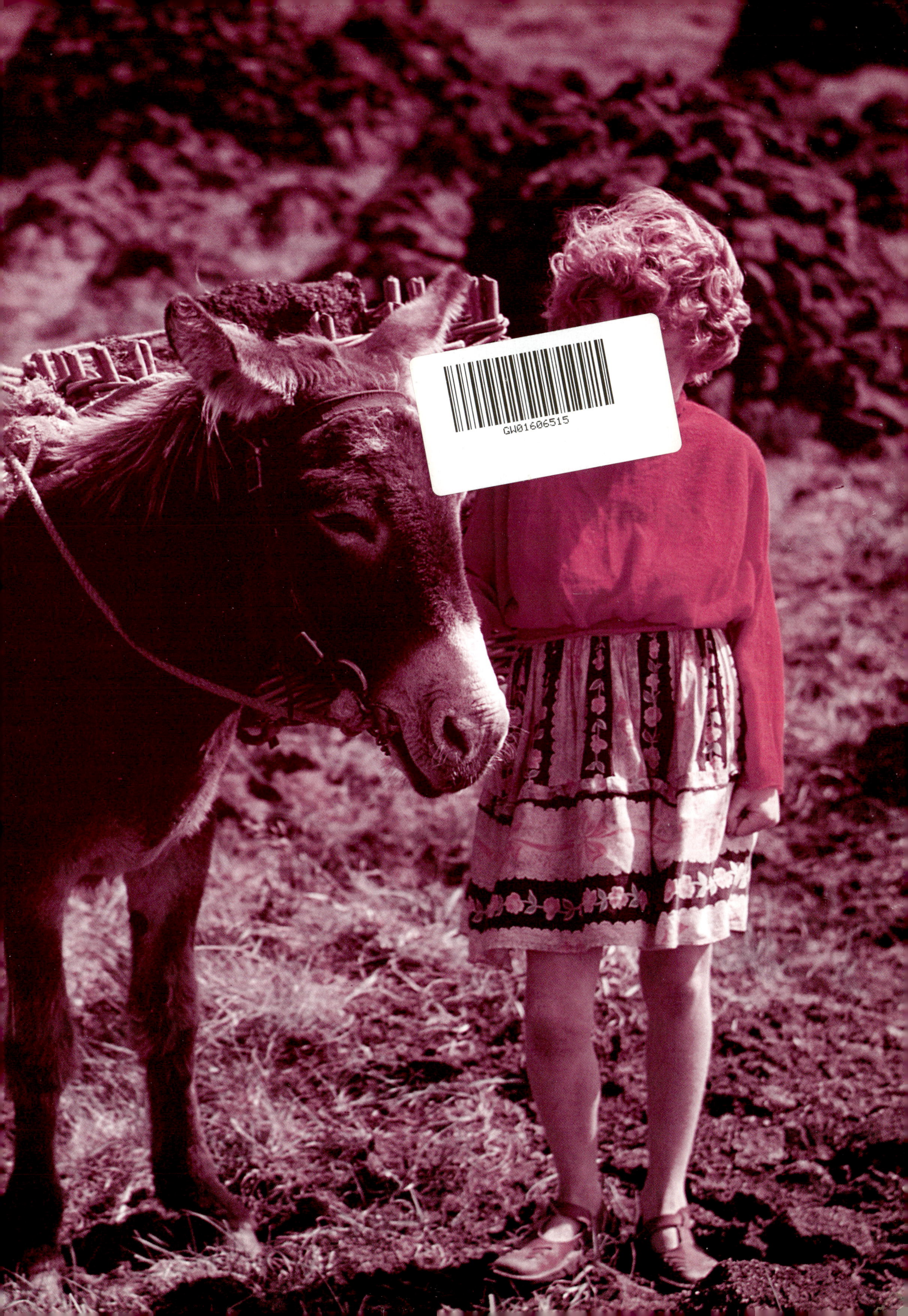

Hinde*sight*

John Hinde Photographs
and Postcards by John Hinde Ltd.
1935-1971

Hinde*sight*

The Irish Museum of Modern Art, Dublin.

Published by The Irish Museum of Modern Art, Dublin 1993
in association with Orchard Gallery, Derry & Cornerhouse, Manchester.

ISBN 1-873654:09-X

Designed and produced by Creative Inputs
Typesetting by Creative Inputs
Separations by Pentacolour, Dublin. Scantrans, Singapore.
Printed in Ireland by John Hinde Ltd.

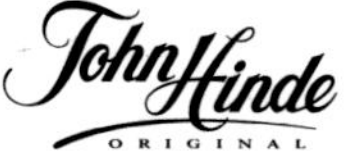

Supported by **JOHN HINDE INTERNATIONAL LTD.**

Contents

Acknowledgements

Without the full co-operation and generosity of John and Jutta Hinde this exhibition would not have been possible. Mr and Mrs Hinde have given unstintingly of their time and John Hinde allowed us unrestricted access to his personal records and photographs. We couldn't have wished for more assistance than was given.

Many have been generous with their time and hospitality during the preparation of the exhibition. Foremost among these are the photographers themselves, those who put John Hinde's ideas into practice: Elmar Ludwig, Edmund Nagele, David Noble, Peter O'Toole and Richard Beer. Journalist Stephen Quinn went to enormous trouble to interview another Hinde photographer, Joan Willis, who now lives in New Zealand. Artist Kenneth Webb and Clare Cryan provided valuable background information about the processes employed at John Hinde Ltd. Without their co-operation at an early stage the exhibition could not have started. Jack Coote, author, photographer, and pioneer in the development of commercial colour photographic processes shared his reminiscences of the 1930s when as Secretary of the colour group at the Royal Photographic Society he was, with his friend John Hinde, one of the few who could make colour prints.

Among the many other individuals who have contributed in various ways, whether through discussion or support, are the following: Emma Parsons, Rosie Lee, Sam Rea, Andre Moller, Julian Germain, Robin Grierson, Christine Redmond of the Irish Gallery of Photography, Brian Redmond, Hilary Roberts of the Imperial War Museum, Paddy Lydon, Ruth Nagele, Pam Roberts of the Royal Photographic Society, Susie Parr, Jean Brooke and Mrs Florence Cole of the Clark's Shoes Museum in Street, Sir Anthony and Lady Parsons, Dr A F J O'Reilly, Mr Jack Lynch, the staff of the British Library including the newspaper section at Colindale, Dorothy Sheridan of the Mass Observation Archive at Sussex University, Sir Stephen Spender, Harry Kerr of the Connaught Tribune, Madge Schelkens and John Joe Boyce.

John Hinde himself would like to acknowledge the particular support and encouragement given by his Mother in the early period and then by his wife Jutta, also Arthur Cox and Arthur Marsden, the late Bruno Vimercati of Milan, the brilliant innovator in photo processes and the many other specialists in Germany, Switzerland and Italy who provided technical support and expertise beyond the call of business.

The Irish Museum of Modern Art is especially grateful to John and Jutta Hinde, John Hinde International, Patrick Crane, Martin Parr, David Lee and Joe Lee.

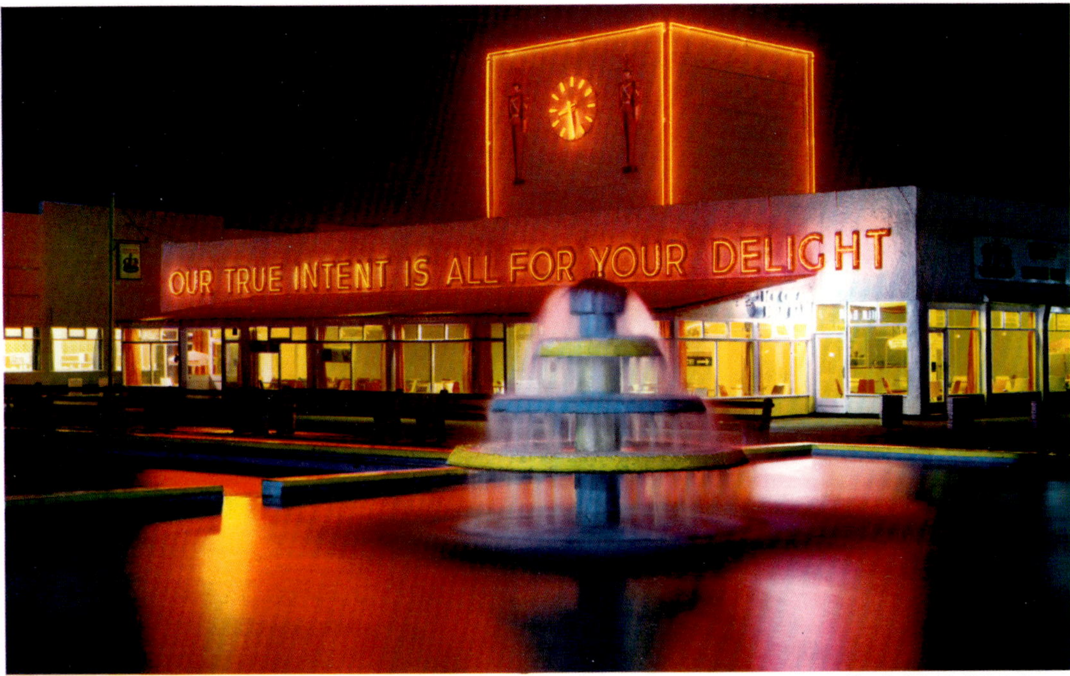

BUTLIN'S SKEGNESS— *Night Scene*

Photo: D. Noble, John Hinde Studios.

"My whole being was obsessed by the need to express myself through the medium of photography, and the style which was to determine the form of this expression gradually crystallised in thought.

"My thinking centred around the premise that a true photographic art form could only evolve as a consequence of using the tools and materials in the most logical way. The camera excelled in rendering fine detail and texture, and in freezing the beauty of action, and the subtleties of facial expression, and in the choice of suitable printing materials and techniques, these attributes could be enhanced. Then, realising that this in itself was insufficient, I added one further requirement - to become conscious of the greatness and fullness of life. By adding this spiritual element to the other practical considerations, the idea became complete.

"I had this sort of vision thing, of the top of the ladder when I was at the bottom, of fantastic colour photographs that I had never seen and that nobody else had ever seen and my whole aim was all the time how to get there, how to achieve it. You ever visualise Heaven?"

John Hinde

Foreword

John Hinde played a major role in the development of colour photography yet his work and career are hardly known even to those who would claim to know about photography and its history since the 1930s and 40s in these islands. This is because he eventually diverted from the purity of photographic practice as previously defined and moved on to become a producer of postcards - virtually a term of abuse within the hierarchy of photography and fine art.

Hinde's imagery is increasingly relevant in the context of the new attitude to colour photography since the mid 1970s, especially among younger photographers working in an art environment. Issues which are now commonplace in photographic practice and debate were present in Hinde's work from his beginning as an individual photographer and as the sensibility underpinning the postcard imagery of the John Hinde Company.

John Hinde seems to have had an unerring sense of what a mass audience wanted. Hinde images outsold all others. His version of an ideal view was no less constructed than that of Capability Brown and his landscaped gardens. Glimpses of wilderness especially from the West of Ireland were circulating widely in the changing world of the late 50s and 1960s.

Much contemporary colour photographic work is created in ways which echo the clear construction of Hinde imagery, from the World War II photographs to the Irish and Butlin's postcards which were ultimately produced by company photographers working to Hinde's compositional and colour formulae. Contemporary debates focus on the fictionalising potential of photography and there is widespread understanding that photographs are made and not taken. Contemporary emphasis on tableaux, exaggerated colour, issues of identity, manipulation of the process echo the work of Hinde.

However, it is important to remember that all of Hinde's images were produced for mass distribution, firstly in books then in postcard form. He had an almost evangelical sense of the role of colour photography in society, Colour was the servant of optimism and positive feeling. Hinde's achievement was firstly to refine the quality of the original photographs and secondly to develop printing techniques, through his own organisation, John Hinde Ltd., to maintain the photographic quality of the original, and to make it available to a mass audience. His enterprise extended technical limits not just for the sake of photography or art but for the purpose of communication.

Hinde documenting Butlins Holiday Camps seems a natural marriage of two similar philosophies born of the post-war period. The fact that both were created for and made available to a mass audience is part of their joint meaning.

Hinde, the man and the company, are best known for the postcards of Ireland which have become synonymous with a rural view of the country as a paradise which in turn became a key part of its official marketing to an outside world. This view has become deeply embedded to a point of iconic invisibility in the minds of anyone who has seen, bought or received a Hinde postcard. It is just as fundamental as the sense of the ideal in 16th and 17th century landscape painting whose compositional structure and aspirational content Hinde employed in his own work.

This exhibition and publication are timely therefore, in our present cultural moment. When artists debate their role in society, when Ireland and other similar countries reconsider the issue of identity constructed over many decades, when the properties of photography are being tested and when an important period of recent social and cultural history is being re-examined it is right that the work of John Hinde and the Hinde Company should be exhibited widely. The Museum and Gallery environment which is now part of widespread cultural debate provide the necessary critical environment and a long overdue acknowledgement of Hinde's own contribution to the development and application of colour photography.

The Irish Museum of Modern Art is extremely grateful to photographer Martin Parr, writer David Lee, and film-maker Joe Lee who brought the project to the museum.

But none of this would have been possible without the unreserved co-operation of John Hinde himself and of the present management of John Hinde International in Dublin.

Declan McGonagle
Director
Irish Museum of Modern Art

(Opposite circa 1942)

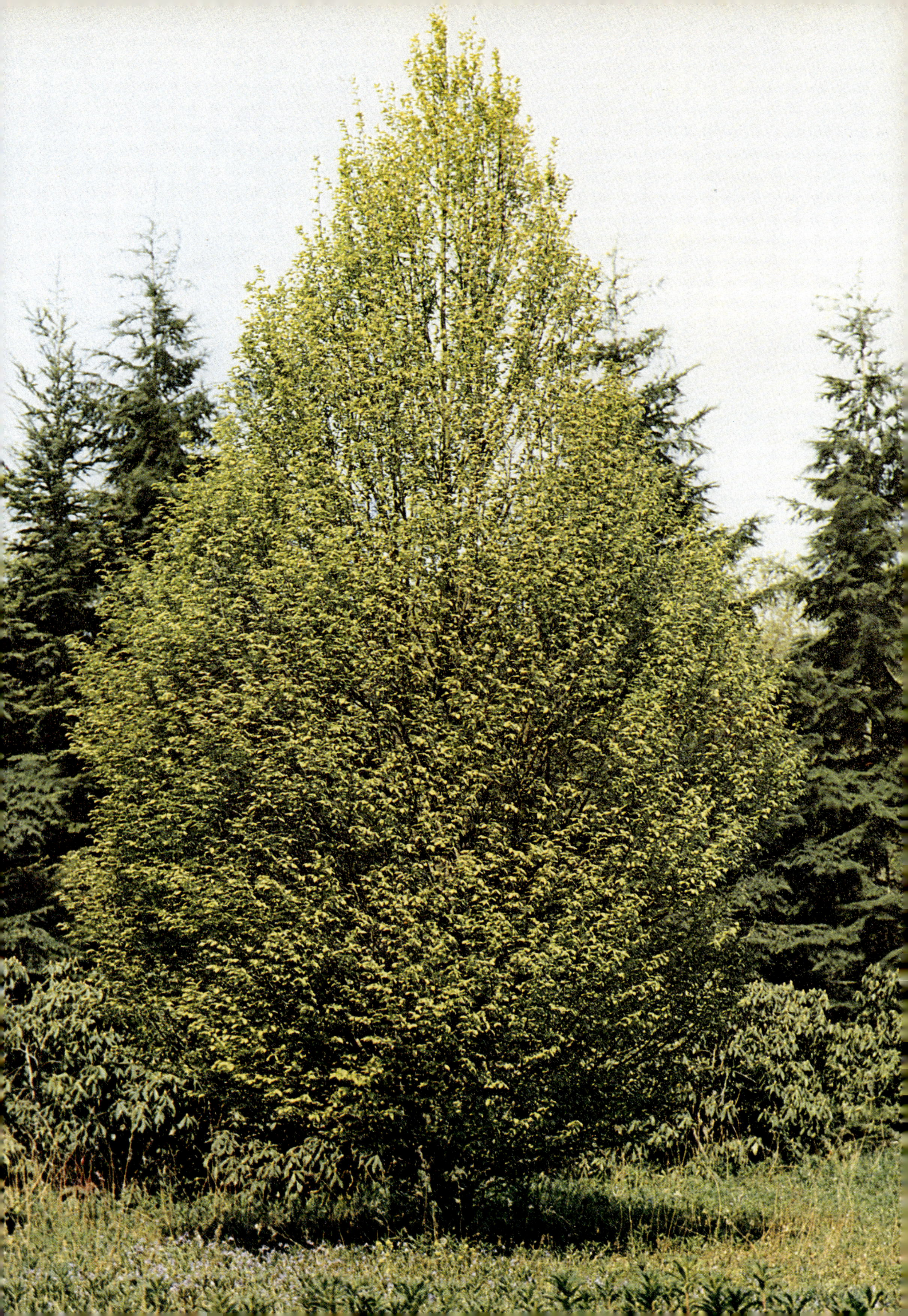

Introduction

David Lee

"Using the medium of colour photography I wish to emphasise the beautiful aspects of the world in which we live and to present these images in a style which would enable them to be instantly understood and appreciated by a mass audience."
John Hinde

When John Hinde started his company manufacturing colour postcards in 1956 it was perfectly timed. All the ingredients - social, personal and economic - required to ensure its success were in place. A period of unparalleled industrial expansion was beginning in Ireland and new policies were being developed to encourage entrepreneurs - such as Hinde - who had good ideas. Also, Ireland was being promoted abroad as a kind of primitive paradise of wild, unspoilt landscapes and charming, yarn-spinning rustics, ideal spectacles for the new kind of mobile tourist who wanted to see life as it used to be lived. Bord Fáilte, the Irish tourist authority, needed allies like Hinde to help them in their sales drive to market Ireland as this type of commodity.

Apart from it being a financially propitious moment to set up a business, Hinde himself had developed over the previous 20 years all the various skills which would enable him to make better postcards than any of his competitors. In terms of practical knowledge, there were few anywhere in the world who could call upon Hinde's experience of making colour photographs. Nor could they match Hinde's ability to reproduce accurately the qualities of a photograph on the printed page, because before Hinde this was precisely where colour photography fell down. It did not reproduce well. Colour photographs printed in books or on posters tended to resemble watercolours or pastels: Hinde wanted them to look as good as the original photographic prints.

But what was most important to the success of his venture was that the time had arrived for Colour, and not just for colour photography. John Hinde Ltd started fortuitously at the beginning of a new Pop culture which would interpret bright colours as synonymous with freedom, choice and optimism, qualities which corresponded precisely with Hinde's own simple, Christian ideals of giving satisfaction to others through visual images. It is not an exaggeration to say that for Hinde colour photography was a life force.

His interest in photography went back to boyhood. From the day the eleven-year-old (in 1927) received in the post a pinhole camera he'd sent for from 'Modern Boy', he was hooked and virtually all his spare time was spent taking and developing pictures. From the beginning he recognised the importance of becoming a master of technique, if he was to command the ability to present his visual images with maximum impact. Hinde is the first to admit that initially his knowledge of composition was gained from studying the pages from 'The Amateur Photographer' and the other prize-winning prints he saw in photographic society exhibitions, which themselves had been constructed according to the same precepts. Over the year as he developed a clearer concept of the purpose he wished his photography to fulfil, he developed a simple but distinctive style of his own. Hinde, and the photographers who would later work for him, used the basic academic compositional formulae originally devised for 17th century landscape painting: vertical markers at the sides with diagonals through the middle. Nevertheless, although his knowledge of photographic art never developed much beyond a textbook level, his artistic awareness was more than adequate for the goals he eventually set himself. In this exhibition and book it is not our intention to trumpet the discovery of a neglected artist so much as of a neglected innovator. Hinde had no desire to be an artist, as such, although in the end, with his postcards, he was self-consciously intent on producing a popular art form for the common man. He wanted instead to appeal to a mass public, for which purpose pretenses to art were no good to him. At least in this century, 'Art' and 'The Public' have tended to regard one another with a deep-rooted mutual disdain.

As soon as he saw the crude attempts at colour photographic printing of the local chemist in Street, Somerset, where he was brought up, Hinde was sold on achieving the perfect colour photograph. Following years of study and the construction of special equipment he had designed himself, not to mention countless failures and setbacks, he became adept at tri-colour carbro, a process so long and complicated and involving so many separate operations that it took two days to make one print. It was typical of Hinde that although carbro was among the more difficult methods, he chose it because it delivered the highest quality results. Nothing was too much trouble for Hinde providing the end product could not be bettered.

It was not until after the second World War 1945-6 that professional photographers and the general public were offered films enabling them to take snapshots in colour. In the 1930s colour photography was in its infancy. There was no shortage of processes - around 400 by 1938 - but each required immense time and labour not to mention biblical patience. The colour photography existing in Ireland and Britain at that time was done either by a handful of 'artistic' pictorial photographers who exhibited their impressionistic efforts at the annual exhibition of the Royal Photographic Society, or by commercial photographers exploiting the considerable potential of colour for use in advertising (in 1936 at the annual advertising industry exhibition one in seven pictures was in colour). Additionally, a small number of chic portrait photographers offered lines in colour. By the end of the decade one company, Colour Photographs Ltd, was alone making 99 per cent of colour prints. The company stopped trading at the start of the war leaving the medium where it had been ten years before. Needless to say colour photography was expensive, with its slow exposure times and the necessity to use costly and cumbersome special apparatus (one-shot cameras or repeating backs) to expose three glass plates simultaneously each through a different colour filter. It was inevitable, therefore, that in much the same way as the development of black and white photography in the 1840s had been left to devoted amateurs, the flame of colour photography was kept alight in the early 1940s by a small coterie of fanatics. Hinde was one of this select band.

Hinde observed with interest (and lectured on) the development of colour photography during the late 1930s. Having seen the stranglehold exerted by Colour Photographs Ltd - colour photography in Britain compared to the progress being made in Germany and America he concluded that the future of the medium depended upon the ability of individual photographers to master the entire process - and that must inevitably include the most difficult part, printing.
By 1940 Hinde was among the most important promoters in Britain of the potential applications of colour photography. However, few took any notice of him and, given the fact that there was a war on, even fewer were prepared to invest in the medium's future.
At this stage in his career Hinde was ahead of his time, and knew it.

In 1941 he started work for Adprint, a publisher's producer, working with William Collins, where he took photographs for a series of books entitled Britain in Pictures. It was during work on this project that Hinde made an important discovery: he realised that his ability to make a near perfect colour print counted for nothing if the quality he struggled to achieve was lost when mechanically reproduced. (It is well to remember that this period marked the beginning of the reproduction of colour photographs in books. The first British book exclusively illustrated by colour photographs was England in Colour, published in 1937. Many of the pictures for this volume were taken by Frank Newens, who was one of the fanatics and had taught Hinde how to make carbro prints at the Reimann School in 1937). Hinde had already investigated continental methods of reproducing colour photographs during a trip to Germany in the summer of 1939 and had returned with samples of colour printing of a quality unattainable in Britain.

During the next six years Hinde worked on a series of books, mainly related to gardening and horticulture, in which he attempted to improve the fidelity of the printed reproduction to the image as photographed. Accuracy of colour reproduction was essential for the purposes of identification. He knew instinctively that a popular audience for colour photography could never be won until the ability to reproduce colour attractively, glossily, caught up with the ability to make a startling colour print. By the end of his learning process in 1945, he knew what conditions were necessary to make photographic print and photographic reproduction all but indistinguishable.

Although he was now in possession of the technical skills, Hinde's personal ambitions were as yet unfocussed. Then, in 1944, he visited a circus in order to take pictures, both monochrome and colour, for his book British Circus Life. He was instantly addicted and he would work for circuses either in a managerial role or as a owner of his own show for much of the next ten years. It was while he was with the circus that he visited Ireland for the first time, although his mother and his own children were born in Ireland and Hinde himself was an Irish national. During that period his photography was sidelined. Why should a man from a privileged background, renowned as an authority on colour photography, suddenly give himself to a popular entertainment like the circus?

Hinde's parents were religious, first as Quakers and later (as a result of an illness which permanently crippled their son) as Christian Scientists. Hinde himself, though not exactly religious in a church-going sense, believes in spiritual values, the perfectability of man, self-improvement through hard work etc. Working on Reco's circus, and later for Chipperfields and Bertram Mills (not to mention his own John Hinde Show) was the first time in his life that he had dealt with, and felt under an obligation to, a large public. As a conscientious objector during the war (a designation he insisted upon despite the fact that his disability would have automatically exempted him from military services) his job with Reco's was a morale booster, not only for him personally but for the thousands of bomb-weary civilians who entered the Big Top. Hinde loved seeing people entertained:

"Working on the circus you saw the pleasure being given to thousands of people of all ages who came to the performances. It gives you a good feeling if you see people going away from the evening, all of them happy. You feel as though you've done something towards creating this situation. The circus was touching the lives of many more people than anything I had done before and I suppose that, in the end, I felt that this was something really worthwhile. And on a more practical level, the need to fill an auditorium with 7000 people twice a day meant that I learnt a lot about communicating with the man in the street."

It is not necessary to labour the obvious connection between the circus and colour picture postcards as popular diversions inspiring clean fun, frivolity, pleasant sentiments and good memories. But the seed on engendering happiness and well-being in a large audience had germinated in Hinde's mind.

When his own short-lived show closed in 1955, Hinde was temporarily directionless. While he was touring Ireland he had been taking colour photographs of beauty spots and it was in these that, almost in

Illustrated Magazine 1944

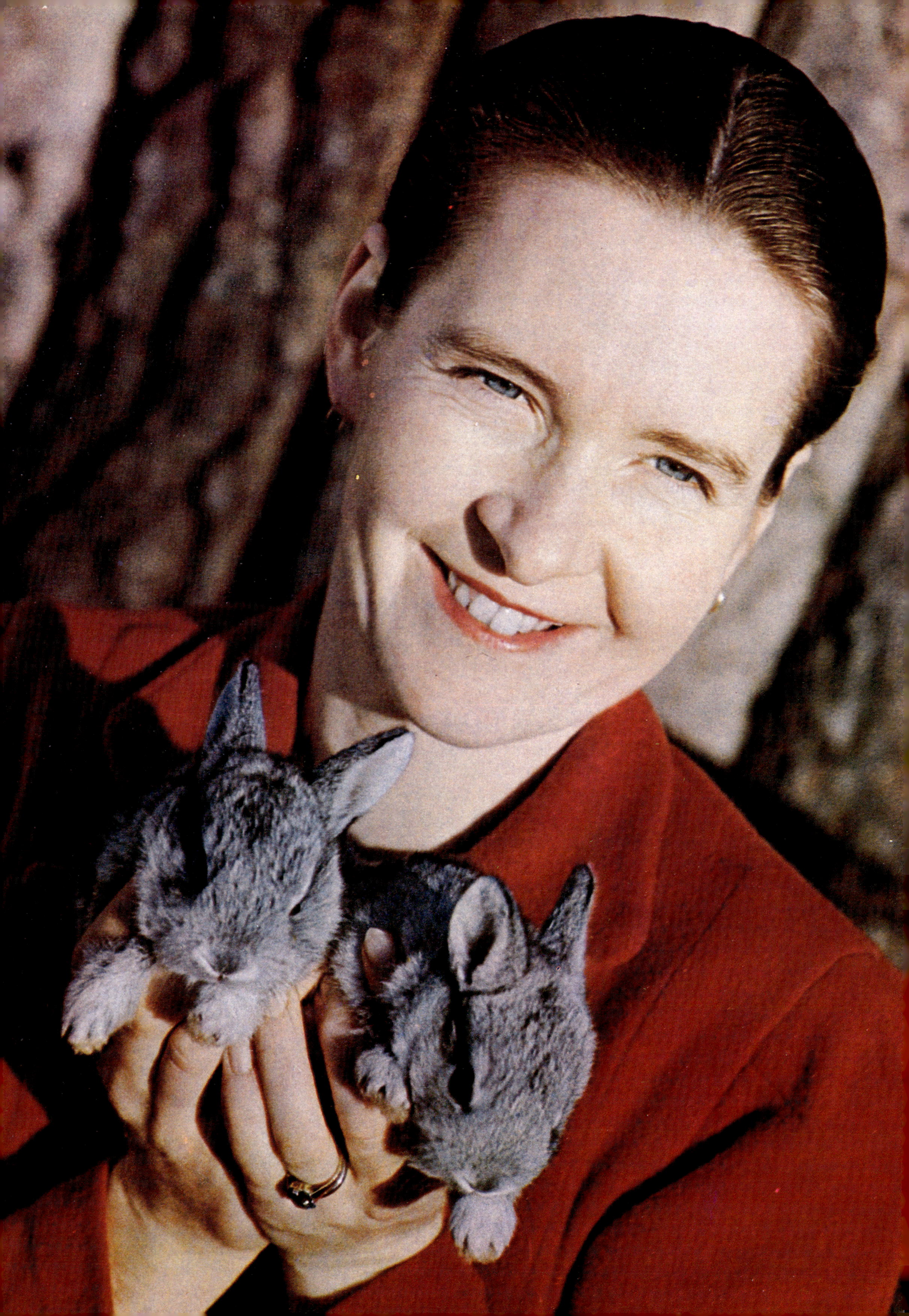

despair at his enforced inactivity, he identified an opportunity. He would start printing his photographs as postcards. With this in mind, over the period of a year, he perfected the mass reproduction of his original colour photographs using a Rotaprint office duplicating machine, which he modified in order to give better results. Throughout, it was always his intention to make the reproduced image look like a photographic print. The printing equipment was installed in his house in Bulloch Harbour on the outskirts of Dublin. This was the start of John Hinde Ltd. He had the photographs, the technical know-how to reproduce them better than any competitor and - the final ingredient - the fervently held belief that he knew what people wanted from a picture.

His initial task with the postcards was to make the picture fit the aim. Hinde had discovered much earlier that unsatisfactory details could be corrected in the reproduced version of a picture by tampering with the separation negatives from which the final image was printed. He brought this idea of improving a photograph to fruition at John Hinde Ltd. For example, he had realised when taking pictures of flowers in the early 1940s that certain subjects have to be encouraged to look their best. As he would say later in a different context: the lily has to be gilded. Petals had to be waxed in position and stalks laboriously reinforced with wire. And equivalent techniques could be applied to landscape. Hinde realised that the reality of a view, and the image of that same landscape in a tourist's memory, were not the same. Colours were stronger in the mind's eye and all best aspects of a location were magically moved into the same picture. Hinde attempted to make his postcards correspond more closely to the image of a place which tourists might carry away in their heads. He did this by stage-managing the photograph down to the last detail and then intensifying colours and erasing unwanted details during the post-production phase.

This process of constructing a photograph seems like a falsification, and indeed it is. But it was not something new. One objective in staging an exhibition of John Hinde's photographs is to convince audiences once and for all that all photographs are constructed. They don't just happen. On the contrary somebody with a definite aim organises them. And this has been true since photography was first announced to the public in 1839. One of the earliest photographs reveals a scene showing the staged 'suicide' of the photographer himself. Hippolyte Bayard did this in 1840 as a joke, and the joke was that photographs could be made to lie. What popular audiences insist on interpreting as photographic truth is always something constructed by the photographer: it is the photographer's own truth and not some universally applicable one. When John Hinde changed the skies in his postcards to something brighter and more summery, he was following a tradition well-established by Victorian landscape photographers. In 19th century pictures the reason for over-printing clouds was forced upon photographers because land and sky required vastly different exposures - details of both could not be achieved in the same picture. Then there was retouching, a practice ubiquitous since 1854. In short, few photographs are what they appear to be at first sight, and John Hinde's are no exception. When David Noble, one of Hinde's photographers, said that "each picture was a bit of a production" he was not exaggerating.

By introducing bright foreground colours into his cards, Hinde was following a naive concept of colour picture-making which was at the same time being discouraged by art experts in magazines. Using blatant primary colours was considered unsubtle and the wrong way forward. Hinde was probably unaware of these strictures and carried on regardless.
He did what experts said was wrong: he stuck primary colours prominently in the foreground to accentuate to viewers that, yes, they were looking at a COLOUR photograph. Critics might have been unimpressed by such garish crudity but Hinde proved that this was what people were prepared to pay for. He was shrewd enough to realise that an audience used to seeing black and white pictures didn't just want to see a bit of colour tinting, it wanted to see A COLOUR PHOTOGRAPH. In Hinde's case this

meant red pullovers, foreground lupins, overhanging rhododendrons, ochre cottages, azure Mediterranean skies (even in Donegal), golden beaches, yellow cars and blood orange sunsets over Dublin Bay. Astonishingly, even this kowtowing to what was perceived as the lowest common denominator of taste was not a Hinde invention. Strident foreground reds were already the stock-in-trade of touristic colour photographers. Hinde was merely responsible for adapting what was already becoming an accepted style in colour photography for consumption by a mass public.

And even if the bright colours were not part of the actual photograph, existing colours could be cleaned during the separation stage before printing, or changed completely. Hinde spared no expense in post-production techniques to ensure that the picture conveyed precisely the optimistic mood that he felt people wanted. In the end, when all the ingredients in the Hinde picture style were in place, and other photographers had begun to take the pictures according to his prescriptions, Hinde himself stopped taking photographs because of business pressures.

Hinde's was a simple style designed to produce a postcard in which colour was equated with happiness. He devised and perfected his 'look' using Irish views and then exported it successfully, first to Britain and then to dozens of carefully selected foreign markets. Hinde tended to be a difficult person with whom to communicate unless it was relevant to an immediate problem. Increasingly throughout his life he depended for his inner strength upon the observation of beauty in nature which he considered to be the work of a Master Artist. This explains his involvement with Africa - its open spaces, its wildlife and its peoples. Hinde has explained this simple philosophy:

"Beauty is an attribute of Good or God. It's one of the things which make up our concept of divinity. We need to be uplifted rather than depressed. To me pictures should always convey a positive, good feeling, something which makes people happy, which makes them smile, which makes them appreciate some tenderness."

How much of an innovator was John Hinde? Colour photography and its reproduction were already well advanced when Hinde issued his first six postcards in 1957. From the early 1950s onwards publishers were beginning to exploit the possibilities for colour at a time when colour was being introduced in other areas of life. Coloured furniture in moulded plastic, coloured formicas, coloured cars, coloured ('designed') packaging for food were all first introduced in the 1950s. Colour supplements arrived in newspapers from 1962 followed by colour TV in 1967. The introduction of colour, the start of John Hinde Limited and a period of economic prosperity and expansion began almost simultaneously and advanced together. Hinde was perceptive enough to realise that the time was ripe for an inexpensive product based on colour photography that was focussed, glossy and depicted a proverbially 'beautiful' subject, produced to the highest quality standards. He was the first popular successful colour photographer in the British Isles.

David Lee is a writer and editor of Art Review.

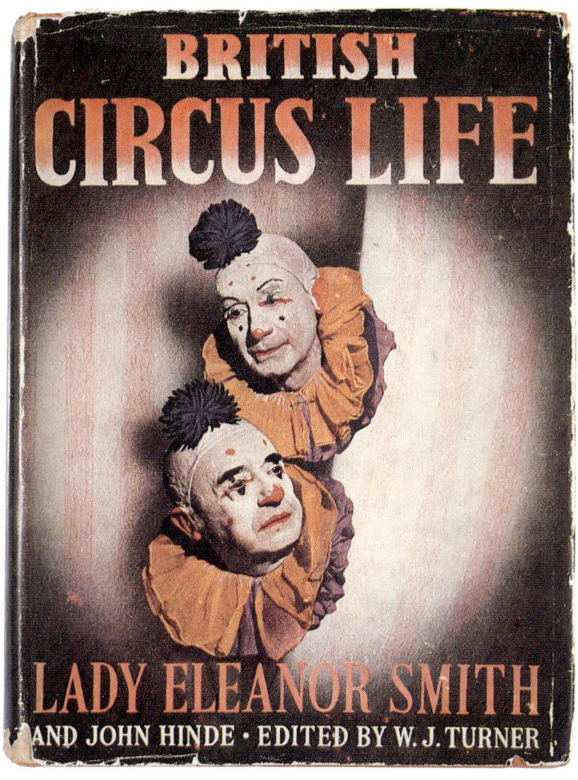

1945

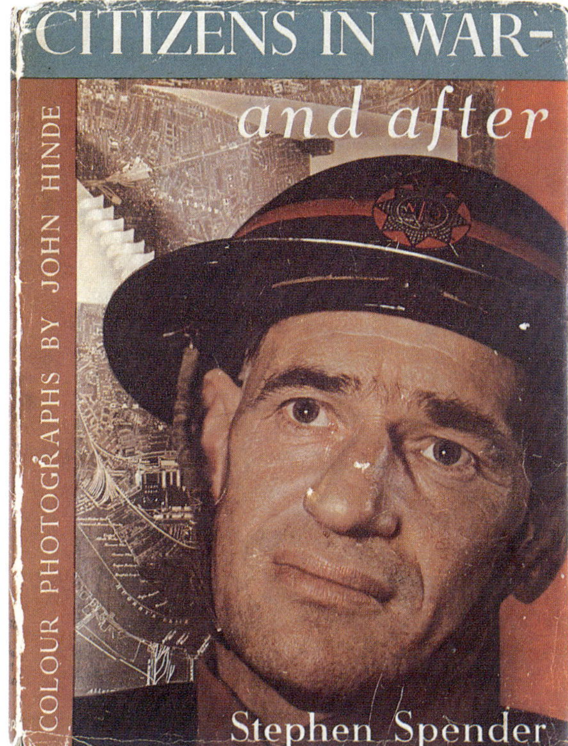

1945

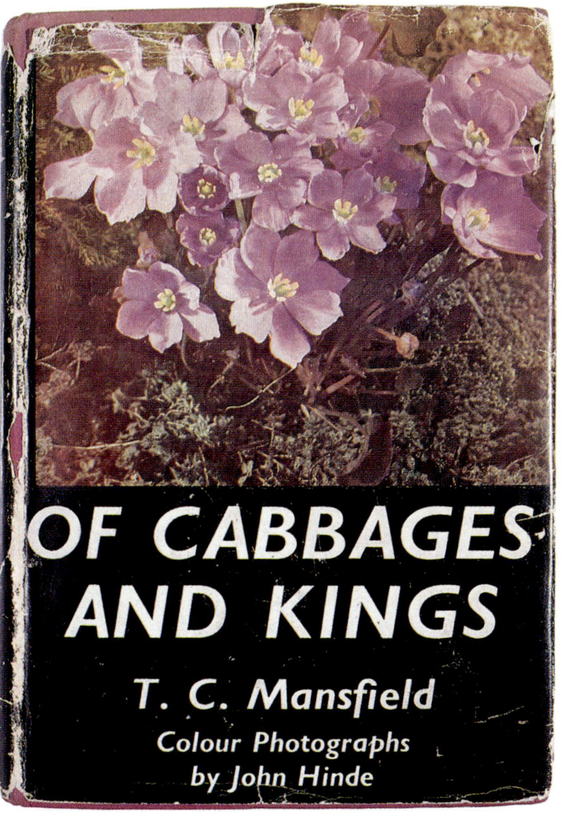

1945

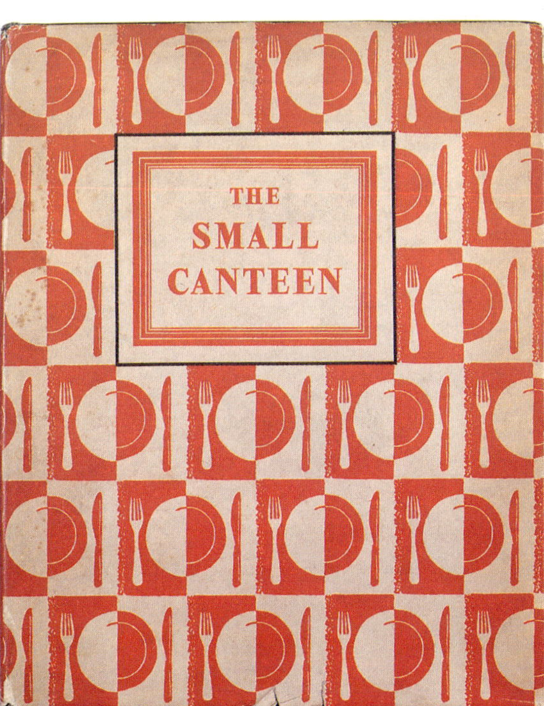

1947

Some of the books published by William Collins and Harrap between 1942 and 1949 containing colour photographs by John Hinde.

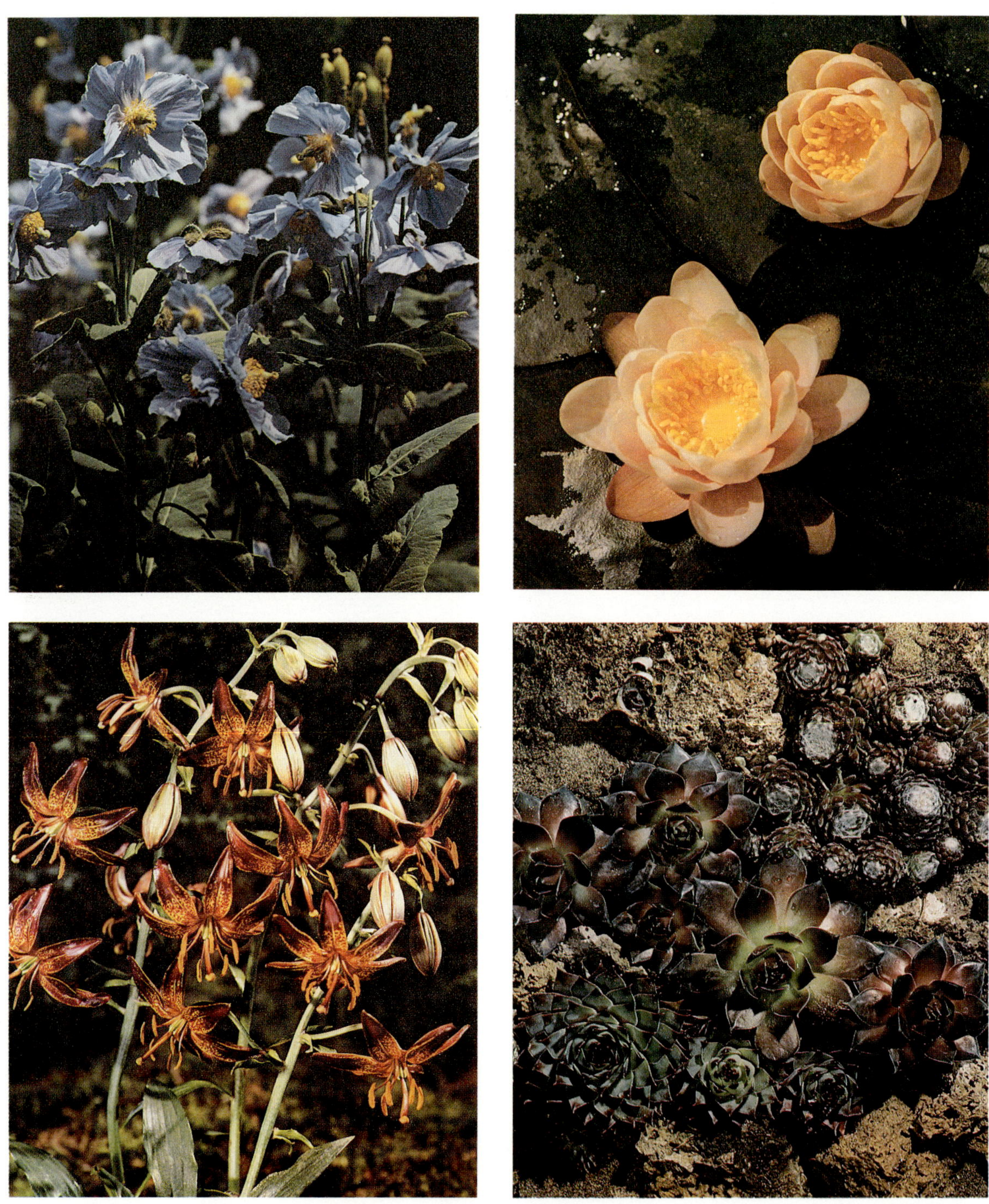

"Of Cabbages and Kings" 1945 (Collins). Photographs by John Hinde.

Above are four of the colour plates reproduced from the original 10" x 8" 3 colour carbro prints. The separation negatives were made in the studio with a 9 x 12cm German Bermphol one-shot camera.

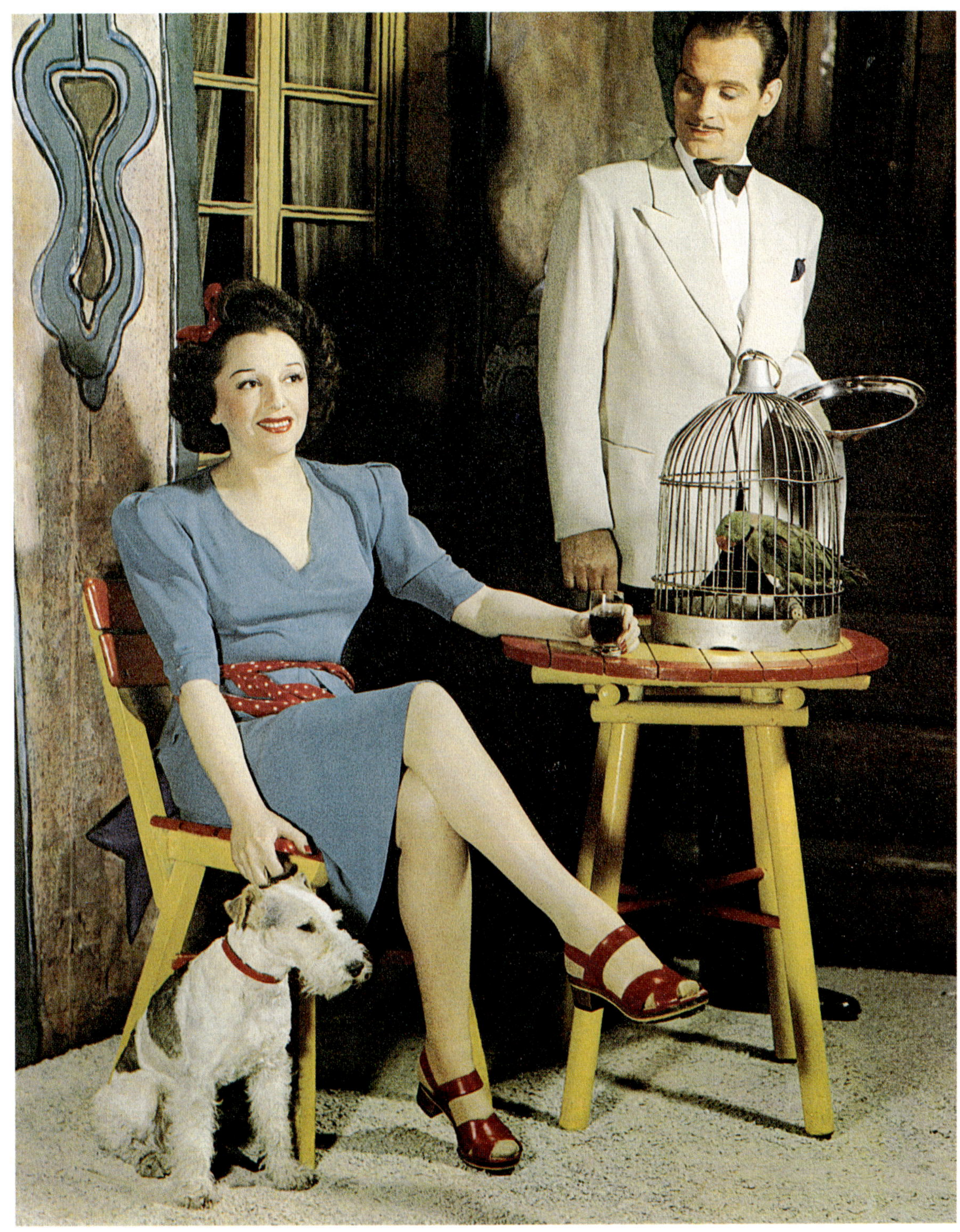

"The series of advertisements (1944) visualised by my cousin Hugh Clark, appeared on the rear cover of the Conde Nast magazine, 'Vogue', then the most prestigious of the high quality fashion magazines... It was essential that the pictorial composition of each picture should be striking, and that the actress and the shoes she was wearing were featured prominently." *John Hinde*

Reproduced from the original 12" x 10" 3 colour carbro print. The separation negatives were made with a $3^1/_2$" x $2^1/_2$" American Devin one-shot camera. The set was illuminated by 50 foil flash bulbs.

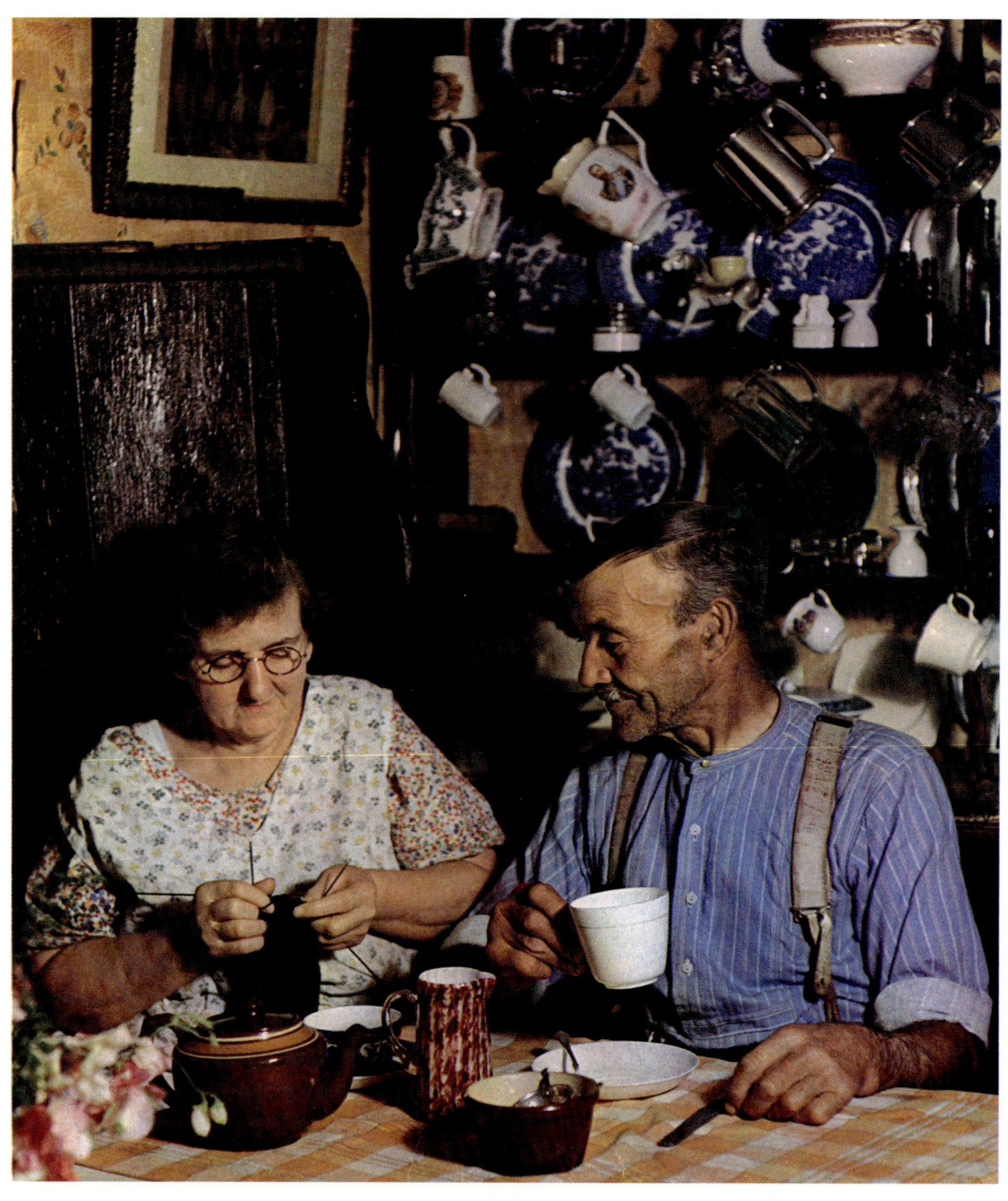

Illustration from "Exmoor Village" 1947 (Harrap). Photograph by John Hinde.

Reproduced from the original 10" x 8" 3 colour carbro print. The separation negatives were made with a $3^1/_2$" x $2^1/_2$" American Devin one-shot camera. Lighting: foil flash bulbs.

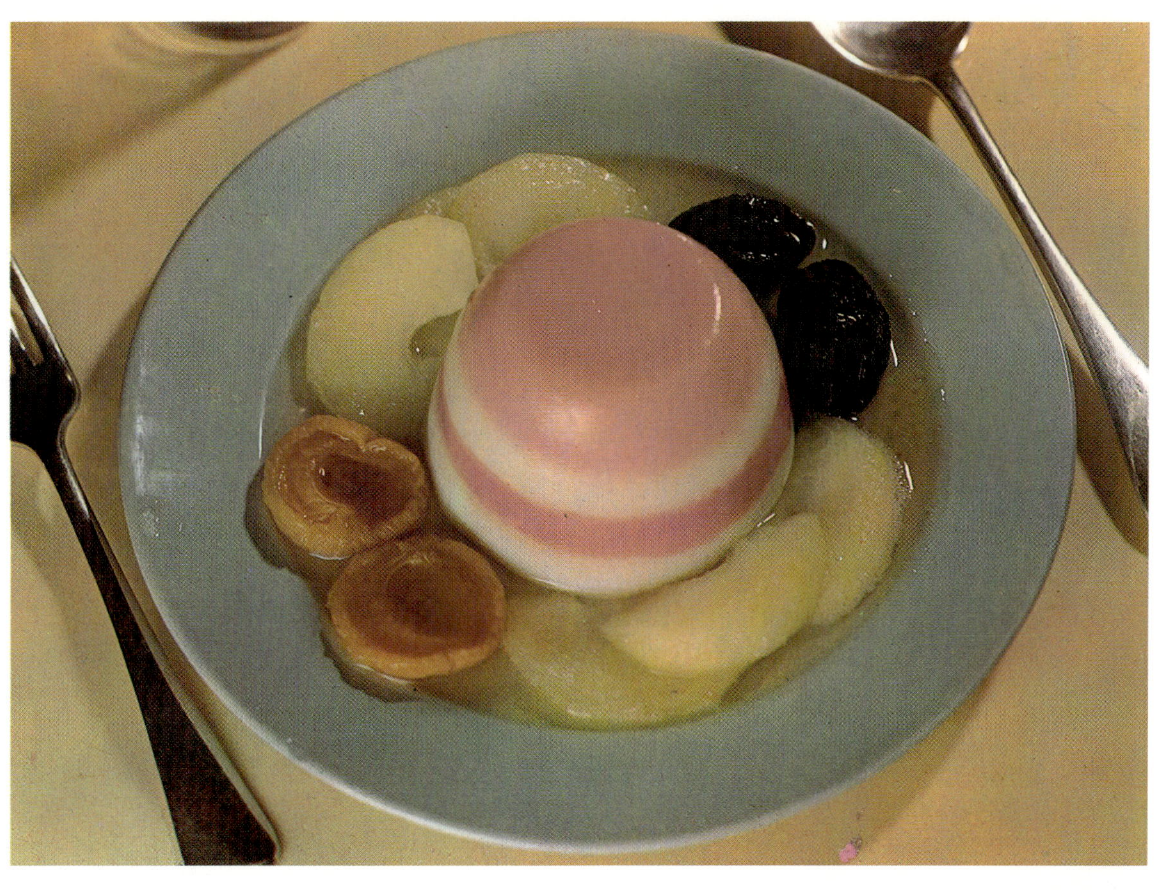

"The Small Canteen" 1947. Photograph by John Hinde.
Reproduced from the original 3 colour carbro print. Separation negatives made with a $3^{1}/_{2}$" x $2^{1}/_{2}$" American Devin one-shot camera.

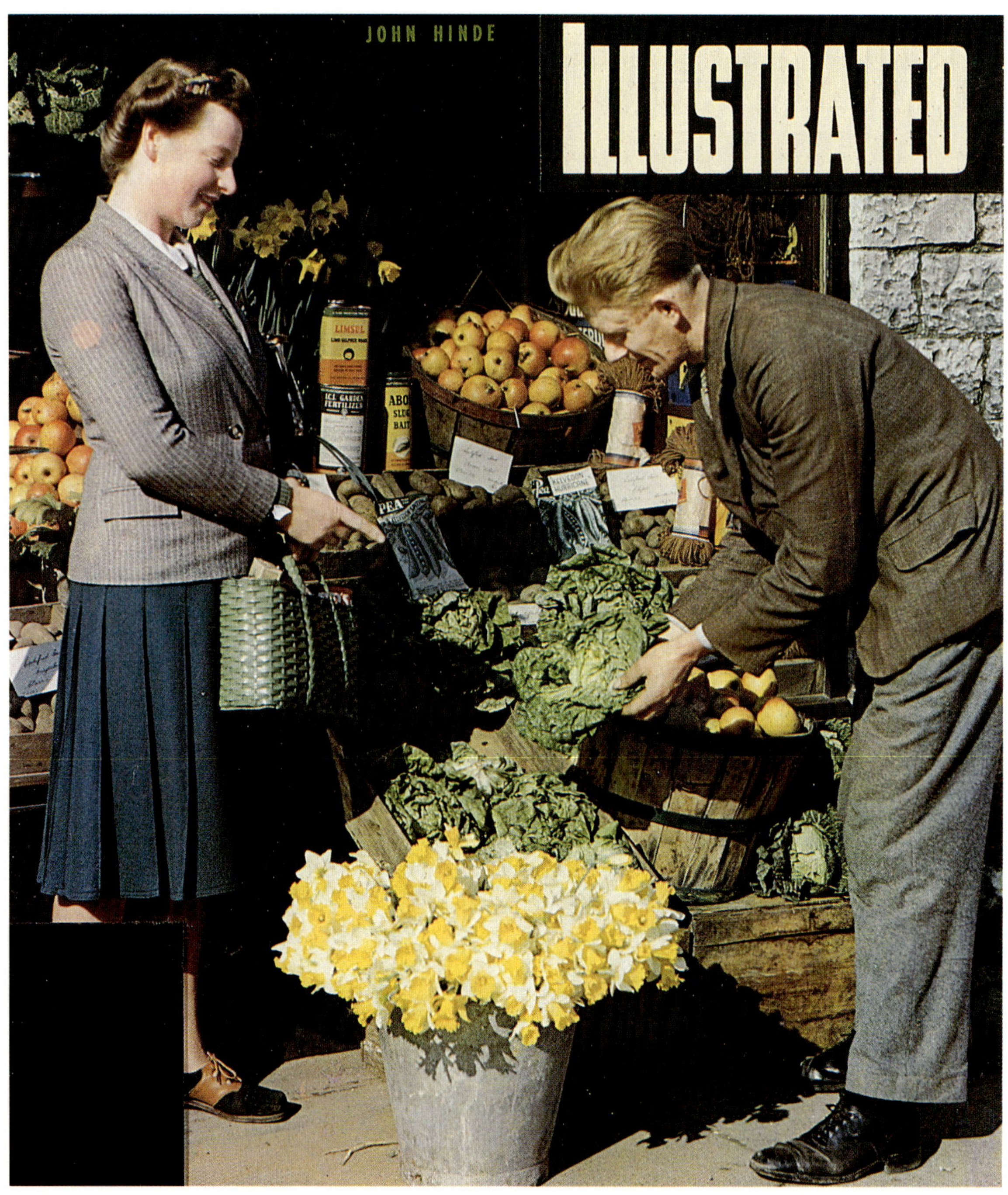

1943 cover picture by John Hinde for the weekly news magazine 'Illustrated' (Odhams Press). This (and the picture on page 27) were among the first colour photographs to be carried by the mass media in Britain.

Reproduced from the original 12" x 10" 3 colour carbro print. Separation negatives made with a $3\frac{1}{2}$" x $2\frac{1}{2}$" American Devin one-shot camera taken on location in sunlight. Exposure $\frac{1}{5}$ sec.

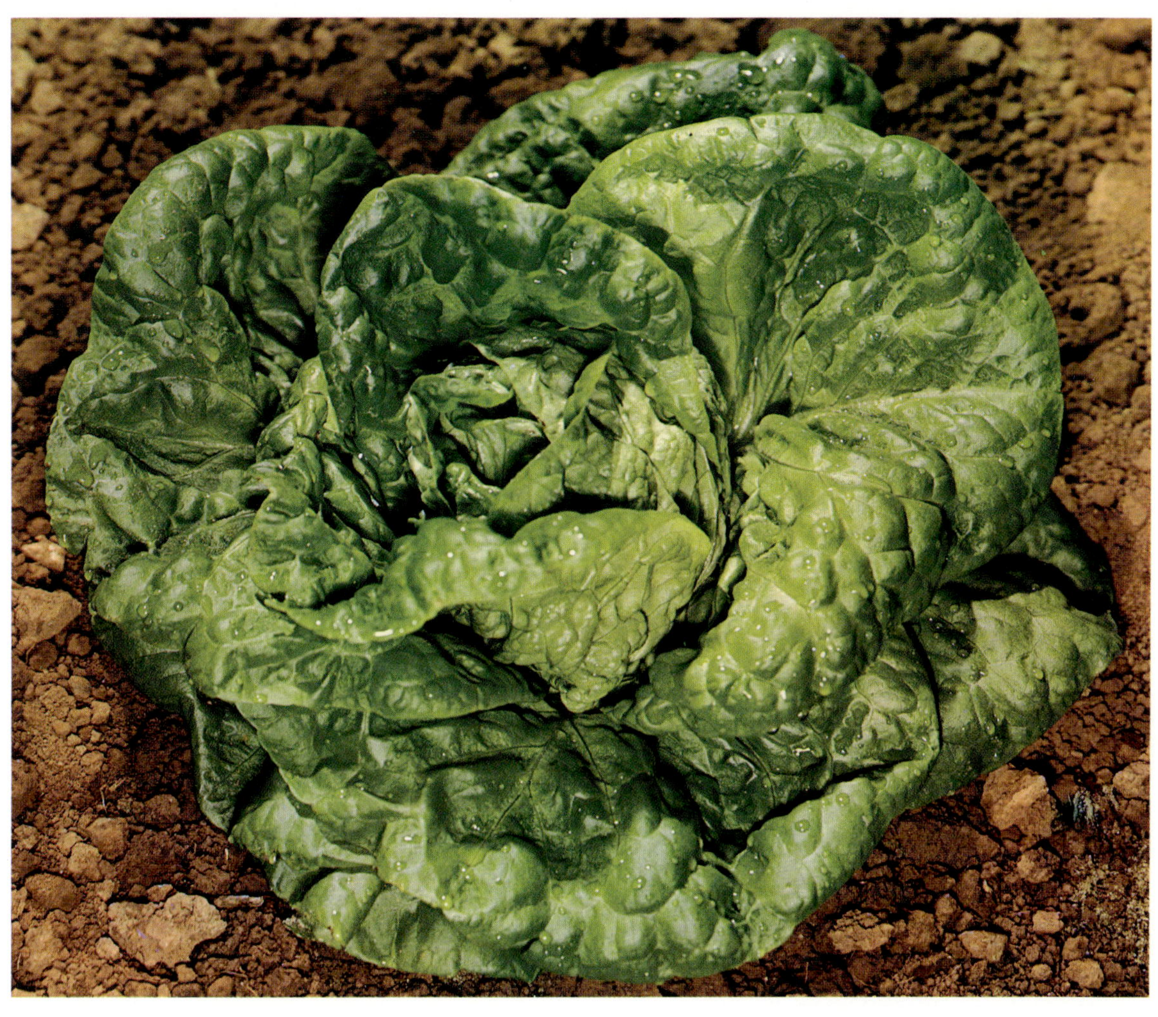

'Illustrated' magazine feature photograph by John Hinde, 1943.

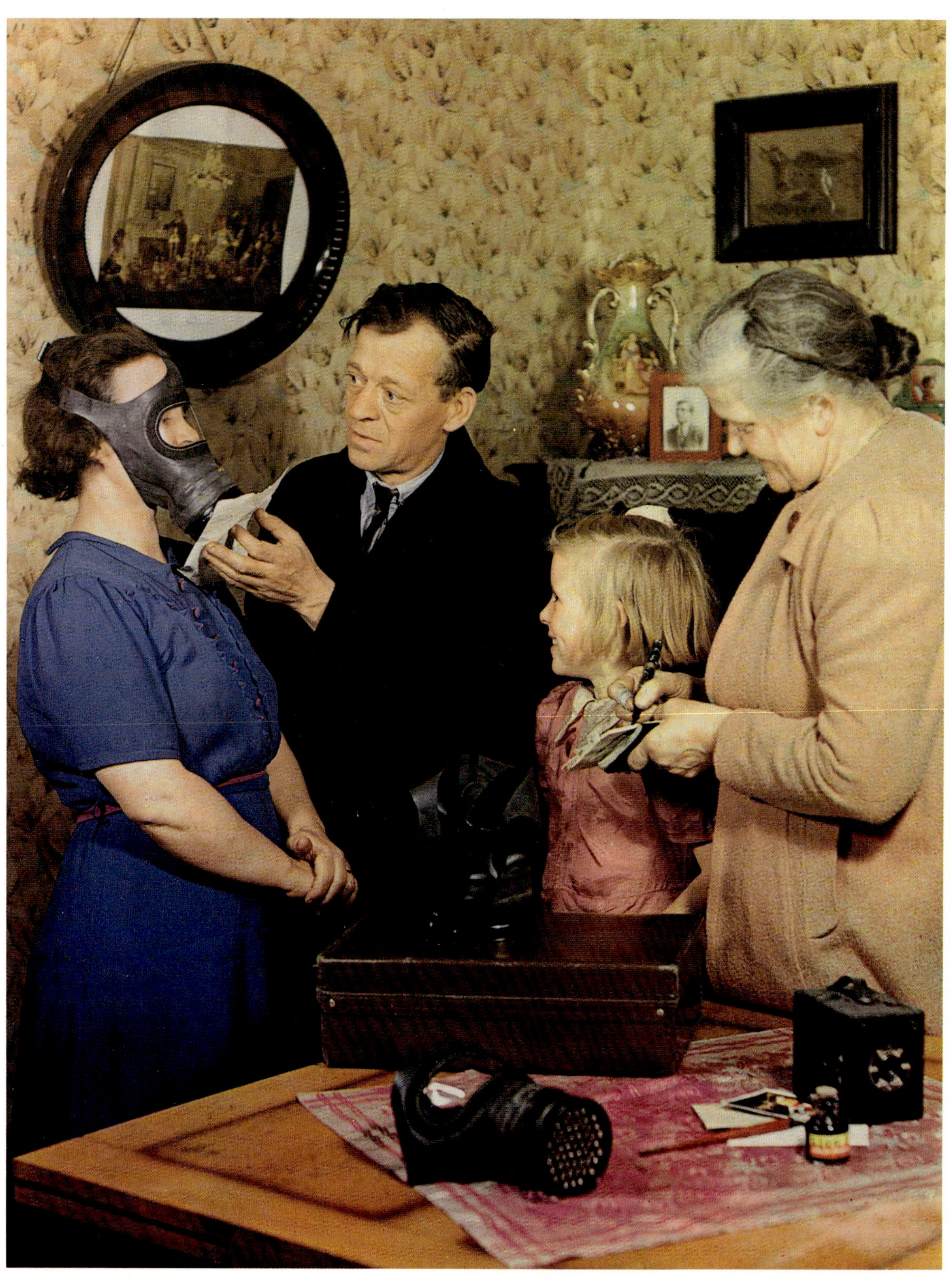

"Citizens in War - and After" 1945 (Harrap). Photograph by John Hinde.

This picture and those on the following 3 pages, reproduced from the original $8^1/_2$" x $6^1/_2$" 3 colour carbro prints, are from a series of 48 photographs taken by John Hinde to illustrate Stephen Spender's "Citizens at War - and After" 1945 (Harrap). The Imperial War Museum believes them to be the only

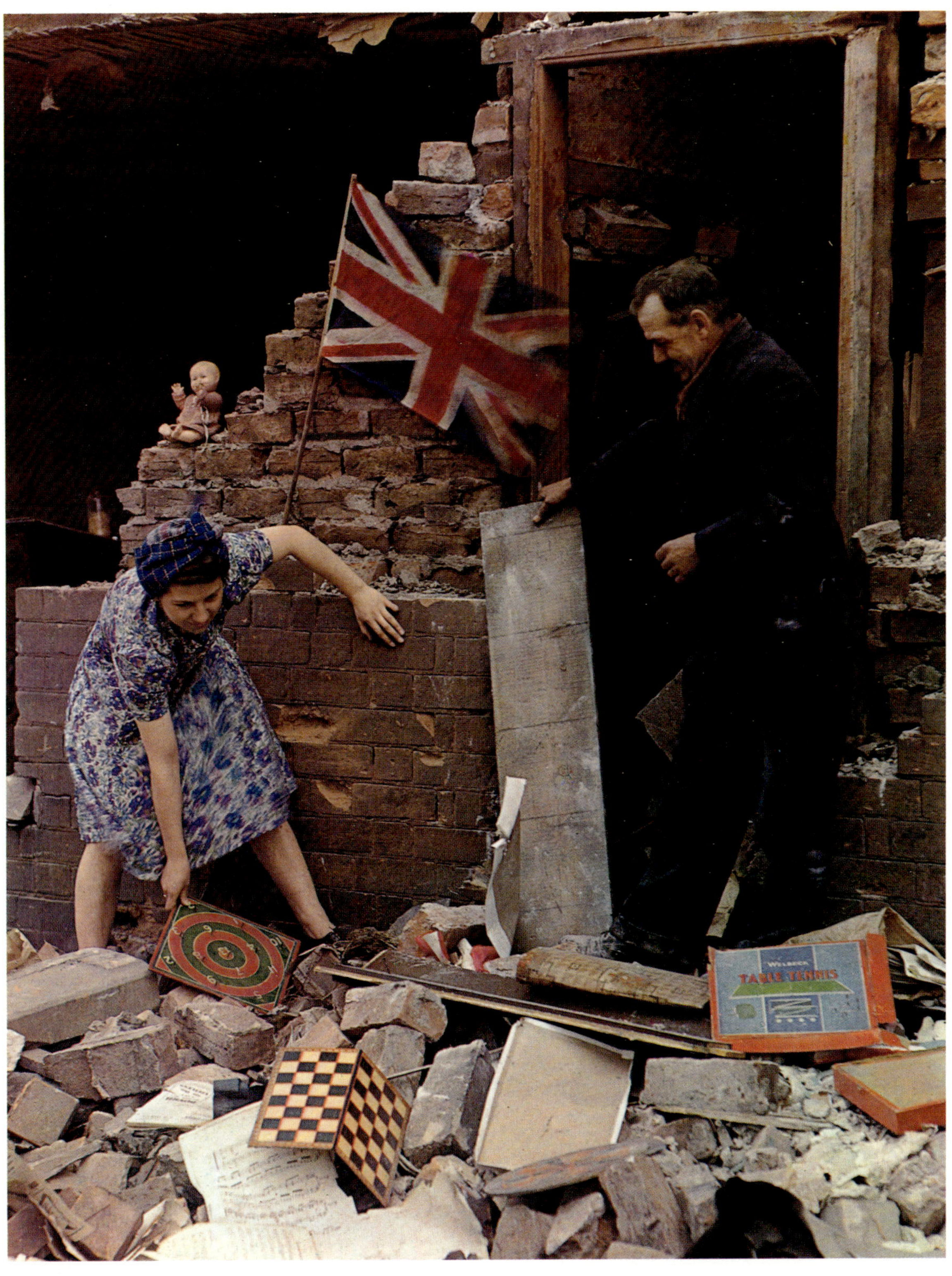

"Citizens in War - and After" 1945 (Harrap). Photograph by John Hinde.

photographs in colour recording the British Civil Defence Organisation (1939-45). The subject matter presented the optimum challenge to the photographer using a $3^1/_2$" x $2^1/_2$" American Devin one-shot camera.

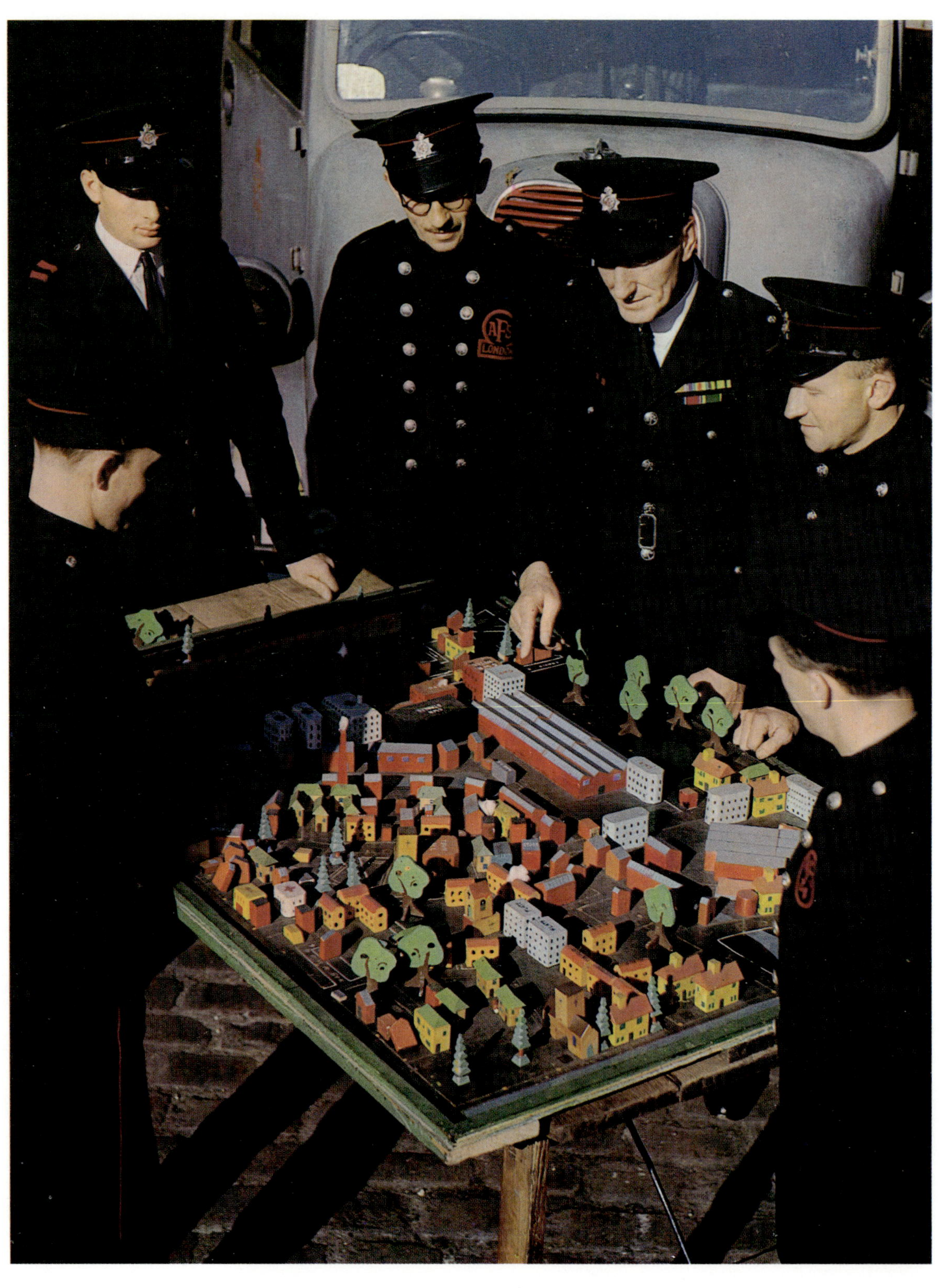

"Citizens in War - and After" 1945 (Harrap). Photograph by John Hinde.

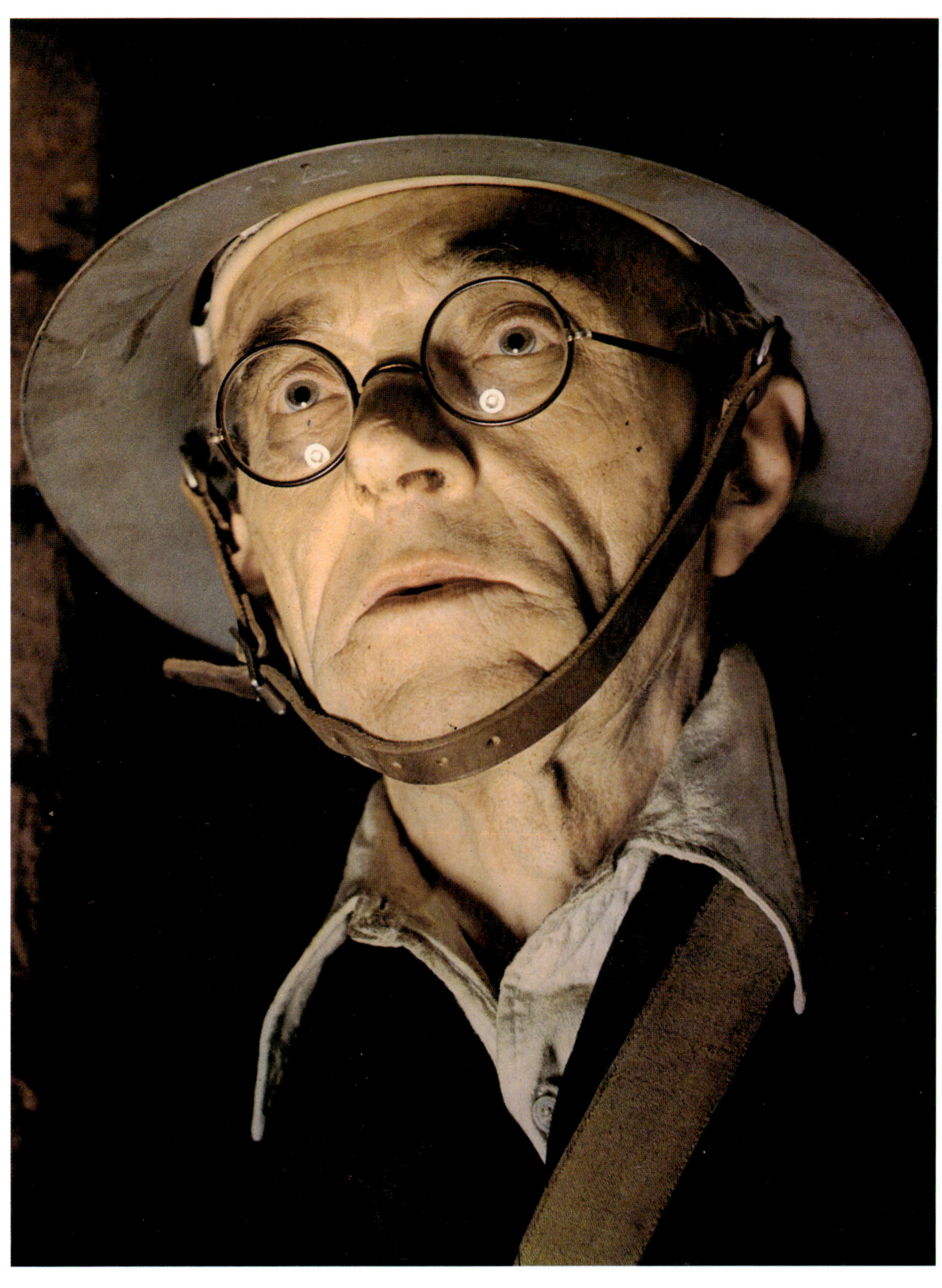

"Citizens in War - and After" 1945 (Harrap). Photograph by John Hinde.

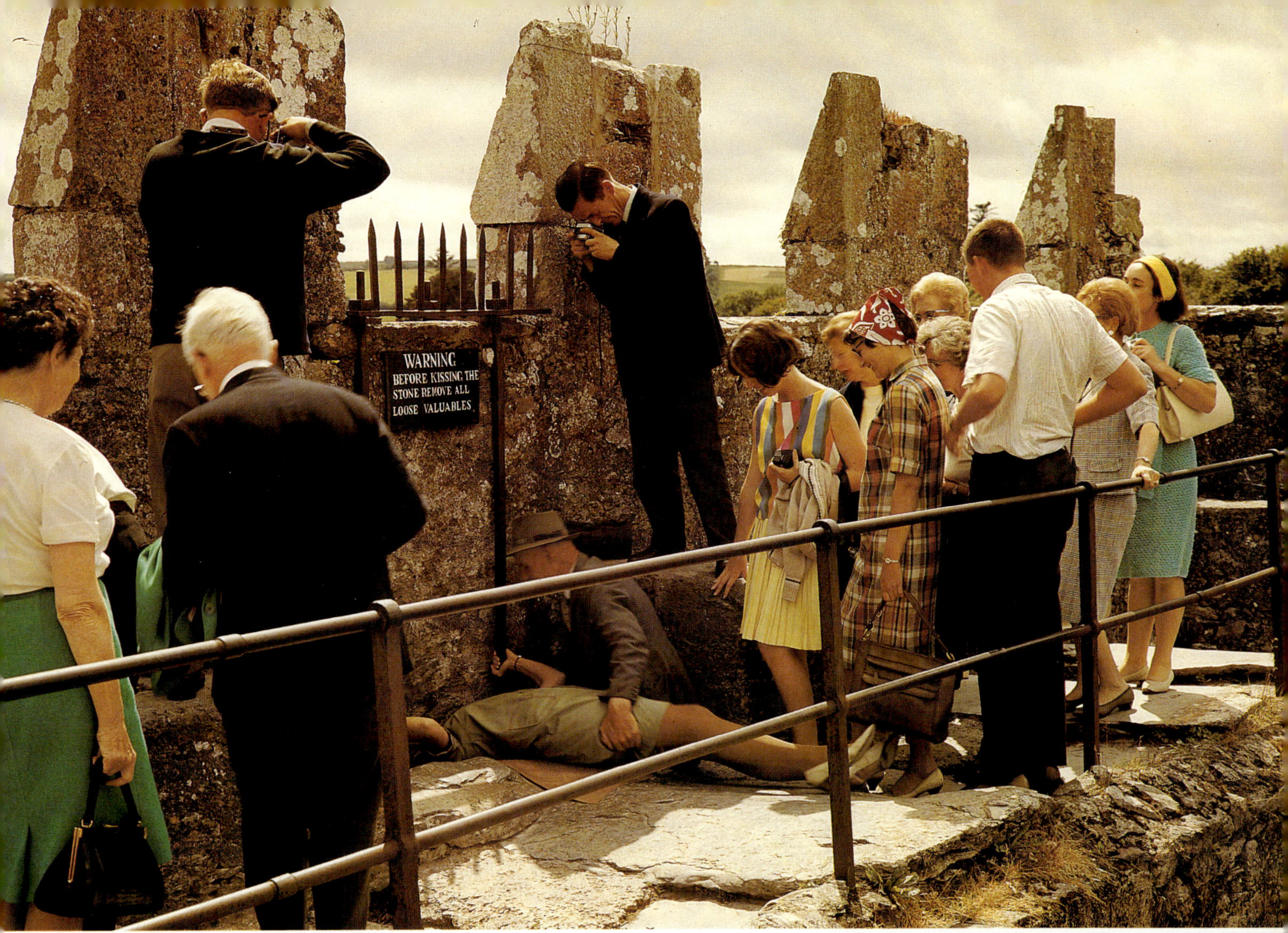

WARNING
BEFORE KISSING THE
STONE REMOVE ALL
LOOSE VALUABLES

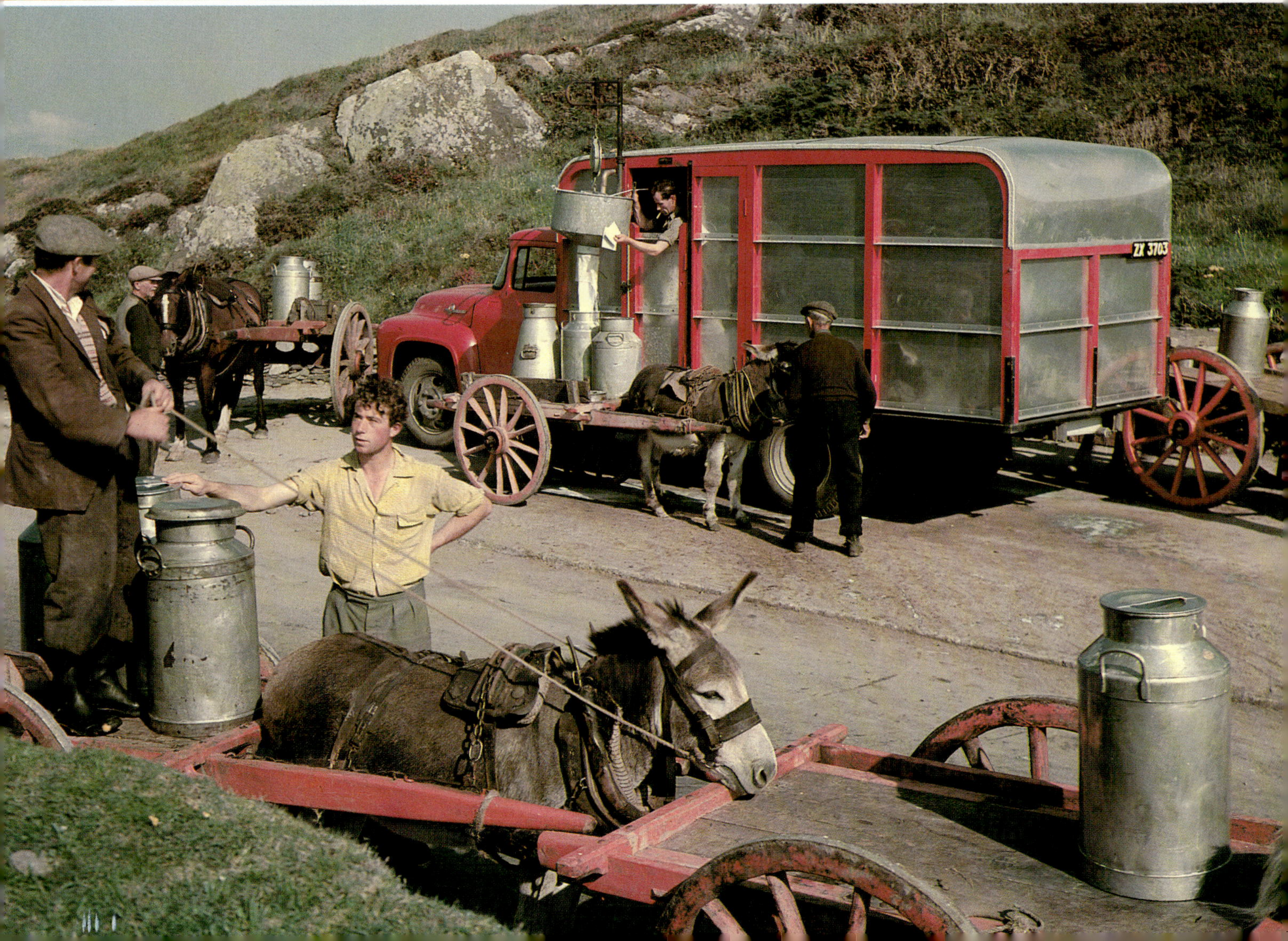

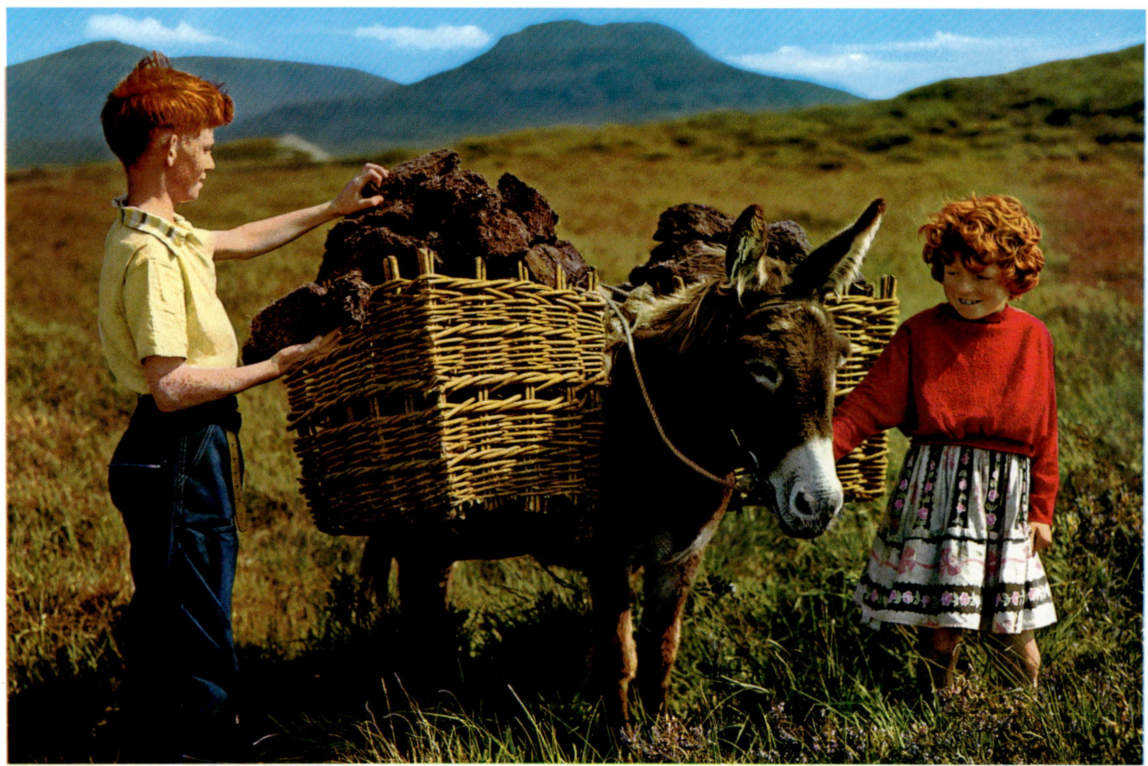

Collecting Turf from the Bog, Connemara, Co. Galway, Ireland. Colour Photo by John Hinde, F.R.P.S.

"Frankly I don't remember how it was taken, I think it is likely that I saw them beside the road and stopped the car to take them. With the non-specific views like the donkey this was perfectly real at the time when we were there. This picture represented the Ireland the visitors looked for, and it did exist. There was a certain resistance to that kind of image of Ireland. About three or four years after we started producing postcards Bord Fáilte discouraged the use of pictures of cottages or donkeys because the government regarded them as the symbols of a backward country. The things they wanted portrayed were skyscrapers. The government then didn't realise that the attraction of Ireland to visitors was completely the opposite."
John Hinde

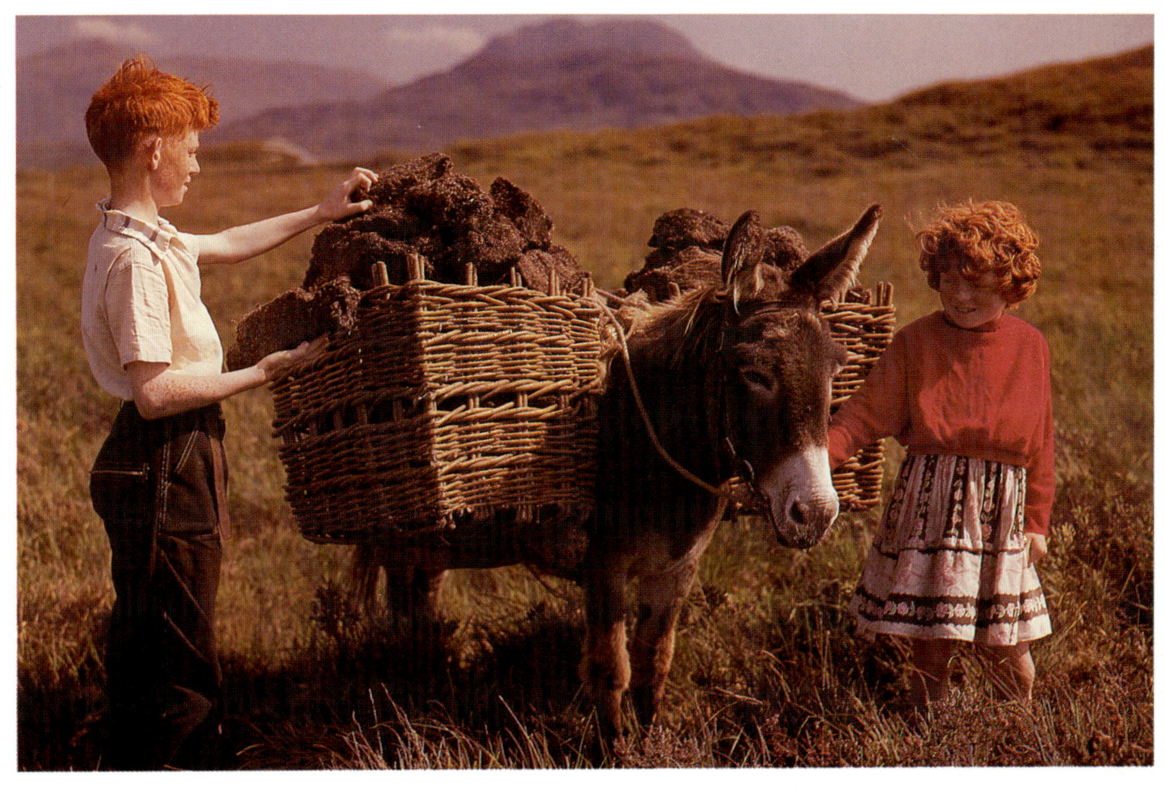

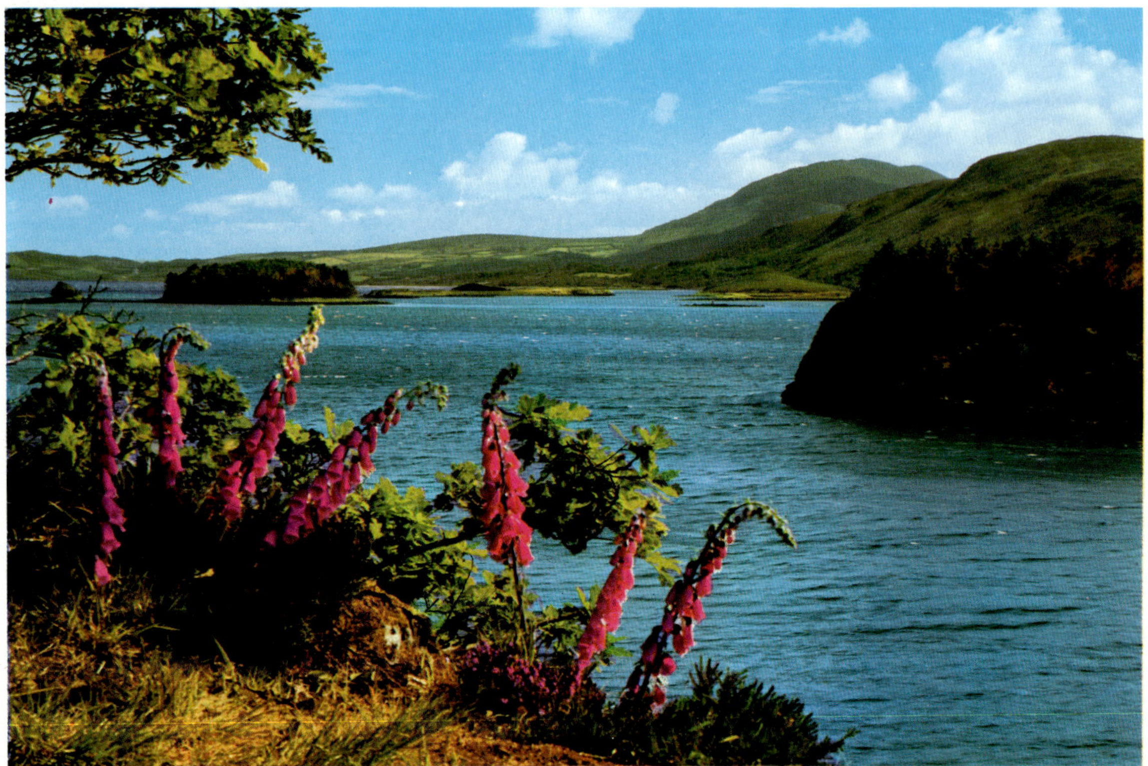

Mulroy Bay near Milford, Co. Donegal, Ireland. Photo: John Hinde, F.R.P.S.

"They were quite strict about what kind of images they required. They wanted them constructed really. You knew that you had to garden, as it were. You knew you had to make the picture a bit more than it was. For example, you'll probably find with that one (with foxgloves in the foreground) that all those flowers were moved there. But they are put in at the photographing stage. There were limits to what they could do in the studio - they didn't have lasers in those days. As the photographer, you understood that a picture had to be constructed. What was nice about working for John Hinde Ltd. was that John Hinde himself was a photographer. The picture was most important to him. When you went round to take a picture of his house, for example, the Rolls Royce would be driven around and parked in front. You'd cut roses and put them on your stand. Then when you wanted to photograph a room, if you needed to take a door off to get the camera in the right position then you took it off. The image had to be perfect."

David Noble

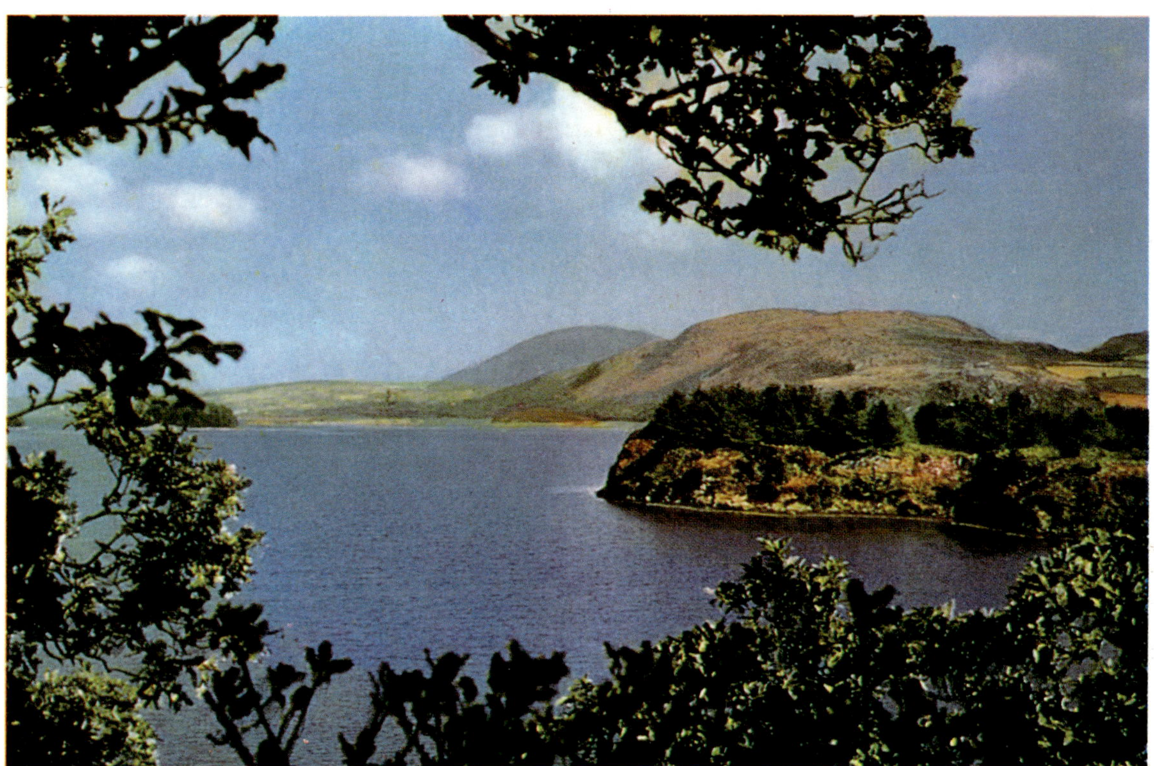

Mulroy Bay, Milford, Co. Donegal, Ireland

Postcard of Mulroy Bay by ***Penman Cards****. circa 1955-60*

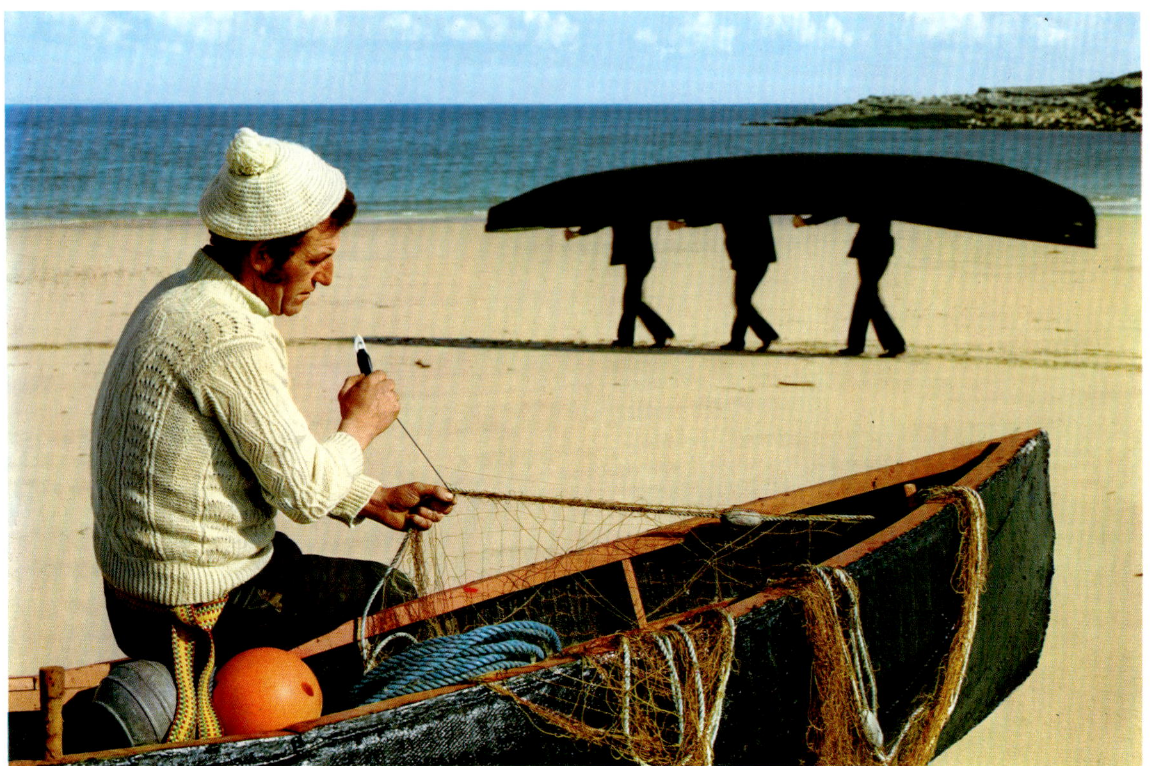

Fishermen on the Aran Islands, Co. Galway, Ireland. Photo: D. Noble, John Hinde Studios.

"Aran Island - I flew in and was there about ten days. I can't remember the full details of the picture where the fisherman's mending his nets but I remember telling them what I wanted and I was very disappointed when the currach carriers turned up on the Sunday morning with their suits on. They'd come straight from church. I wanted them to turn up in their wellies and their sea-going gear. And then I said to the fisherman, well you've got to be wearing an Aran sweater. Nobody had an Aran sweater on Aran. Eventually they found one and it was miles too small for him and had a hole in it. That's why he's posed like this to cover up its smallness. In the end it took the whole morning to get it right and it would have taken some days in advance to prepare for. You're talking about half a day to shoot it and a day to prepare in advance.

"There's an interesting story about another picture I took on Aran. While I was going around the island I came across a perfect cottage, thatched everything, sat right in front of the horizon of Connemara. It was a perfect picture so I set up and took it. I found out afterwards it was the cottage that Flaherty had had built for the family who appeared in his film 'Man of Aran'. He'd deliberately chosen the spot to build the cottage because it made a good picture."
David Noble

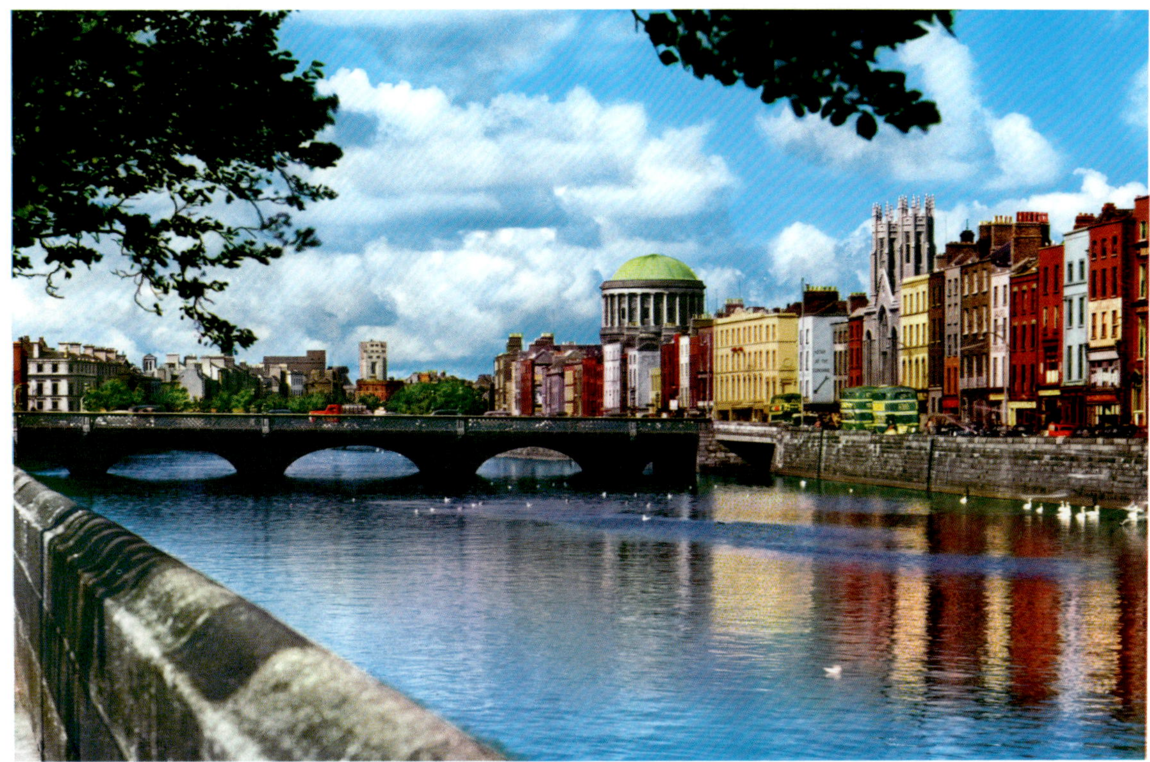

River Liffey, looking towards the Four Courts, Dublin, Ireland. Colour Photo by John Hinde, F.R.P.S.

"Have you ever been to our capital Dublin? If you have there is running through the centre of Dublin, as through the centre of London, a river. In our case it is the River Liffey, from which - we are told - our Guinness is made. The River Liffey is very much the same colour as Guinness. Naturally, our visitors to Dublin would prefer to see a blue/green river rather than a Guinness-coloured river. I mention this to illustrate a point. With our view cards, which are directed not towards the critical photographer but to the man in the street, in some cases the lily is gilded ... slightly."

John Hinde. From a lecture to the Royal Photographic Society, London. 1967

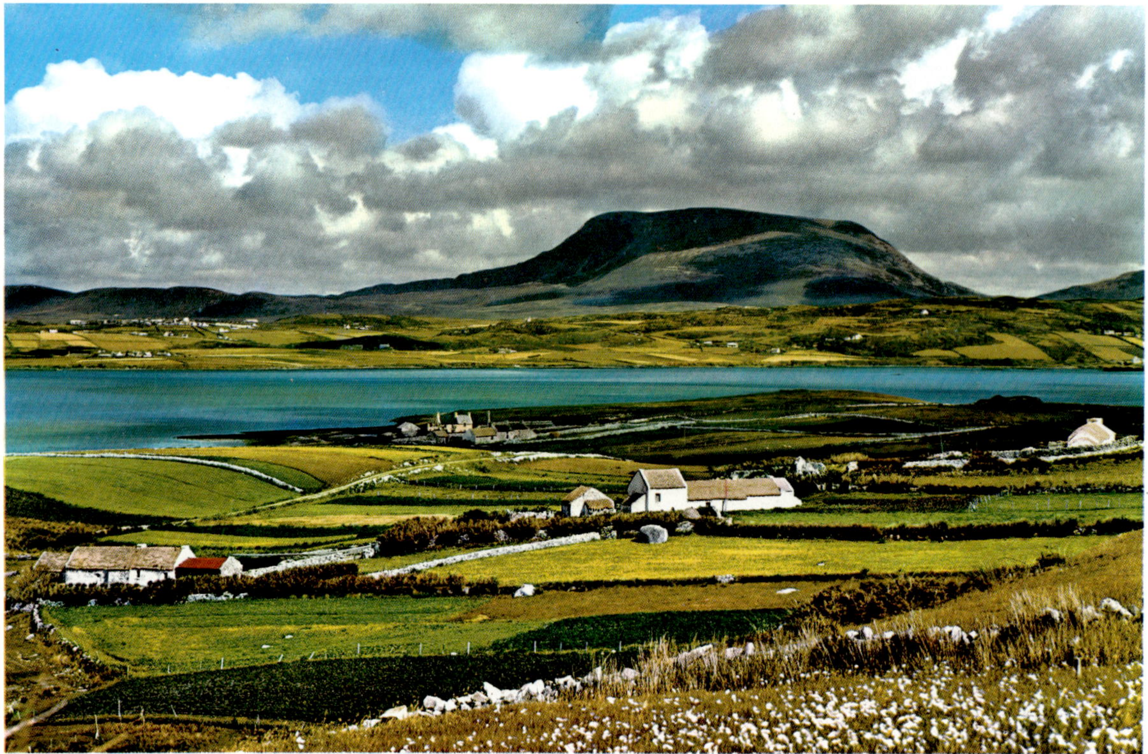

Muckish Mountain, Co. Donegal, Ireland. Colour Photo by John Hinde, F.R.P.S.

"Of course most landscapes in Ireland have no colour. It's these touches of colour in our cards which actually make our postcards attractive. This was where the colour corrections came in. And where possibly I was the only person who could decide what was required to give the card that extra oomph."

"On the separations I developed colour variations in the fields in the landscapes because I didn't want to convey a flat, all-green scene nor a muddy blue sky. It was in a sense a sort of formula that developed in my mind which I felt was right for a postcard."
John Hinde

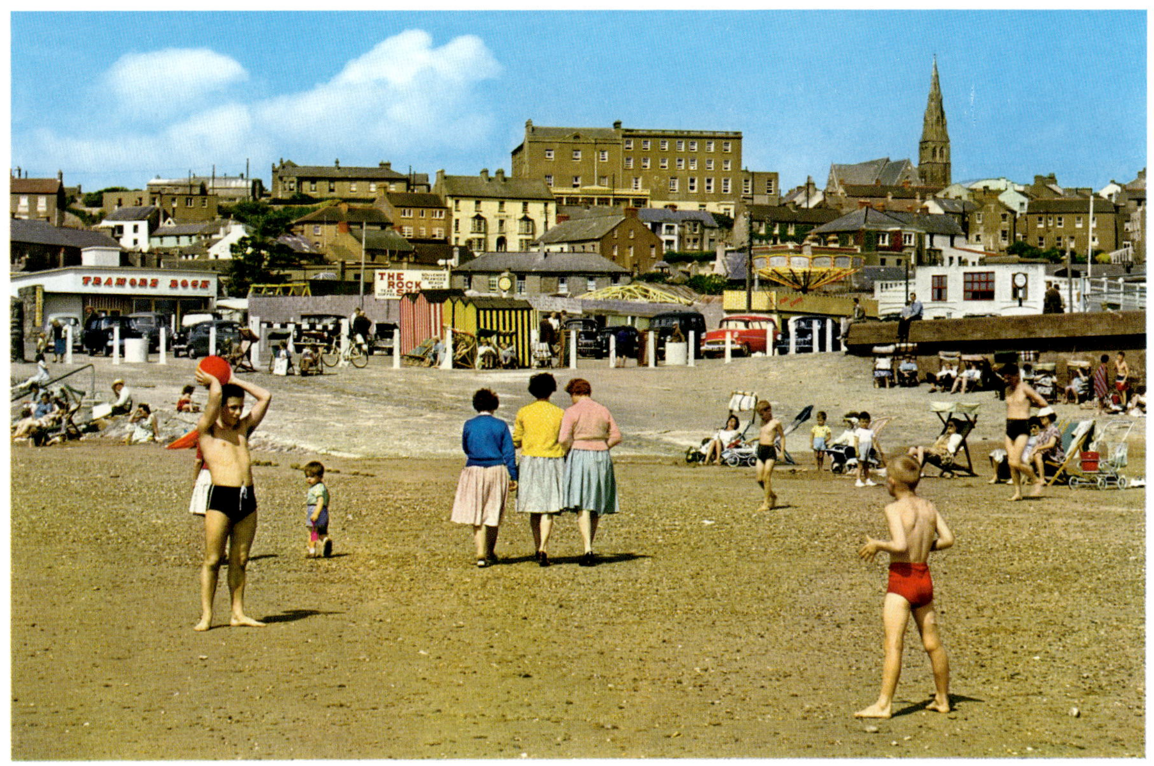

The Beach, Tramore, Co. Waterford, Ireland.

Colour Photo by John Hinde, F.R.P.S.

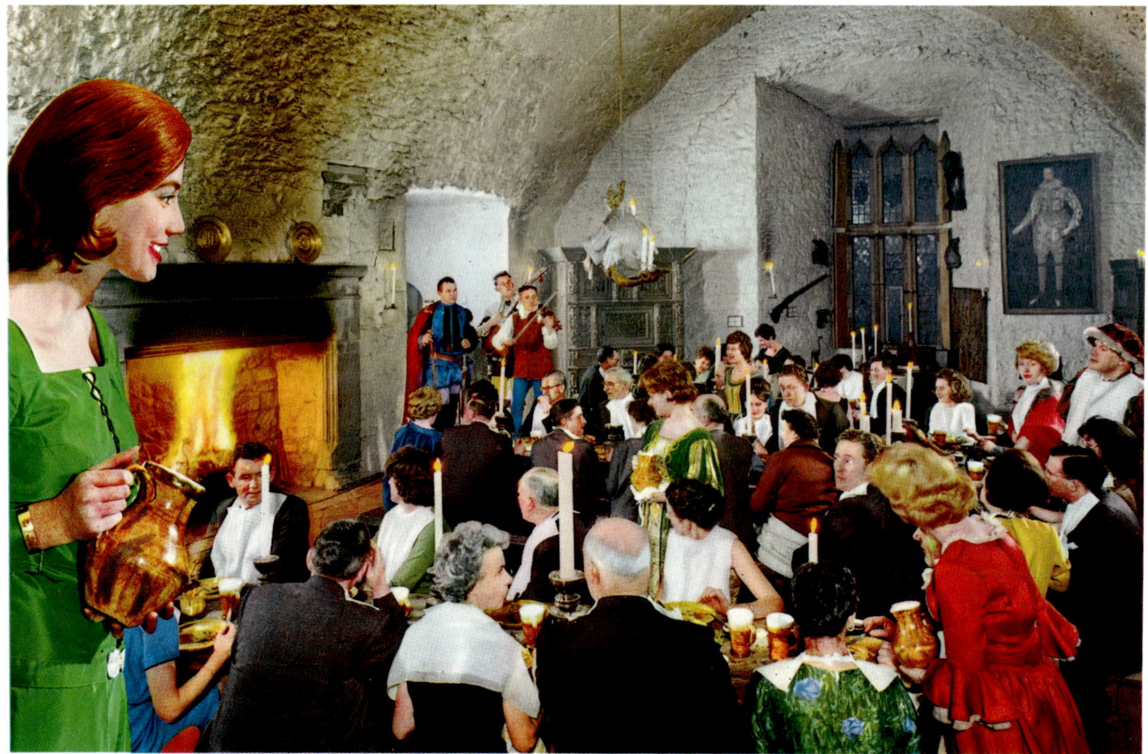

Mediaeval Banquet, Bunratty Castle, Co. Clare, Ireland. Photo: E. Ludwig, John Hinde Studios.

"He was very certain, not that he thought his photography was artistically wonderful but that it was exactly what the market needed. To me it was a very Victorian way of thinking about the market, but there is no doubting its success. I say Victorian because it seemed to me to be arrogant at the time to be so sure that you knew exactly what people wanted. But he did and at the time he was right, they did want idealised pictures with overblown colour. He had a puritan ideal, a bit like De Valera with his sweet maidens and comely lads dancing at the crossroads, that sort of thing."
Clare Cryan

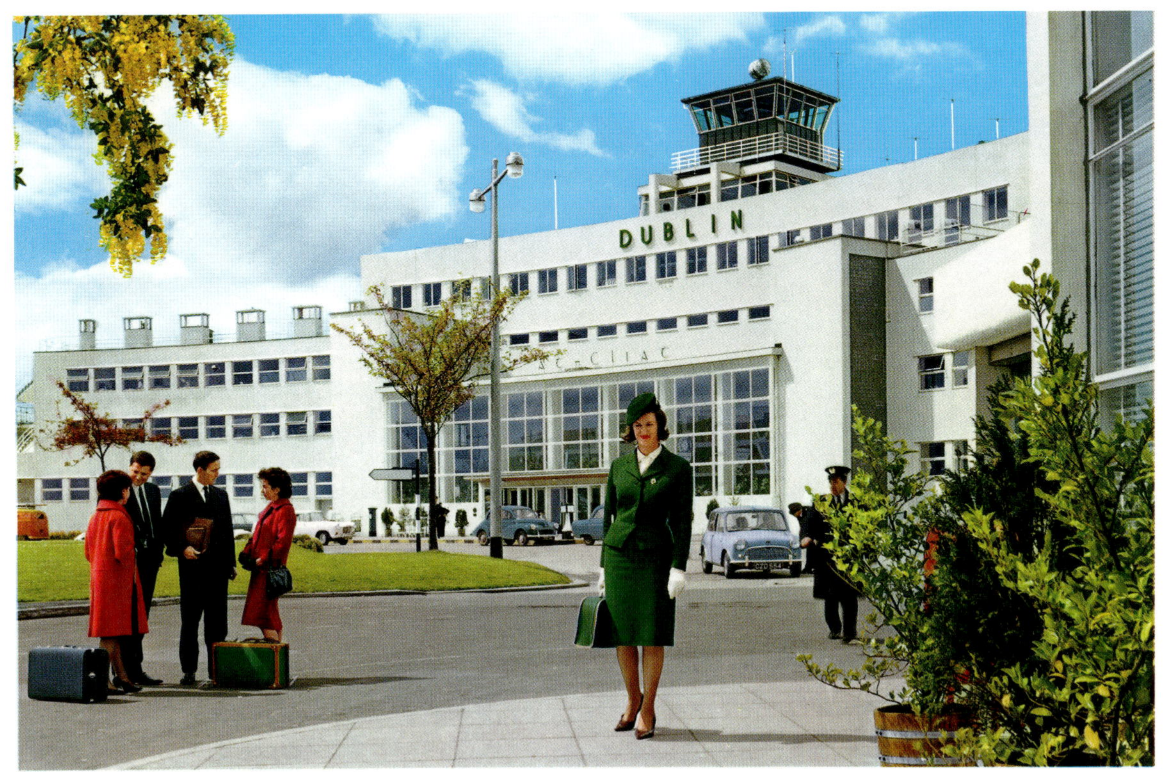

Terminal Building, Dublin Airport, Ireland. Photo: E. Ludwig, John Hinde Studios.

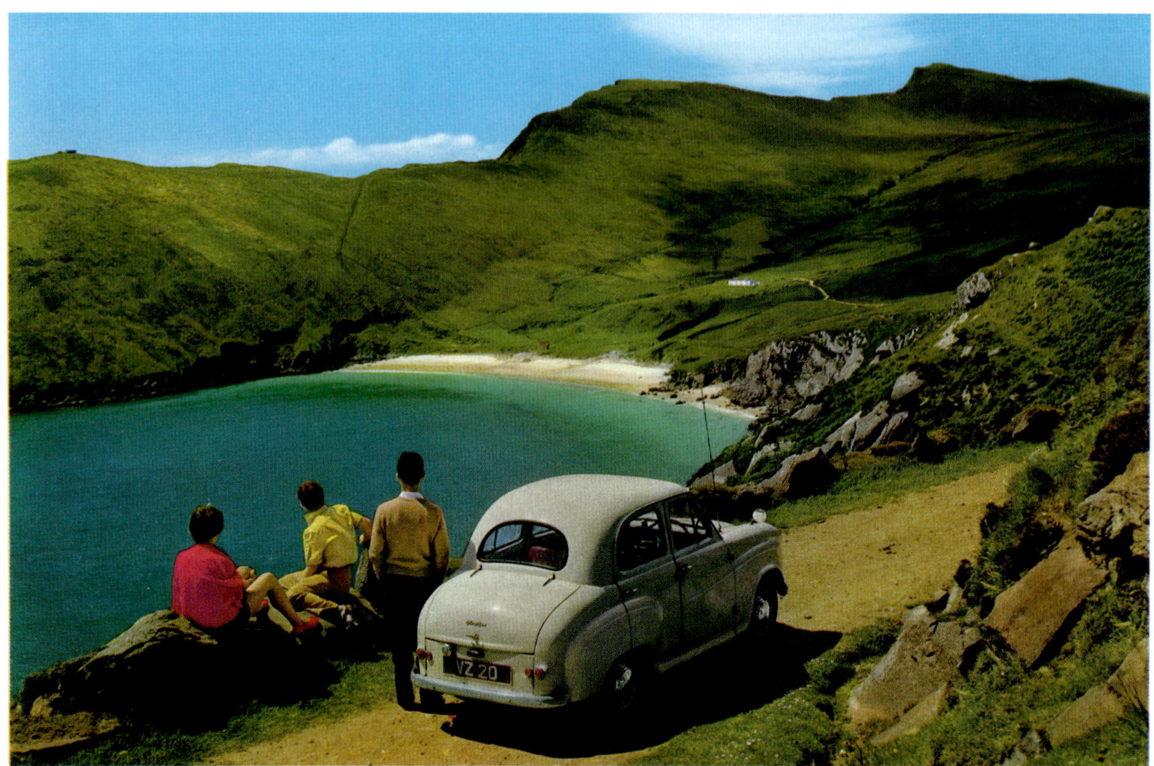

On the road to Keem Strand, Achill Island, Co. Mayo, Ireland.

Colour Photo by John Hinde, F.R.P.S.

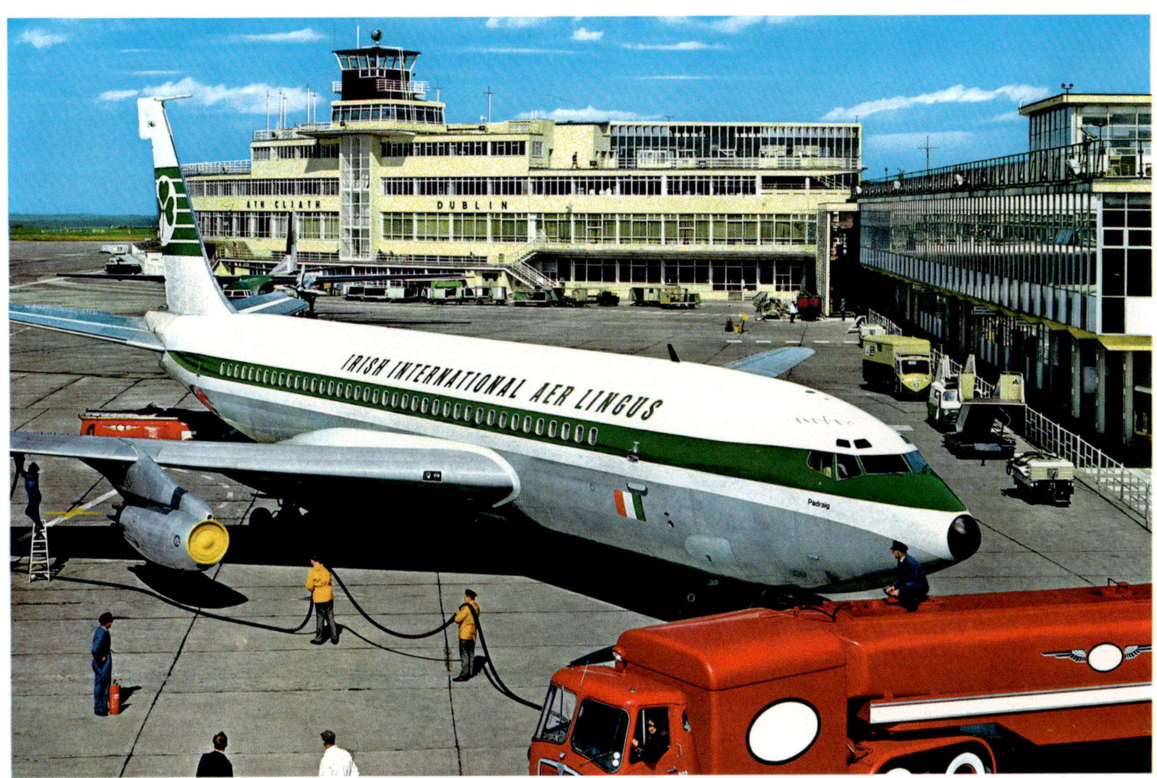

The Apron, Dublin Airport, Ireland.

Photo: E. Ludwig, John Hinde Studios.

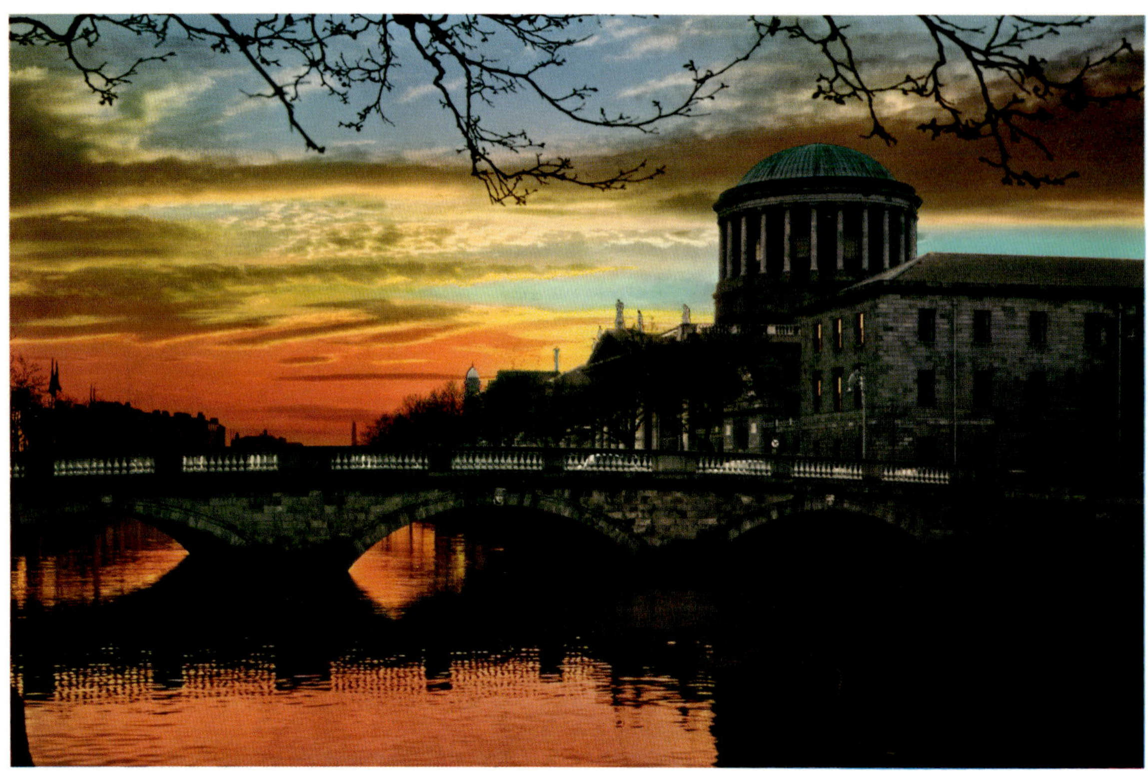

Sunset over the River Liffey and Four Courts, Dublin, Ireland. Photo: E. Nägele, John Hinde Studios.

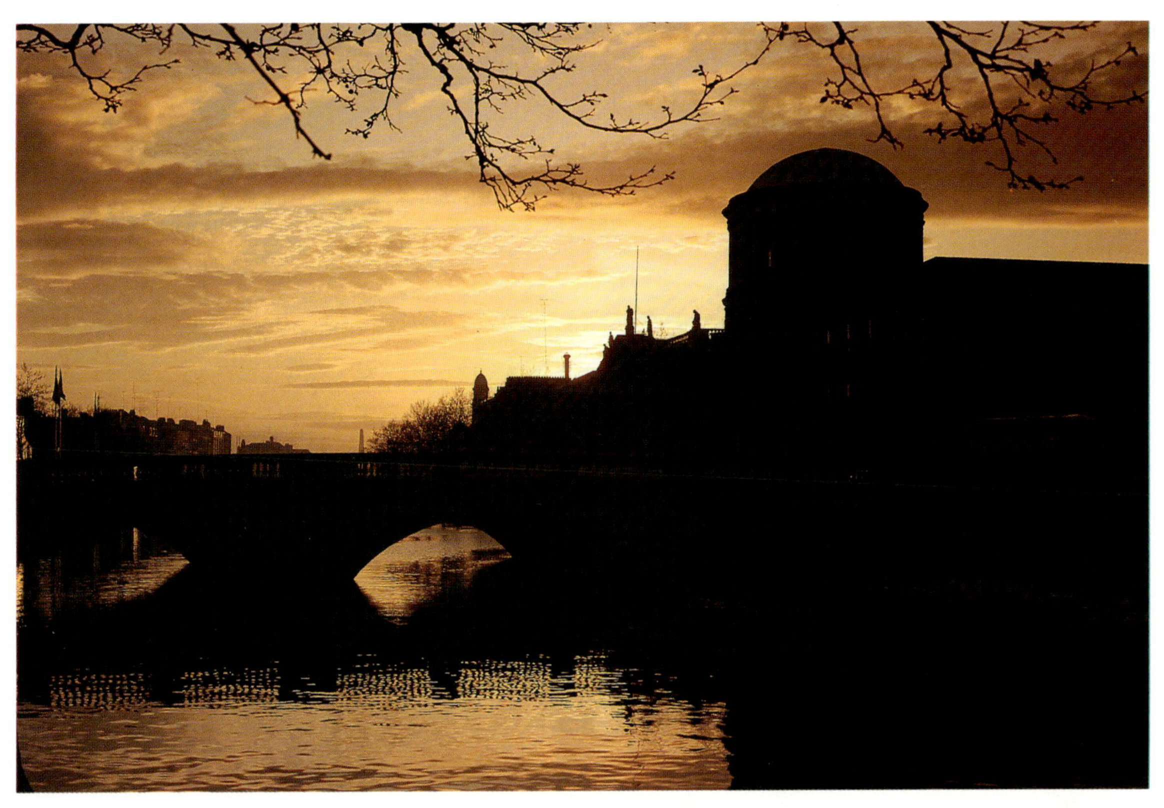

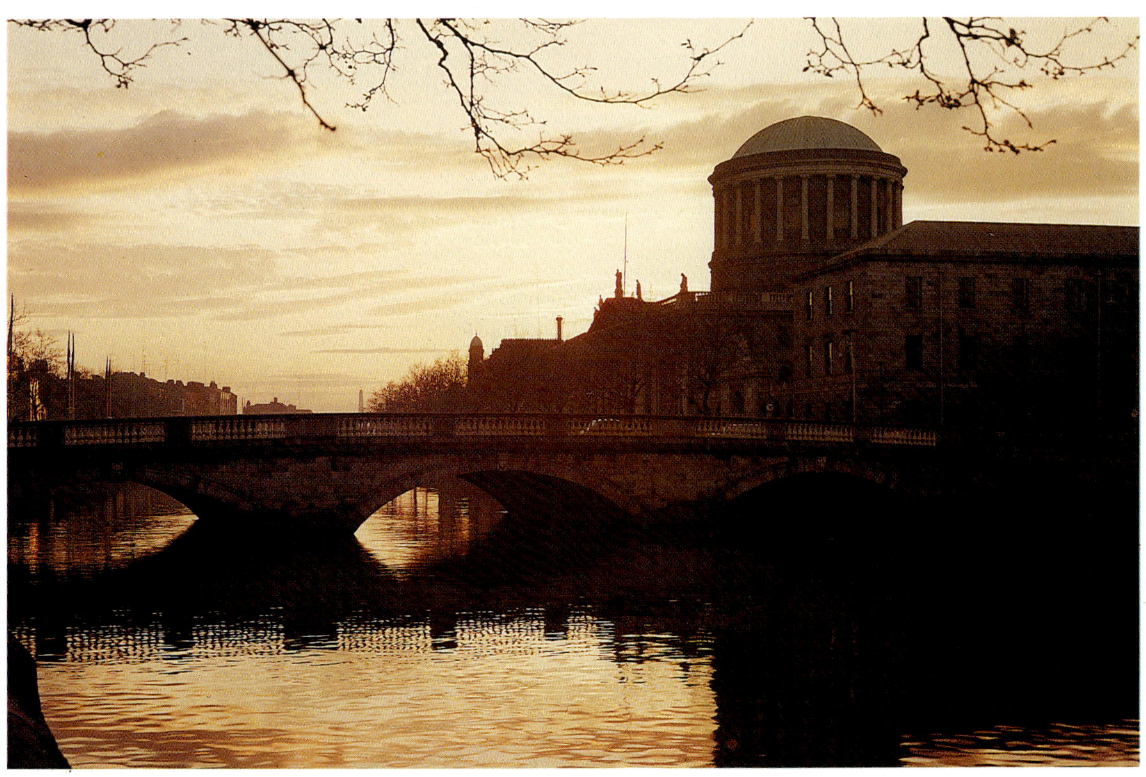

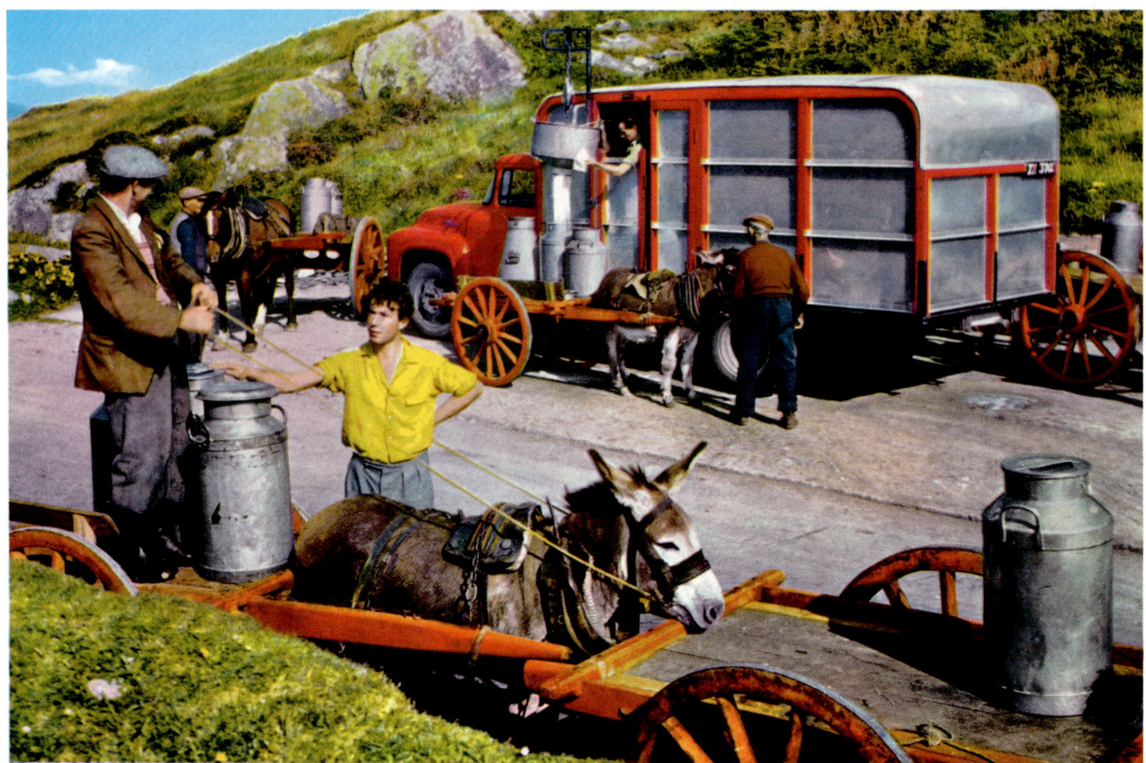

Irish Farmers Meet a Creamery Lorry. Colour Photo by John Hinde, F.R.P.S.

1957 Reproduction of one of the first six postcards. The original photography, colour separations, preparation of the screen positives and their colour correction, the making of the offset printing plates and the final offset-litho printing was carried out entirely by John Hinde working singlehanded at his small house at Bulloch Harbour, Dublin.

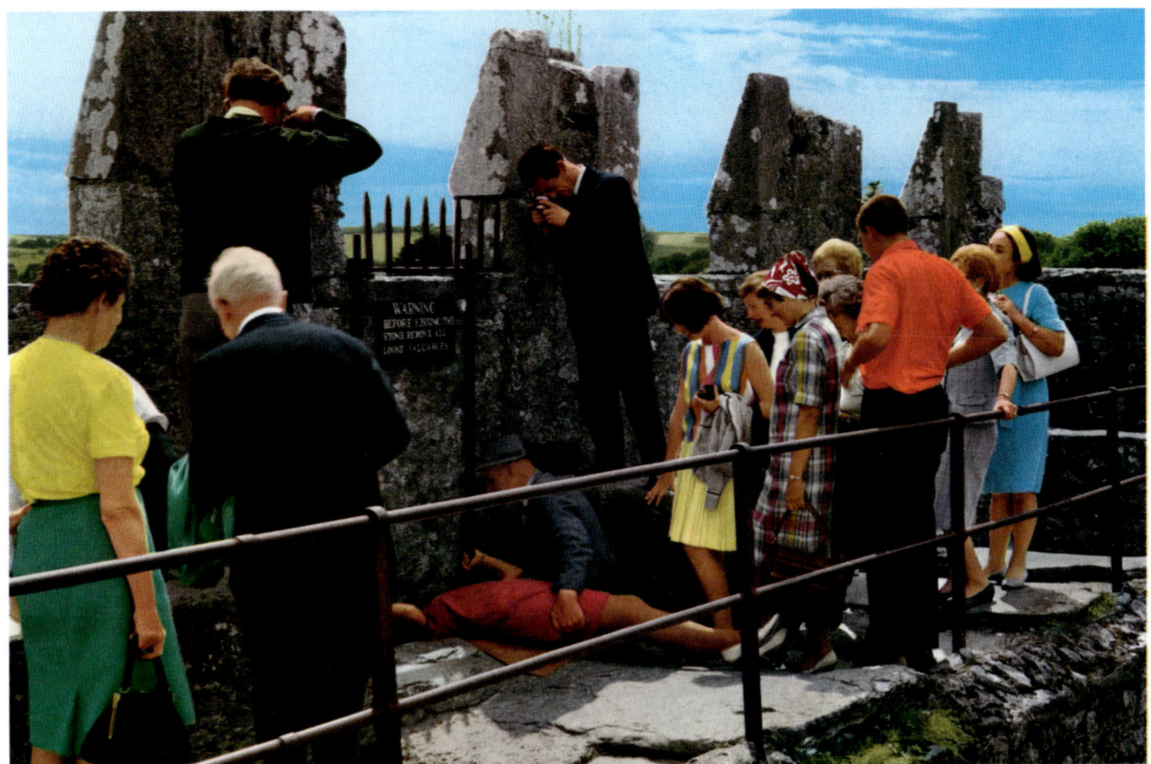

Kissing the Blarney Stone, Blarney Castle, Co. Cork, Ireland. *Photo: Joan Willis, John Hinde Studios.*

"The next question was selling these cards and of course I thought of Shannon Airport, because in those days every flight coming from the States arrived at Shannon. I went up to Shannon and I met the man who was in charge of the duty free shop. He said he'd never seen anything like this at Shannon. We set up a stand displaying the 6 giant postcards and this first night I was allowed to stay in the Duty Free Shop all through the night. And I sat with my back kind of half to the stand - it was only a little stand - to listen to the various comments that people made about the cards. That is how the John Hinde operation started. Of course the Americans like anything which is giant-sized so our giant cards went down very well. That was the beginning, I have a very good knowledge of the problems of reproduction. I'd had work reproduced before but I'd never had a hand in the physical operation itself. Here I had to do it all myself. I got to understand what the problems were and also I gained an image in my mind of the kind of effect which I felt was appropriate for the kind of postcards we wanted to produce. In these first cards there is a semblance - not yet the quality - but a semblance of a John Hinde card."
John Hinde

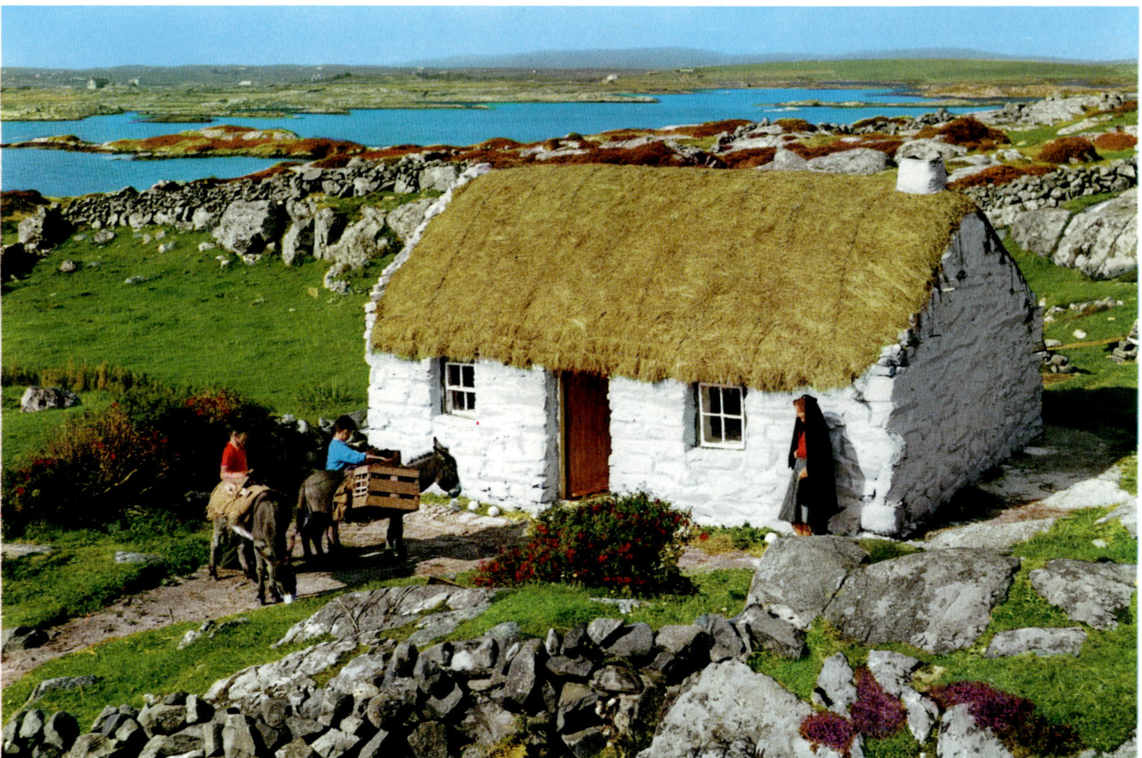

Thatched Cottage, Connemara, Co. Galway, Ireland. Colour Photo by John Hinde, F.R.P.S.

"People buy postcards when they are on holiday - and this is virtually the only time they do buy postcards - they buy them to send to their friends. And very often they put a message on the back to the effect that we are having a wonderful time here. There are two factors here; they want to buy a postcard which is so beautiful that it justifies the choice of the place that they decided to go for their holiday. People often make a mistake. They go for a holiday somewhere and realise that they made the wrong choice. But they'll never admit that to their friends and they want something to fully support their attitude in going to this place. They have to justify their decision to their friends and, whether it's true or not, they have to tell their friends that they really are enjoying it and isn't it a lovely place as you can see from the picture. There was another factor. My wife and I thought Ireland was extremely beautiful. These were the early days of Irish tourism and we were genuinely anxious to present to the world an image of Ireland as an exceptionally beautiful country so that more people could enjoy it. I would think that our contribution to publicising Ireland was at least equal to anything done at that time by Bord Fáilte, because millions of our postcards have gone around the world and been pinned up and framed and incorporated as souvenirs. And that to some extent was more lasting publicity for Ireland than press advertisements, posters and whatever."
John HInde

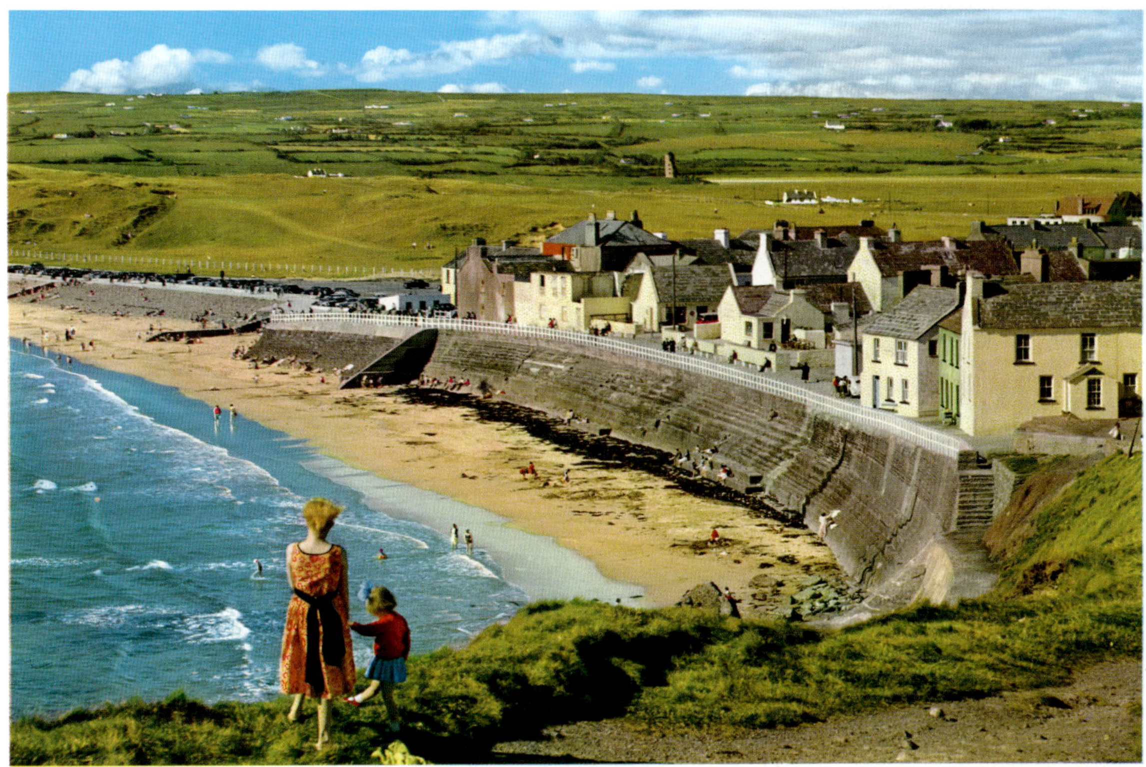

Lahinch, Co. Clare, Ireland.

Colour Photo by John Hinde, F.R.P.S.

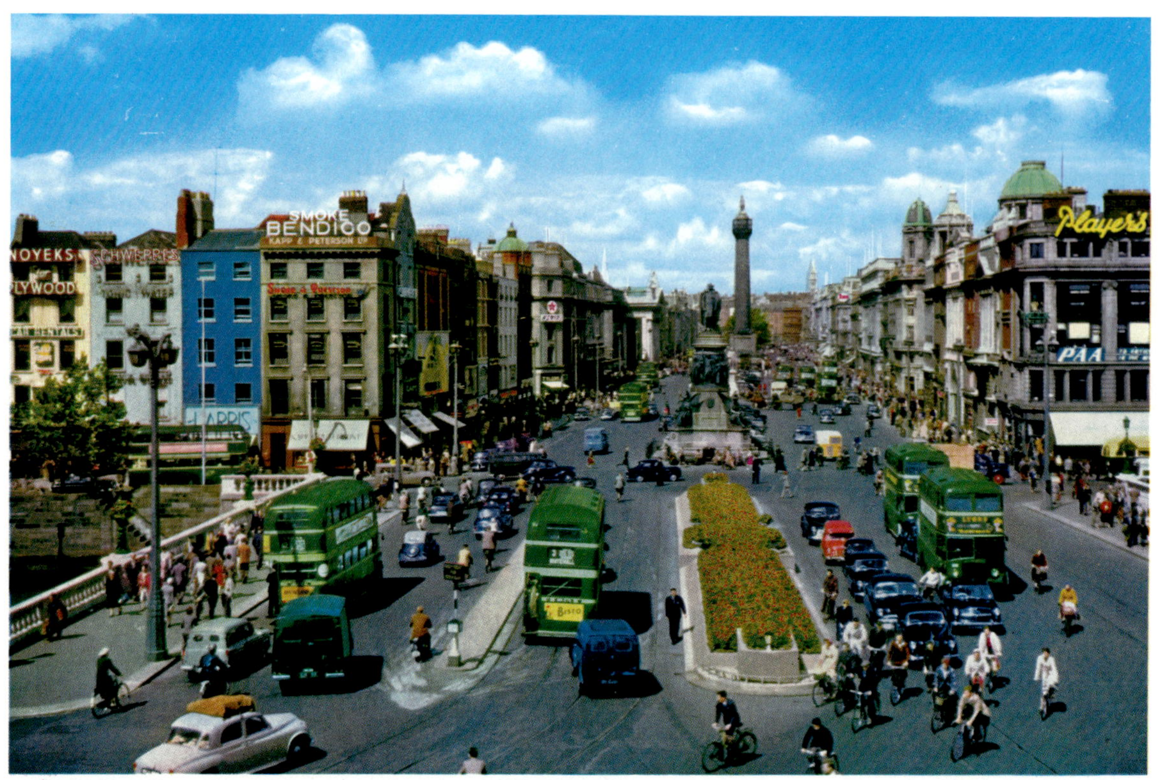

Nelson's Pillar, O'Connell Street, and Bridge, Dublin, Ireland.

Colour Photo by John Hinde, F.R.P.S.

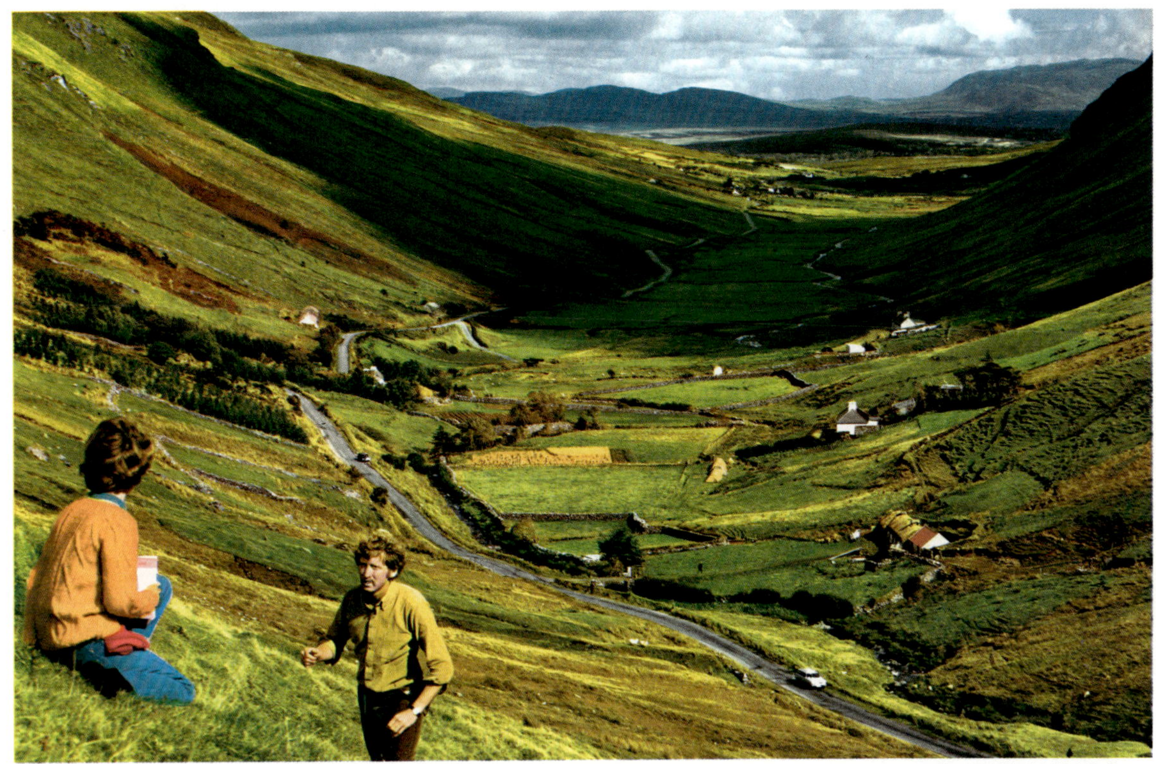

Glengesh Pass, near Ardara, Co. Donegal, Ireland.

Photo: D. Noble, John Hinde Studios.

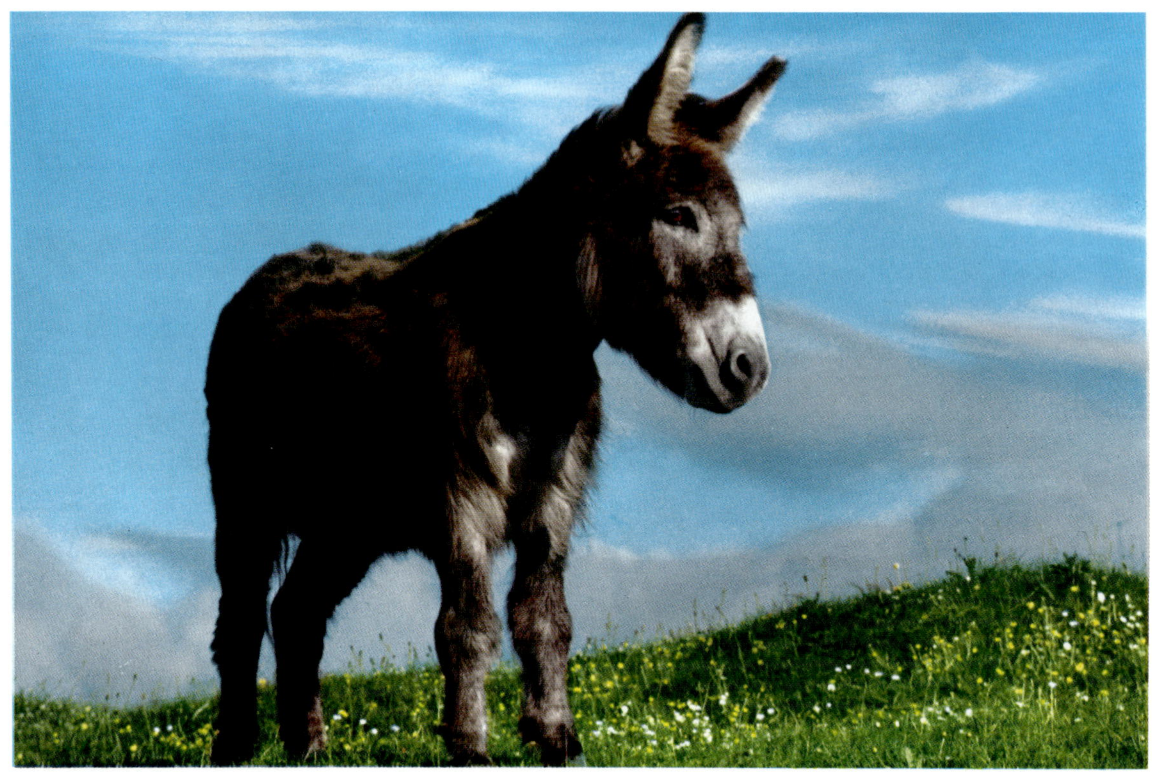

An Irish Donkey. Photo: Joan Willis, John Hinde Studios.

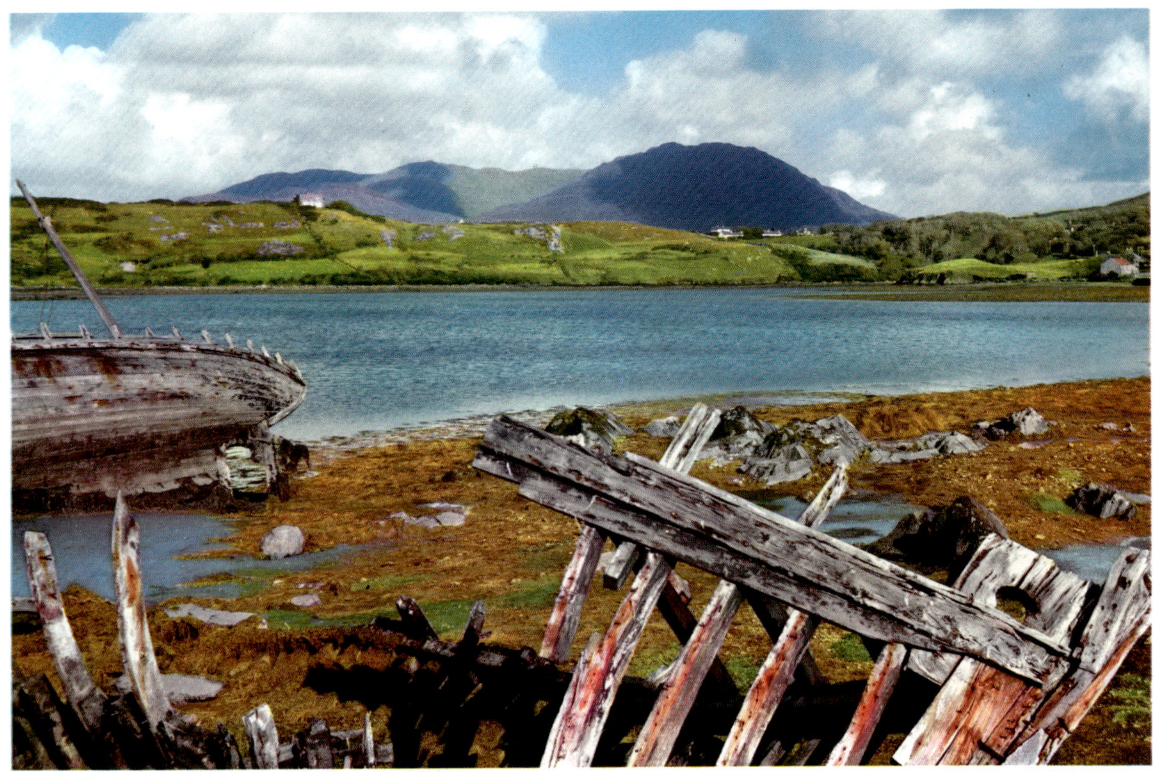

Letterfrack, Connemara, Co. Galway, Ireland.

Colour Photo by John Hinde, F.R.P.S.

John Hinde on Photographic Safari, East Africa 1966

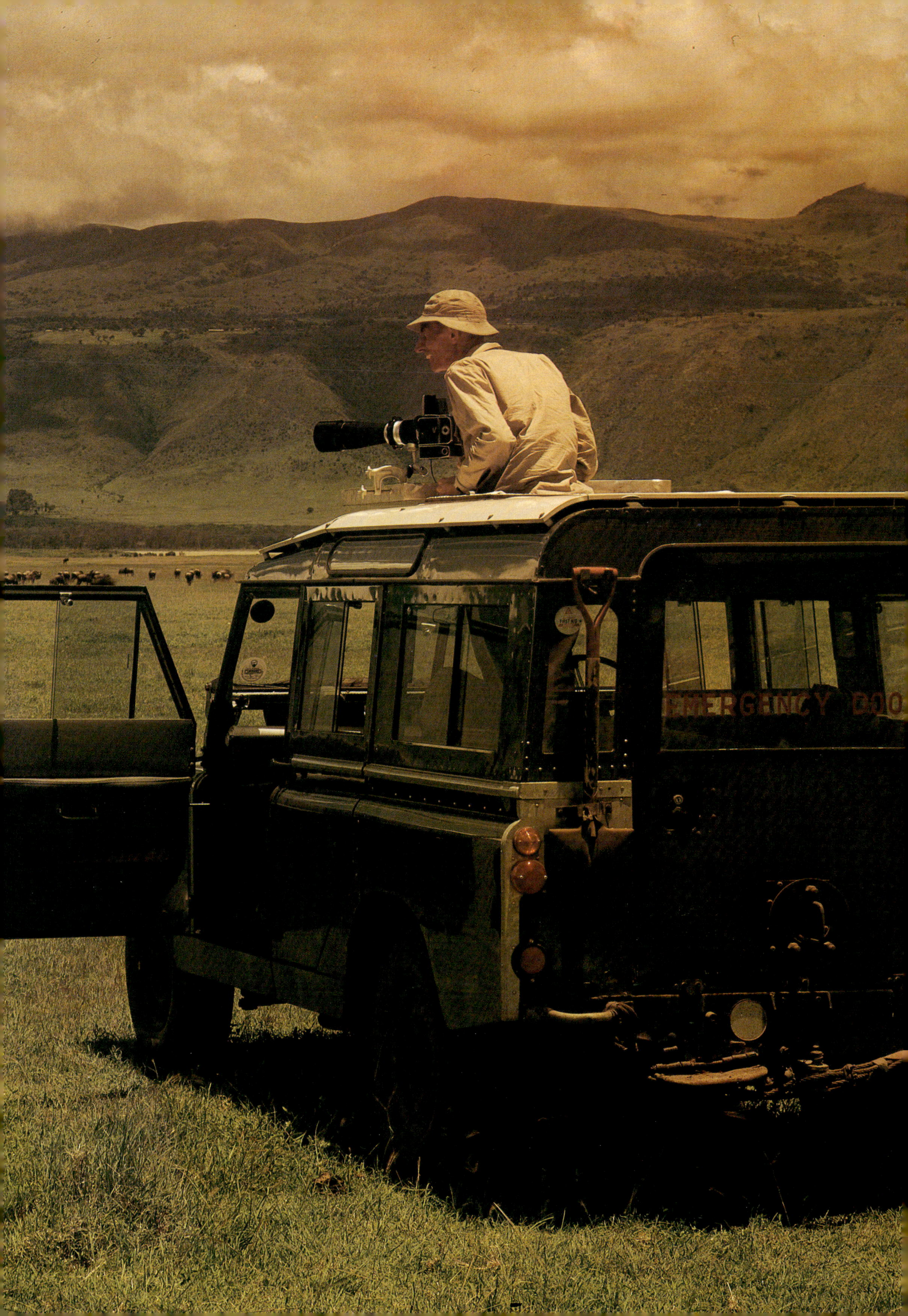
EMERGENCY DOO

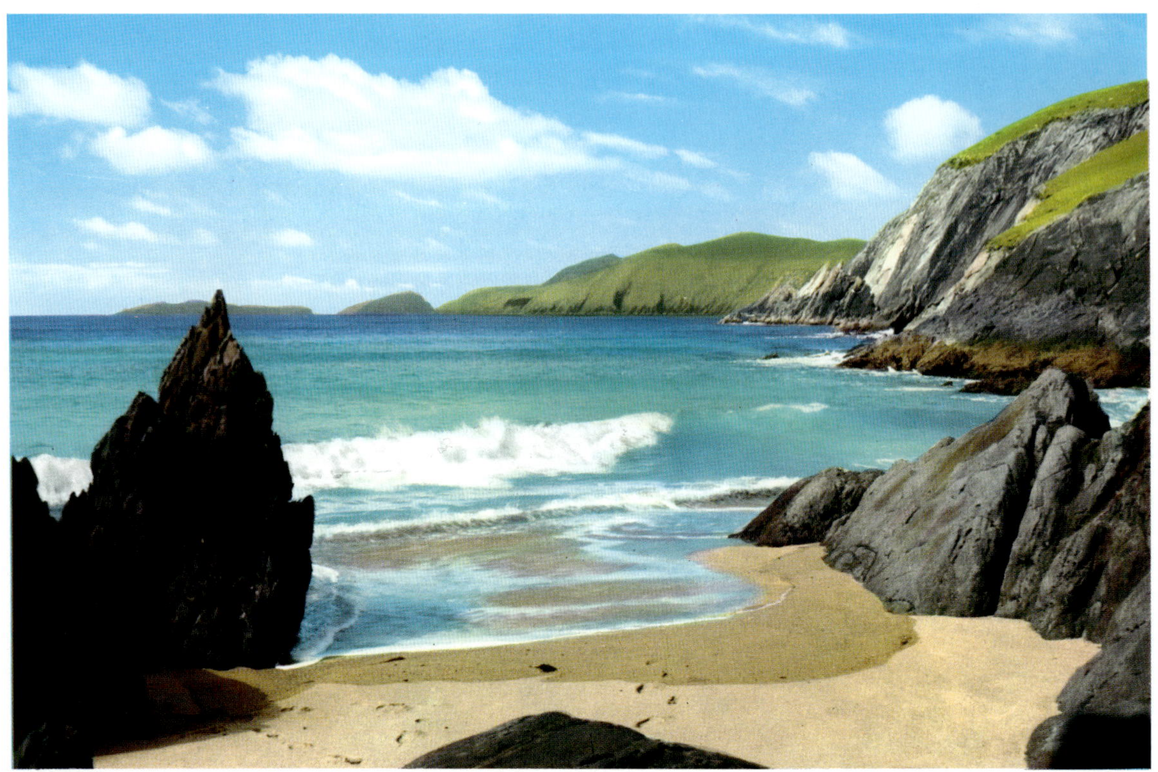

Blasket Islands from Dingle Peninsula, Co. Kerry, Ireland. Colour Photo by John Hinde, F.R.P.S.

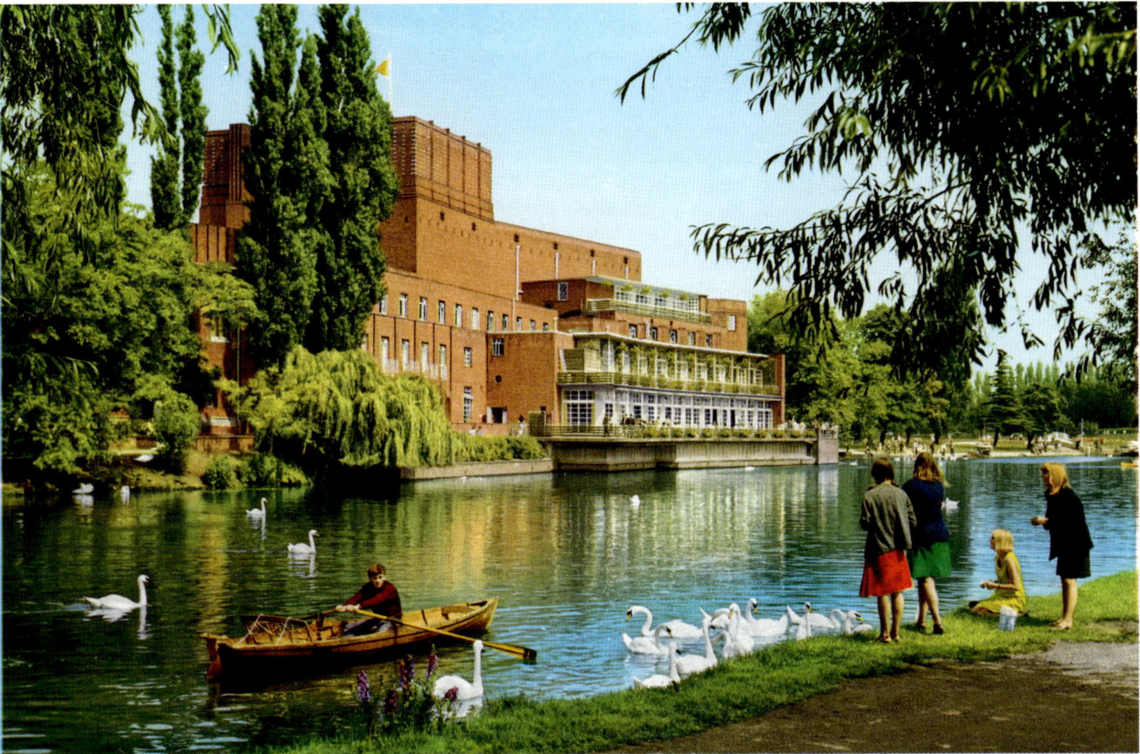

The Royal Shakespeare Theatre, Stratford-upon-Avon. Photo: Joan Willis, John Hinde Studios.

"The very first shot I did in Stratford upon Avon looks very simple but in fact I had to hire a rowing boat and get a man to row it up the river. I had to take bread with me in order to bribe the swans to come in close. Everything in the picture is contrived, the row boat was hired, the girls were co-opted from further down near the bridge where they were picknicking. Even the purple flowers were planted in there. Whoever saw delphiniums growing on a river bank? Without any of that confection it was a pretty bland shot. That was all the sort of thing you planned so that when you actually came to take the shot it is purely the mechanics of tripod, camera, lens, meter and click ... It was more or less standard practice to include figures in the foreground. You always tried to get somebody in the foreground if there was somebody around, anything that would bring a bit of interest. I carried all the usual things around in the car with me, flowers and the like. I also carried a little hatchet so I could chop down gorse bushes and things like this, so I could move them from one side of the hill to another."
Joan Willis

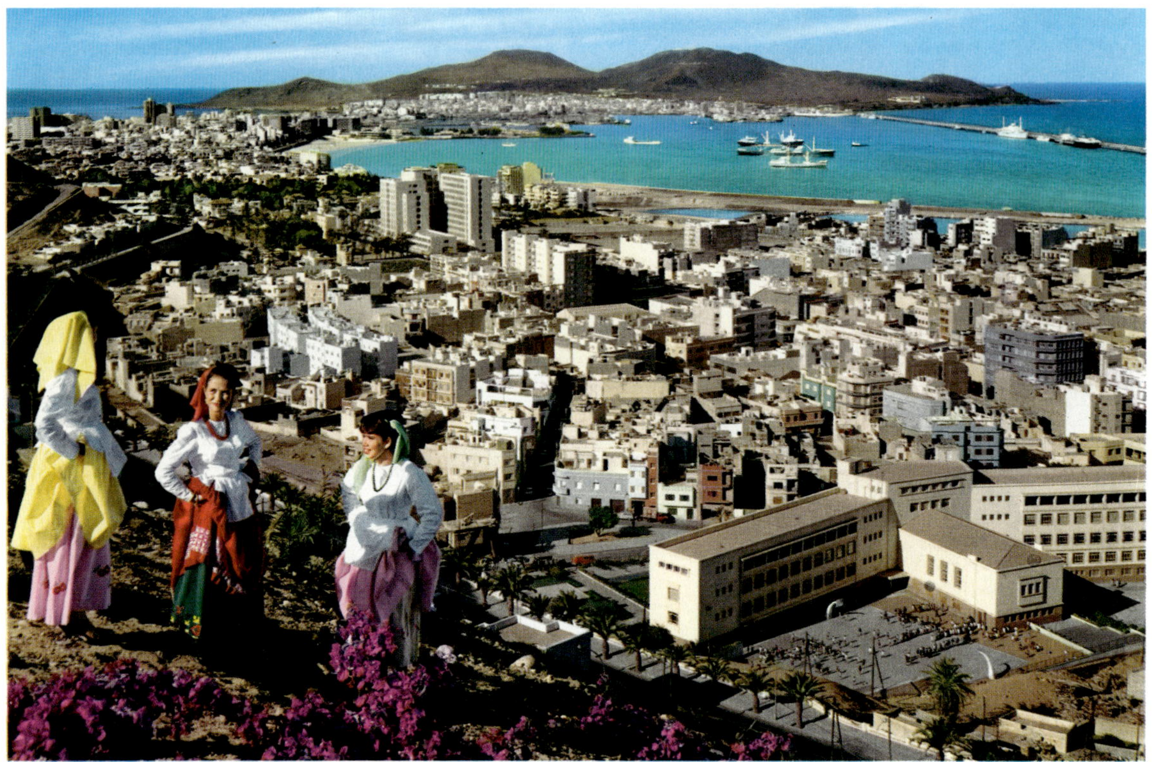

Las Palmas de Gran Canaria.

Photo: E. Ludwig, John Hinde Studios.

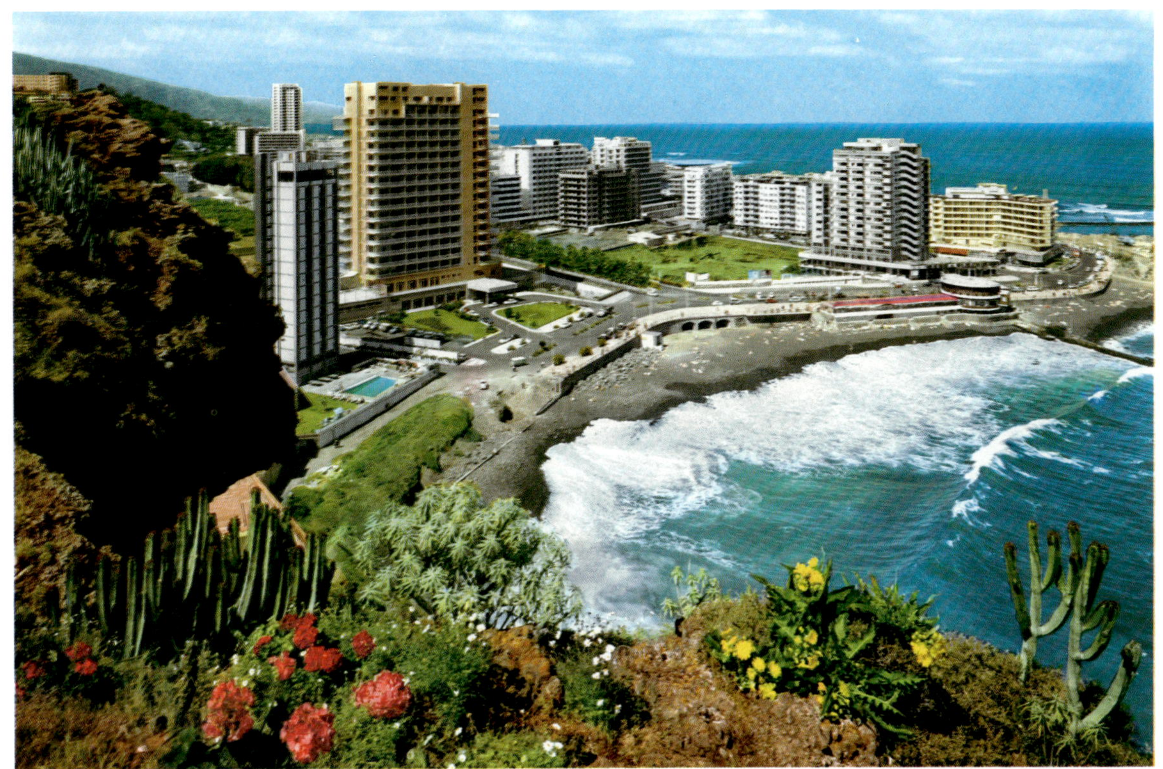

Puerto de la Cruz, Tenerife, Canary Islands. Photo: E. Ludwig, John Hinde Studios.

"Elmar Ludwig was brilliant, amazing. In the Canary Islands there's actually one picture where he planted a full cactus garden in the foreground in order to get the picture right."

David Noble

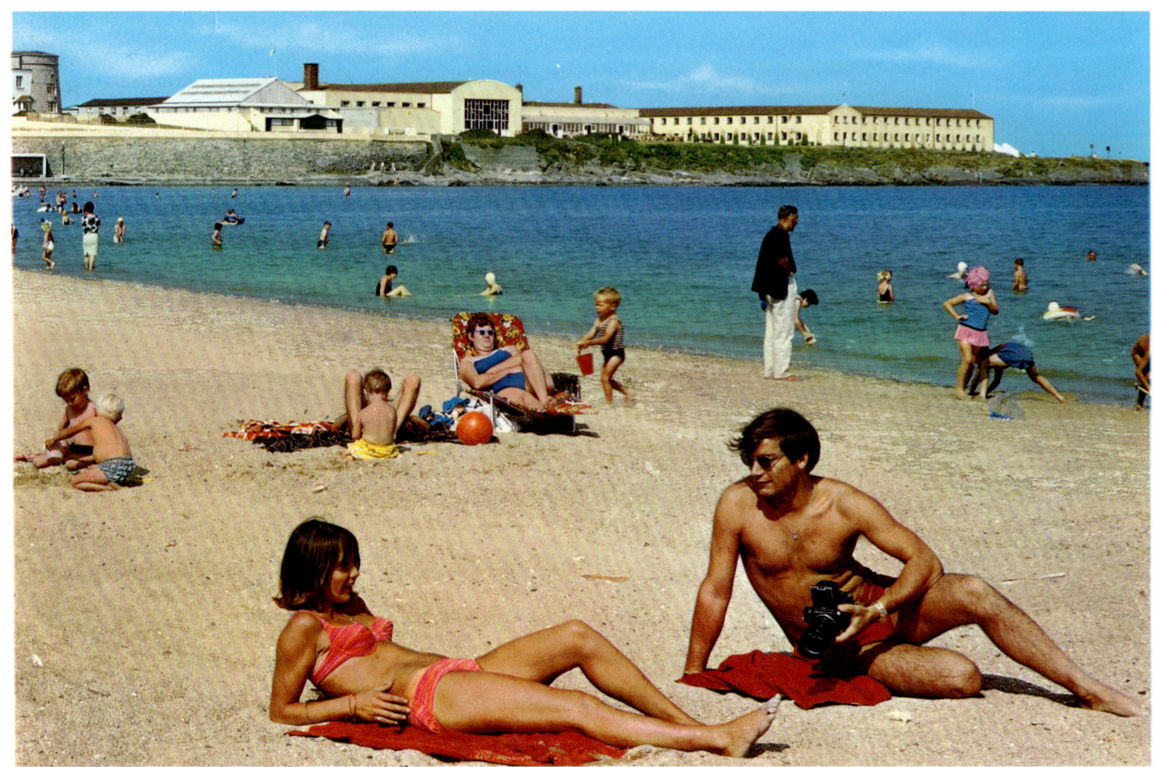

On the Beach, Skerries, Co. Dublin, Ireland. *Photo: E. Nägele, John Hinde Studios.*

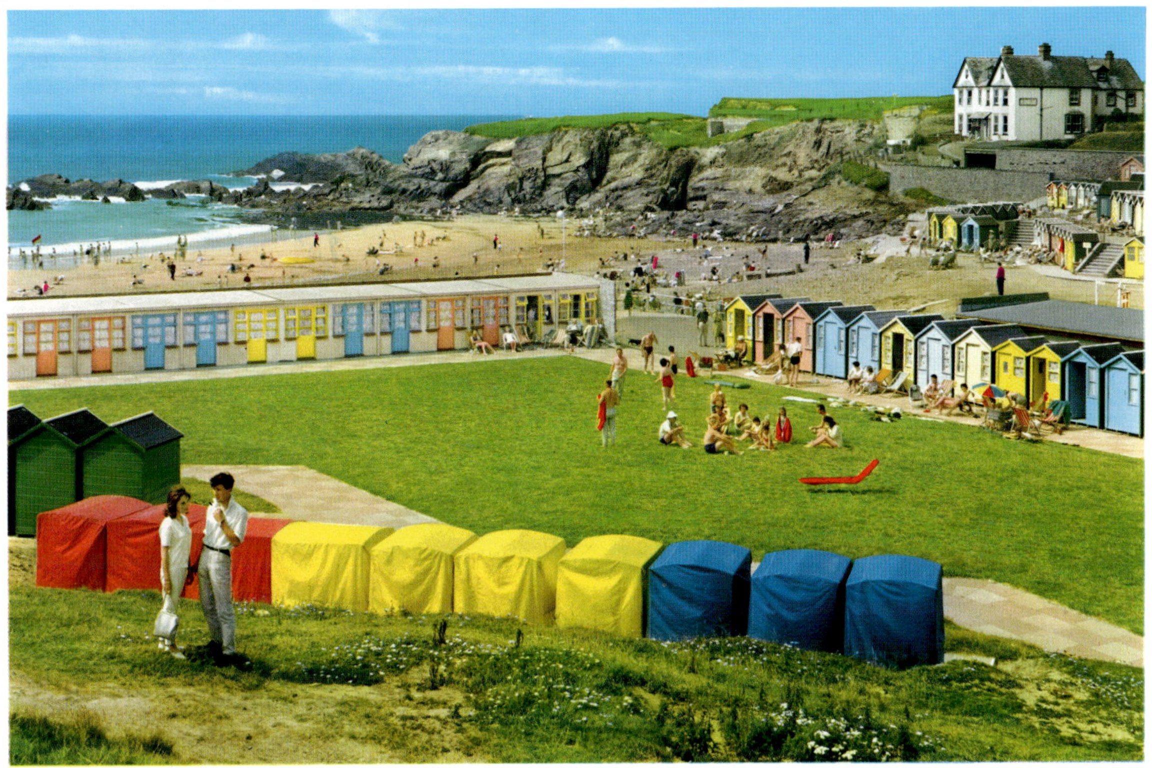

Crooklets Beach, Bude, Cornwall.

Photo: E. Ludwig, John Hinde Studios.

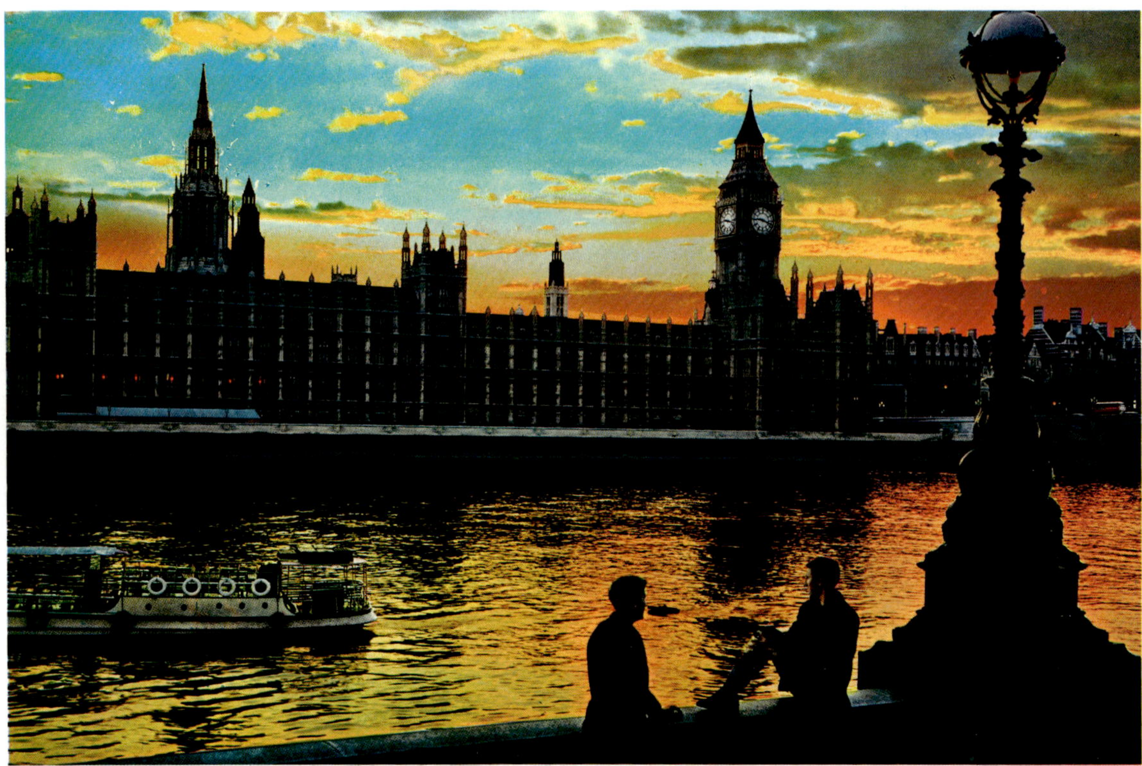

Sunset over the Houses of Parliament, London. Photo: E. Ludwig, John Hinde Studios.

"Sunsets always sell." *John HInde*

"He liked sunsets, sunsets always sell, there's nothing better than a sunset. You wouldn't believe it, these things sell like mad. You can't really have enough sunsets. You see on a lot of these sunsets the sky is completely put in." *Elmar Ludwig*

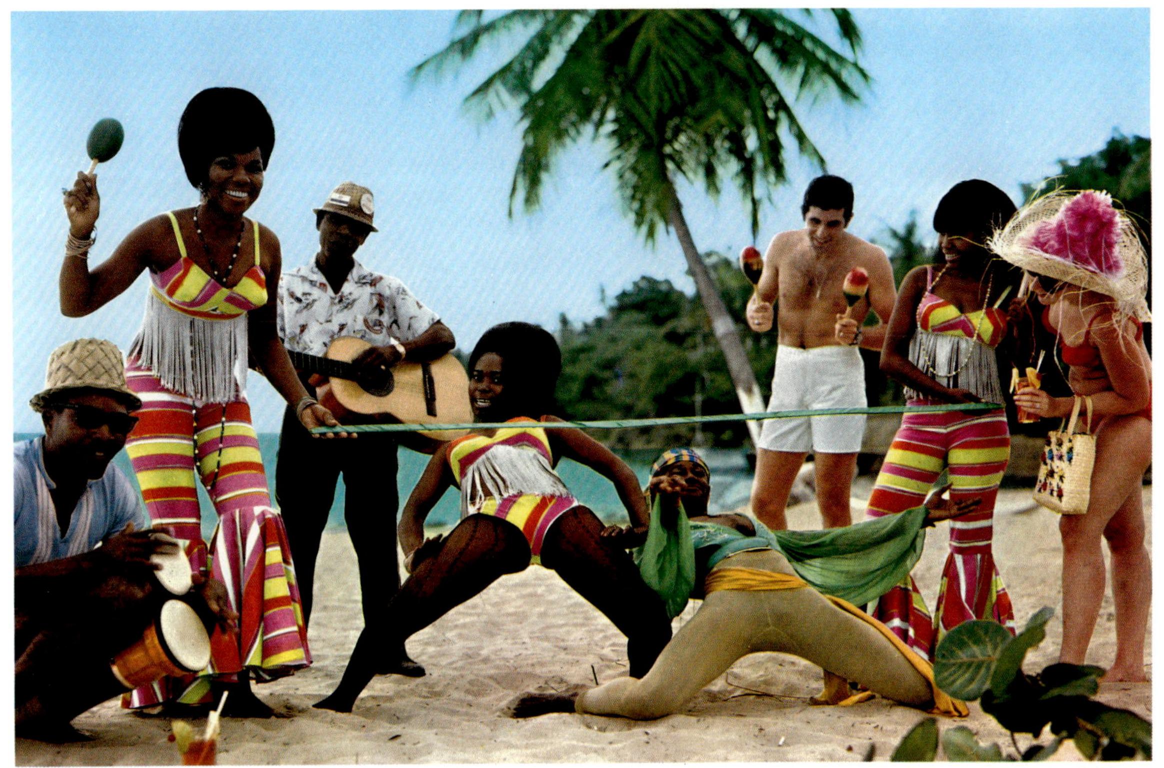

Limbo! Limbo! On the Beach—Jamaica W.I.

Photo: E. Ludwig, John Hinde Studios.

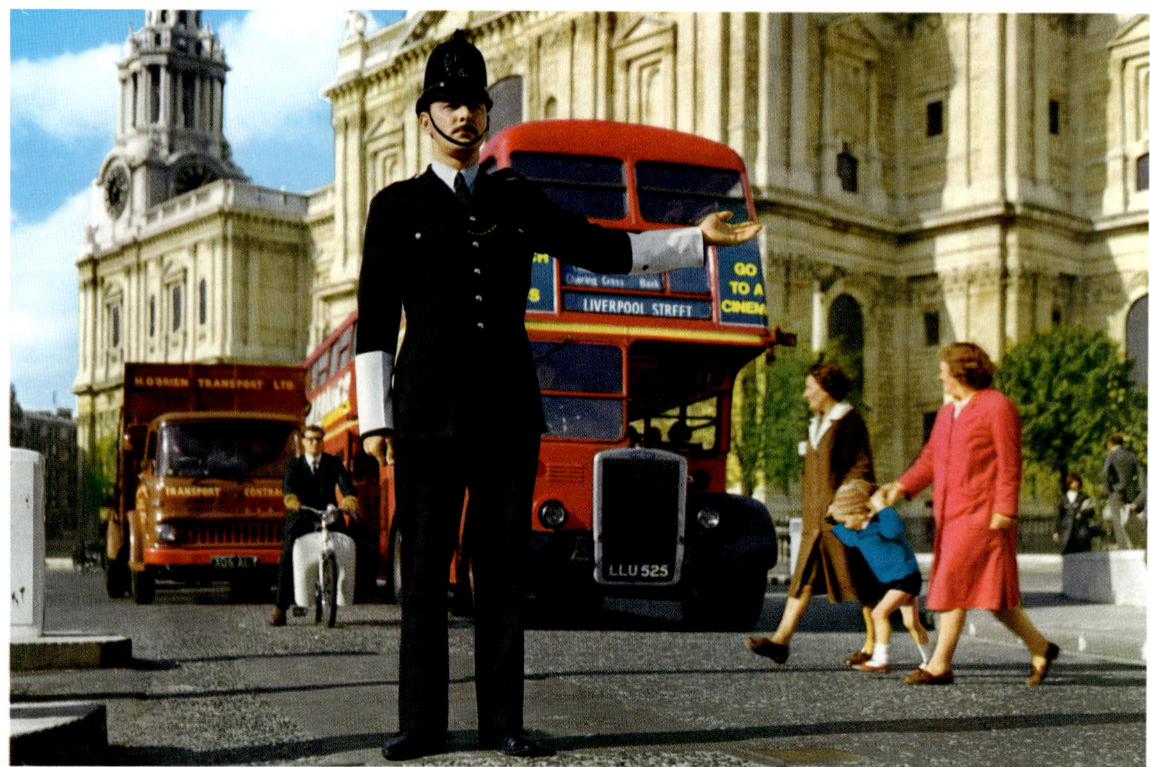

City of London Policeman.

Photo: E. Ludwig, John Hinde Studios.

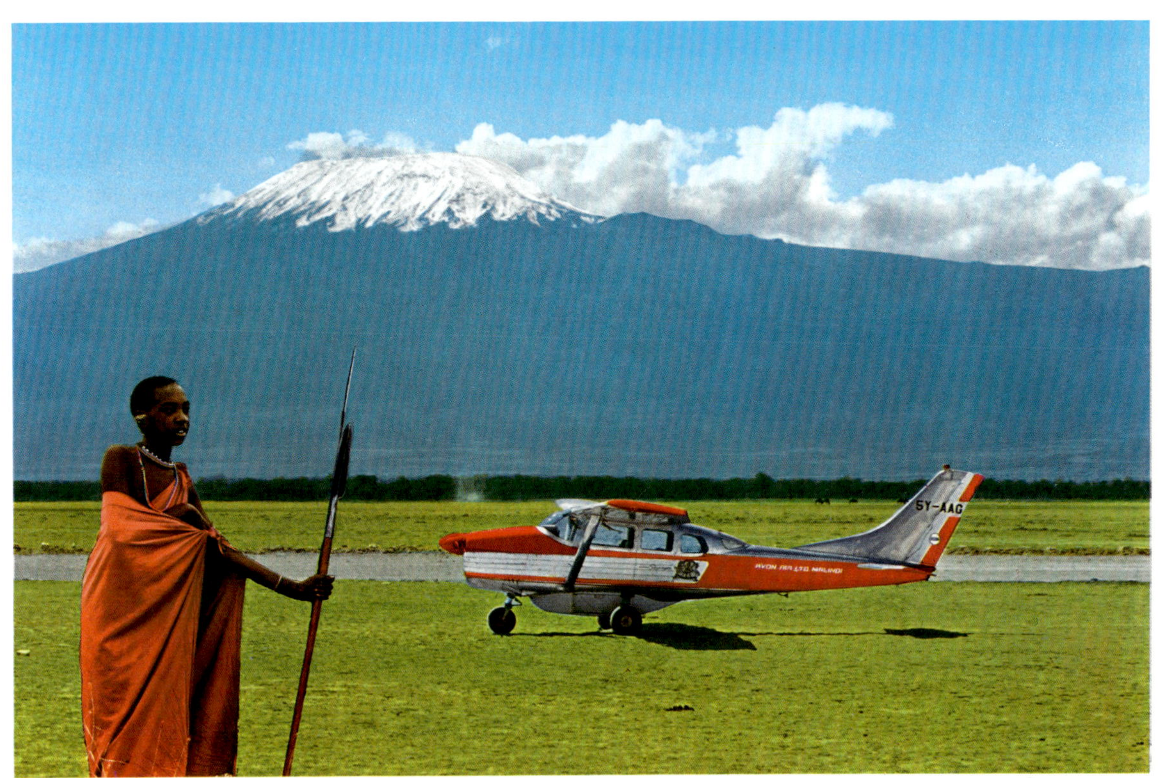

Airstrip—Landebahn—Piste d'atterrissage, Amboseli Game Reserve, Kenya.

Colour Photo by John Hinde, F.R.P.S.

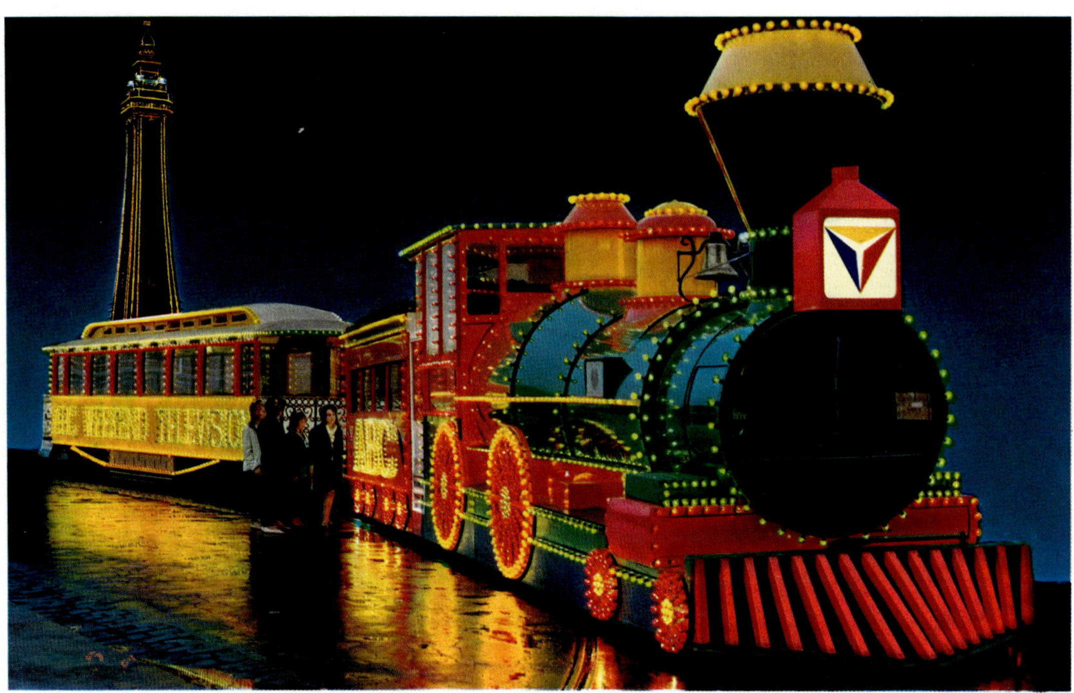

Blackpool Illuminations. The world's most famous Free Show. Photo: E. Ludwig, John Hinde Studios.

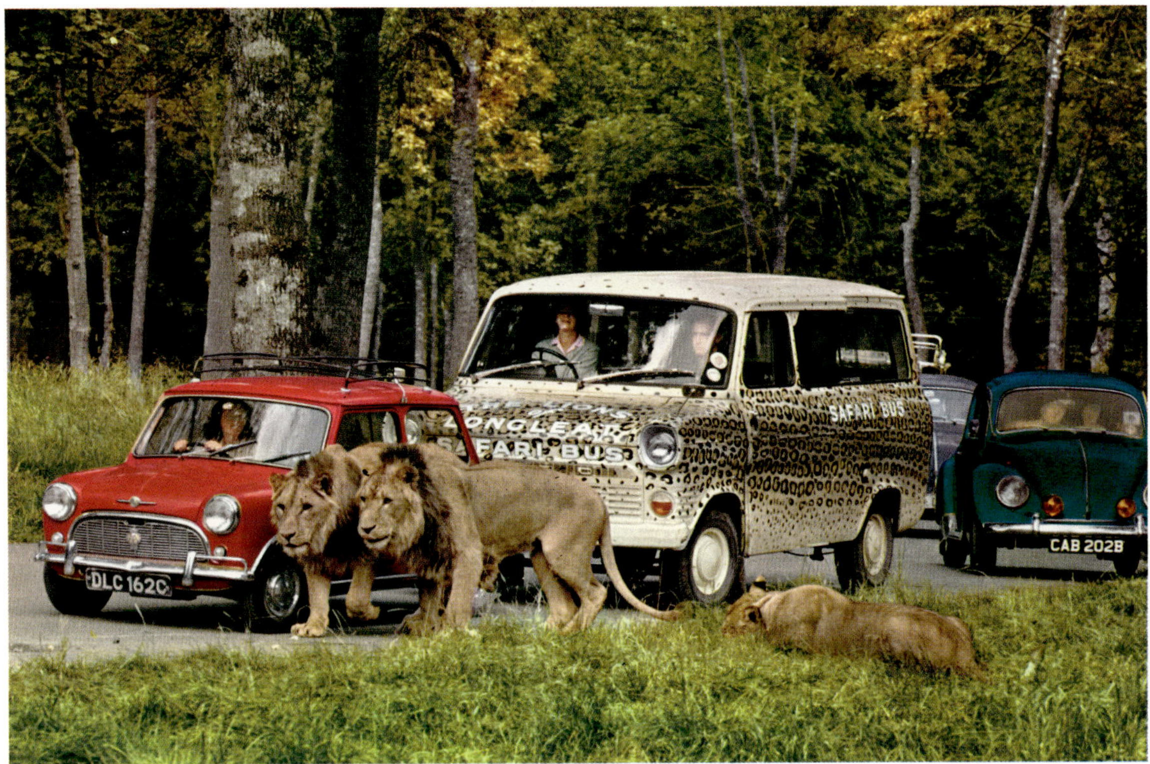

The Lions of Longleat, Warminster, Wiltshire.

Colour Photo by John Hinde, F.R.P.S.

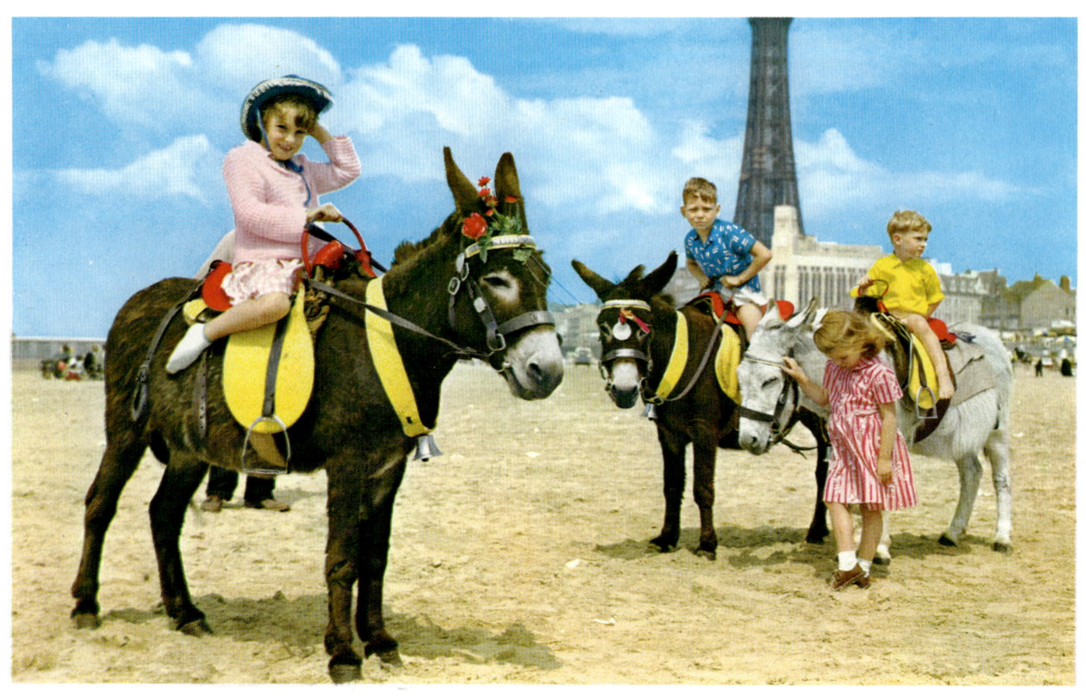

Donkey Rides, Blackpool Sands.

Photo: E. Ludwig, John Hinde Studios.

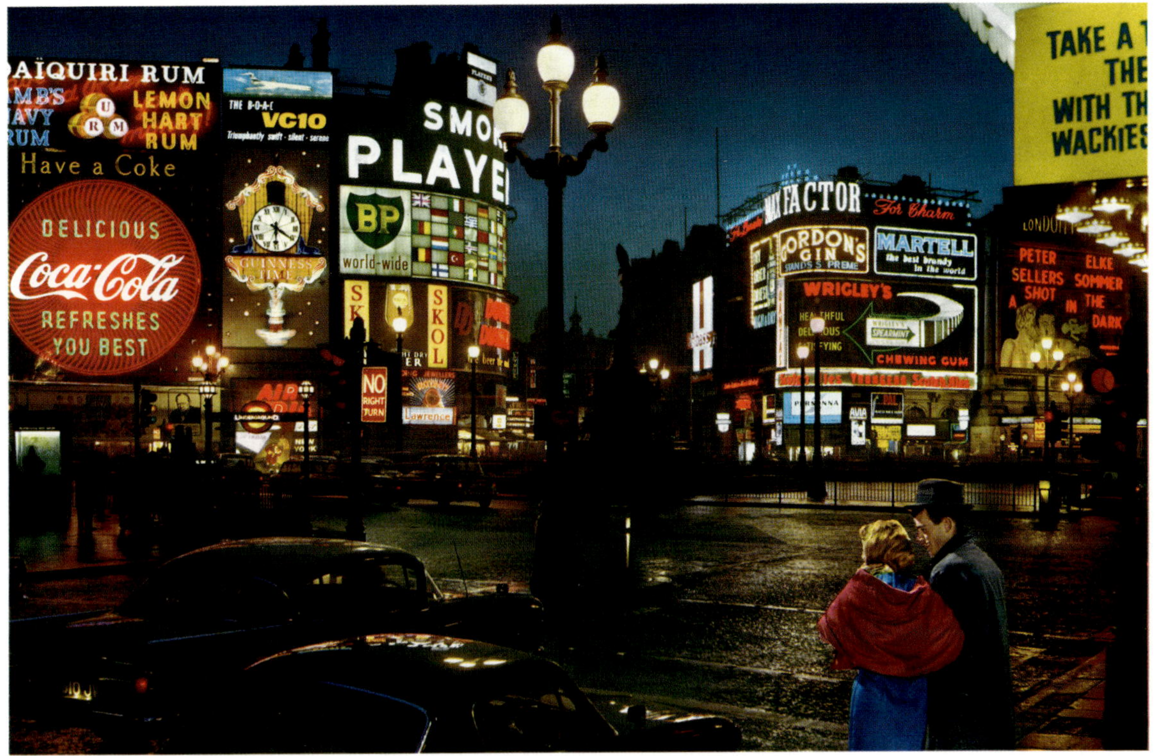

Piccadilly by Night, London.

Photo: E. Ludwig, John Hinde Studios.

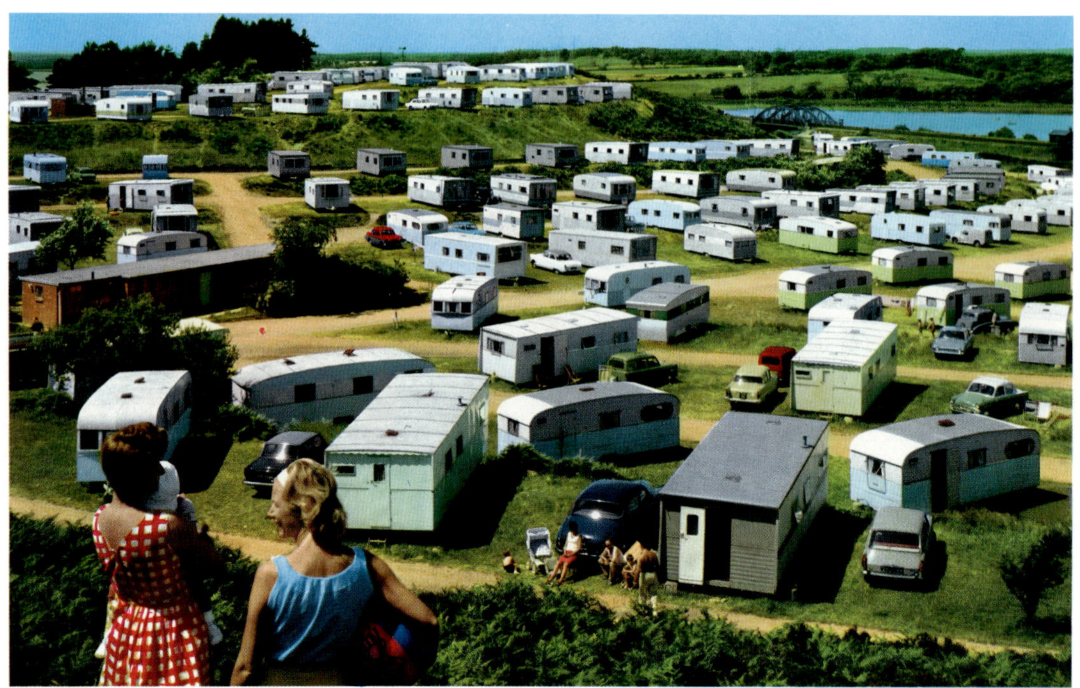

Rockley Vale, Rockley Sands, Poole, Dorset. *Photo: E. Nägele, John Hinde Studios.*

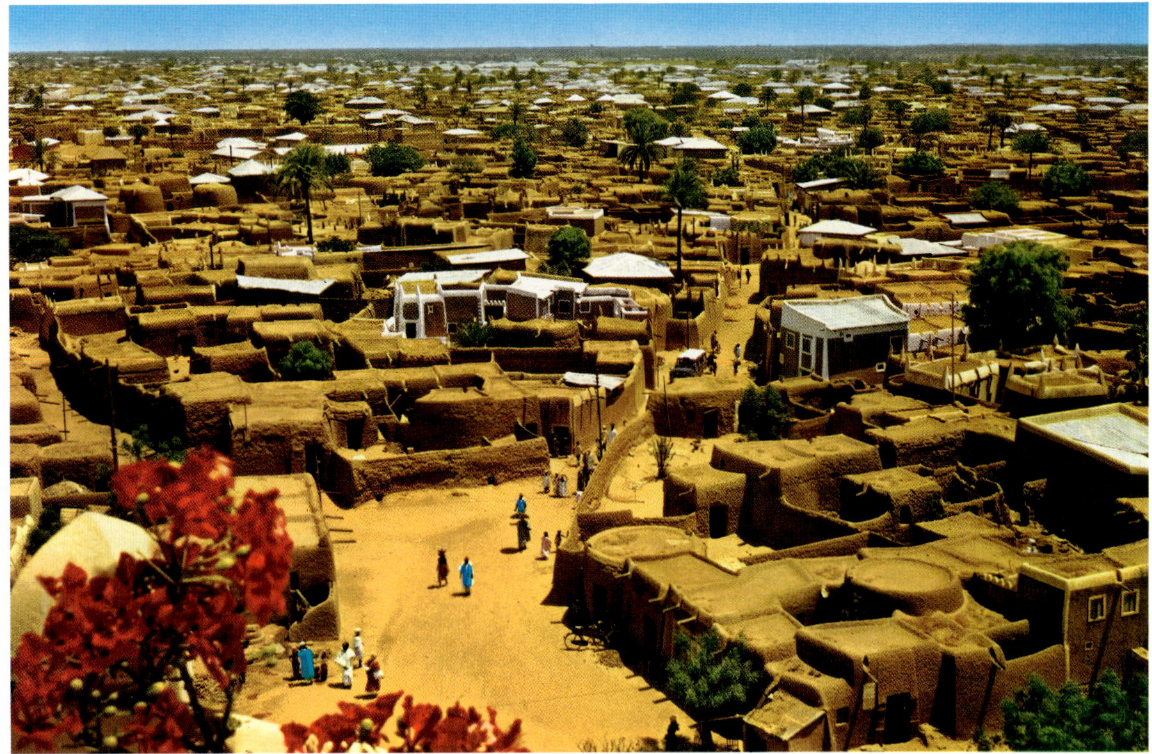

Historic Kano City, Northern Nigeria.

Colour Photo by John Hinde, F.R.P.S.

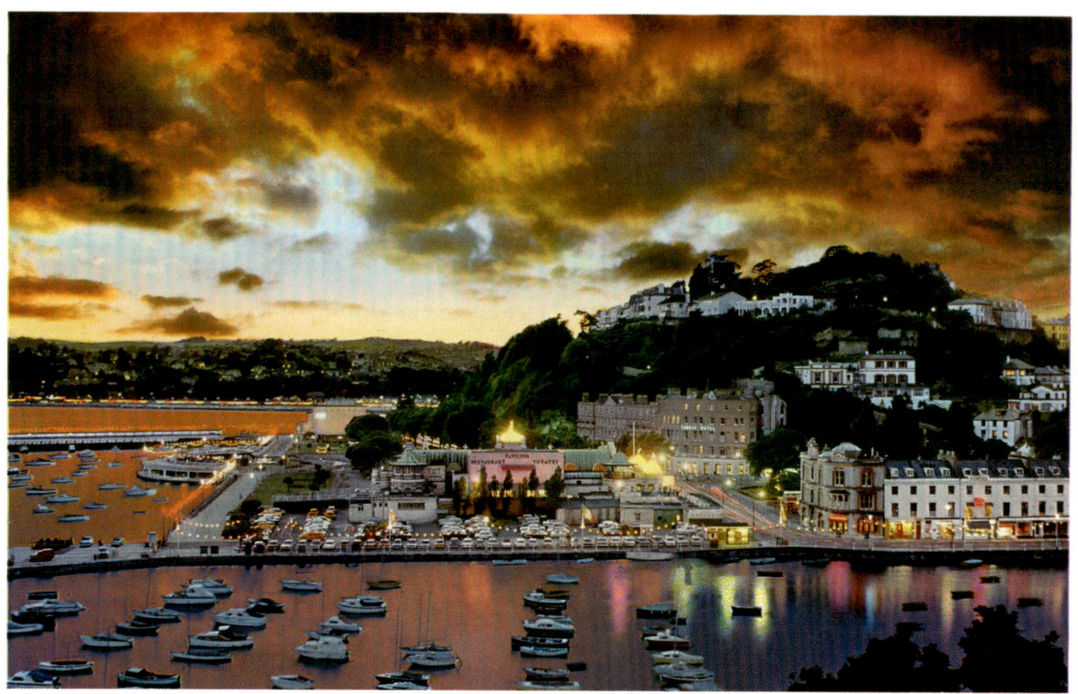

Twilight over Torquay Harbour, South Devon.

Photo : E. Nägele, John Hinde Studios.

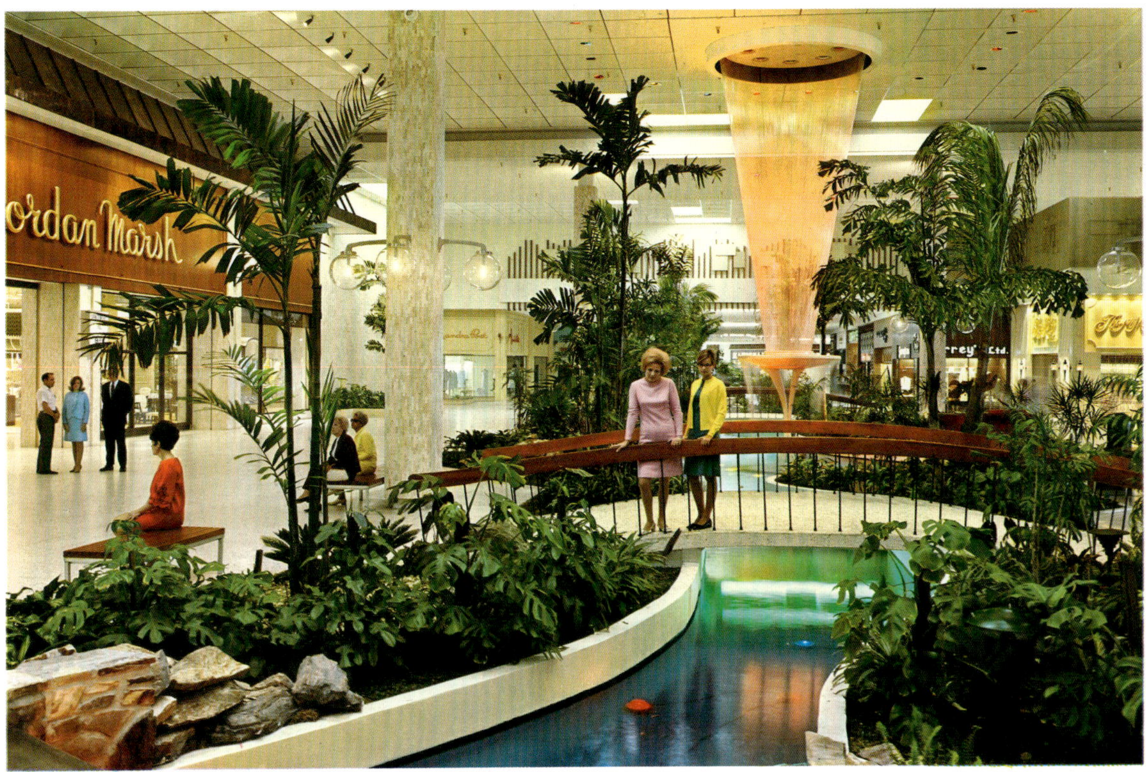

Palm Beach Mall, West Palm Beach, Florida.

Photo: E. Ludwig, John Hinde Studios.

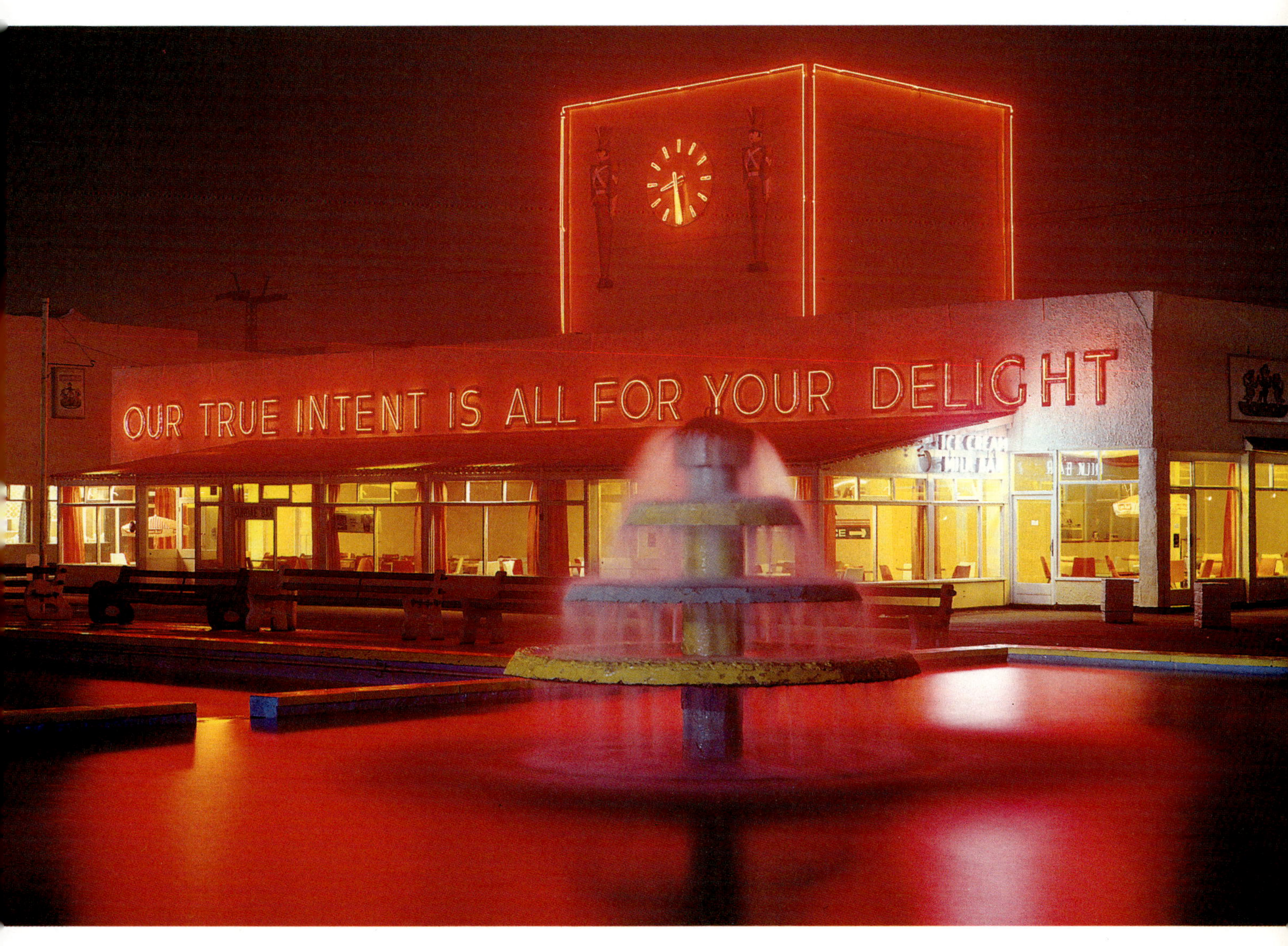

"The idea of these pictures - Butlins - was that anybody looking at them should have thought that this was a great place to have a holiday in."
Elmar Ludwig

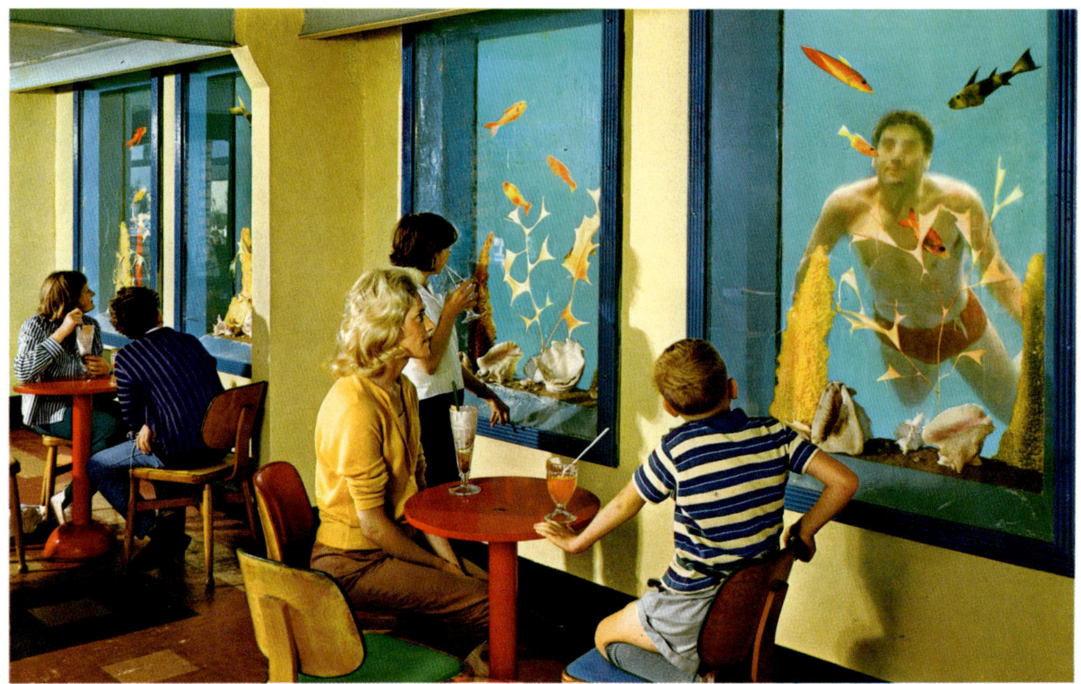

BUTLIN'S AYR—*Lounge Cafe and Indoor Heated Pool (Ground Level).* Photo: E. Ludwig, John Hinde Studios.

"Butlins was considered a bit of a nightmare for everyone *(the photographers)*. The only good thing that could be said about Butlins was that you were guaranteed to get a good few shots out of it, and as much food as you could eat. From a photographer's point of view it was a tough assignment with a lot of interior set-ups, fixing up flashbulbs, stands, changing bulbs, managing people etc. And the rooms were so big it was a problem. And they always had to have people in them, so you needed plenty of light. You've got to use a slow exposure to get the details and flash to get the people sharp. A lot of the people were put in. They were people who either worked there or volunteered. Some of them would be punters but, by and large, they were set up. You can only take two shots of each set-up because you've got three or four flash heads, three bulbs in each and they probably cost a pound each."

Peter O'Toole

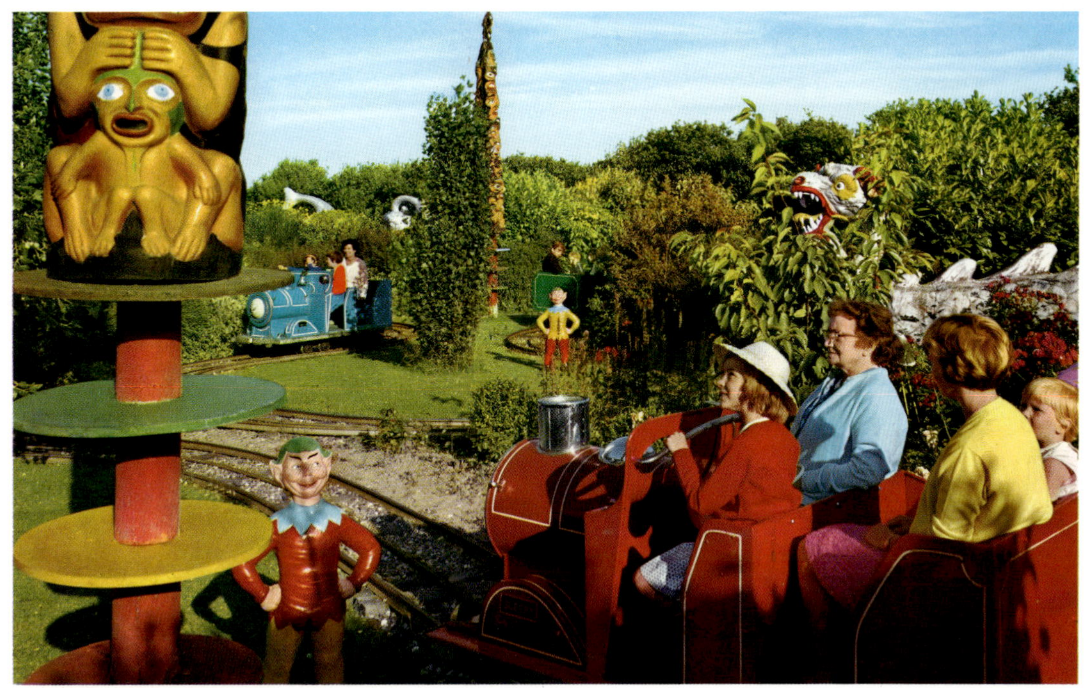

BUTLIN'S FILEY—*Peter Pan Railway.* Photo: E. Nägele, John Hinde Studios.

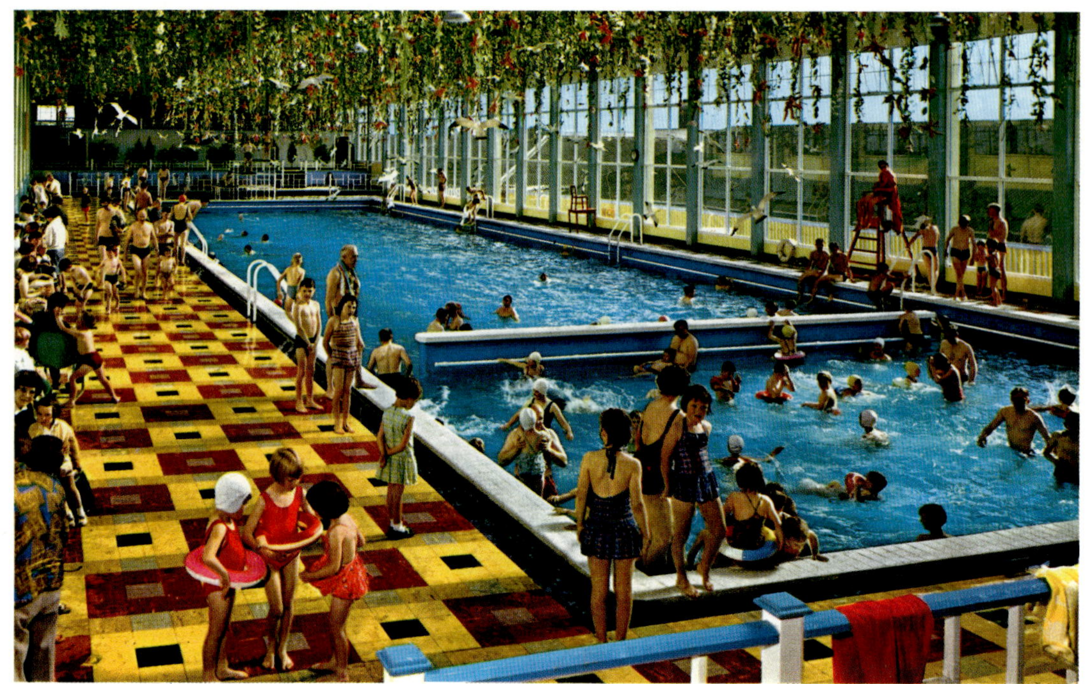

MOSNEY – *The Indoor Heated Pool.* Photo : E. Nägele, John Hinde Studios.

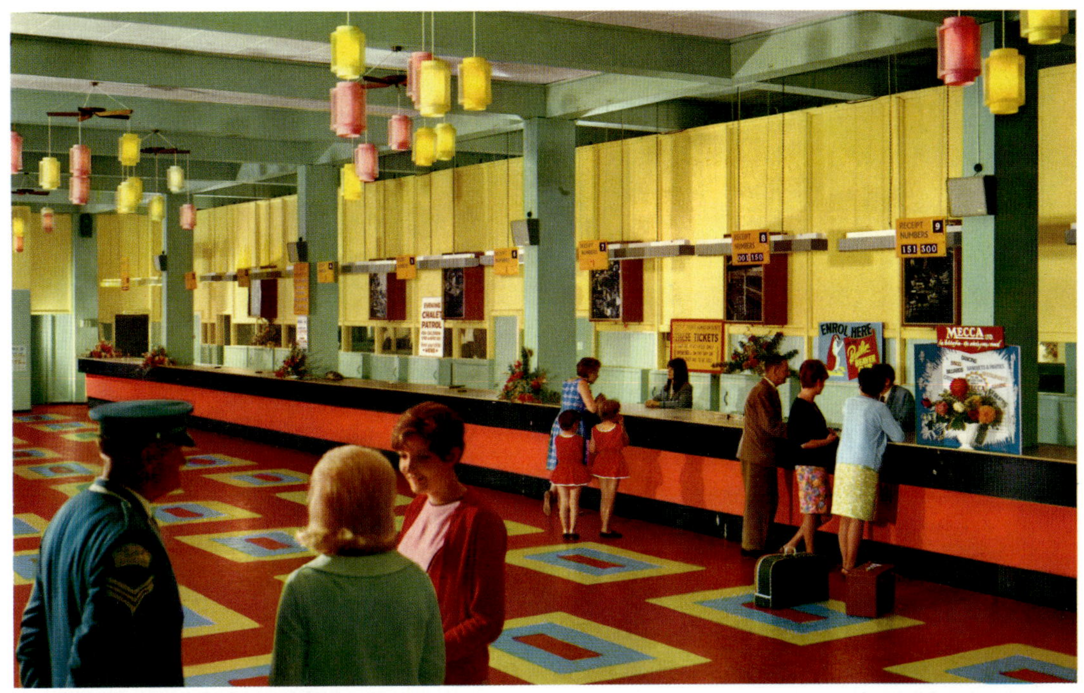

BUTLIN'S BARRY ISLAND—*The Reception Hall*

Photo : E. Nägele, John Hinde Studios.

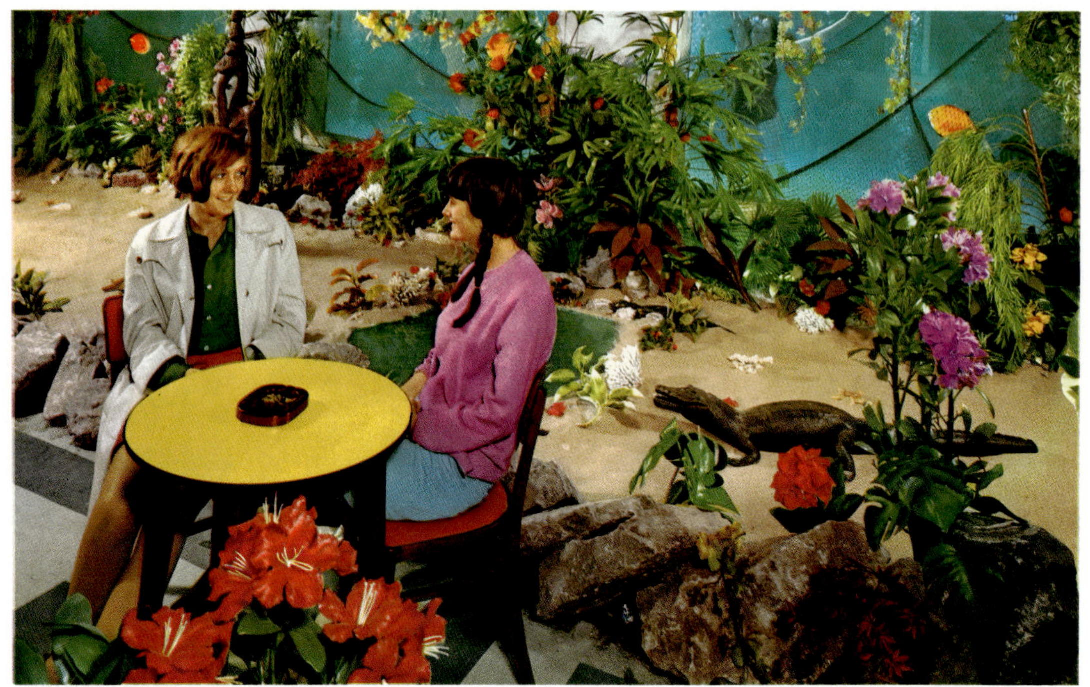

BUTLIN'S BARRY ISLAND—*A Lounge Grotto*

Photo: E. Nagele, John Hinde Studios.

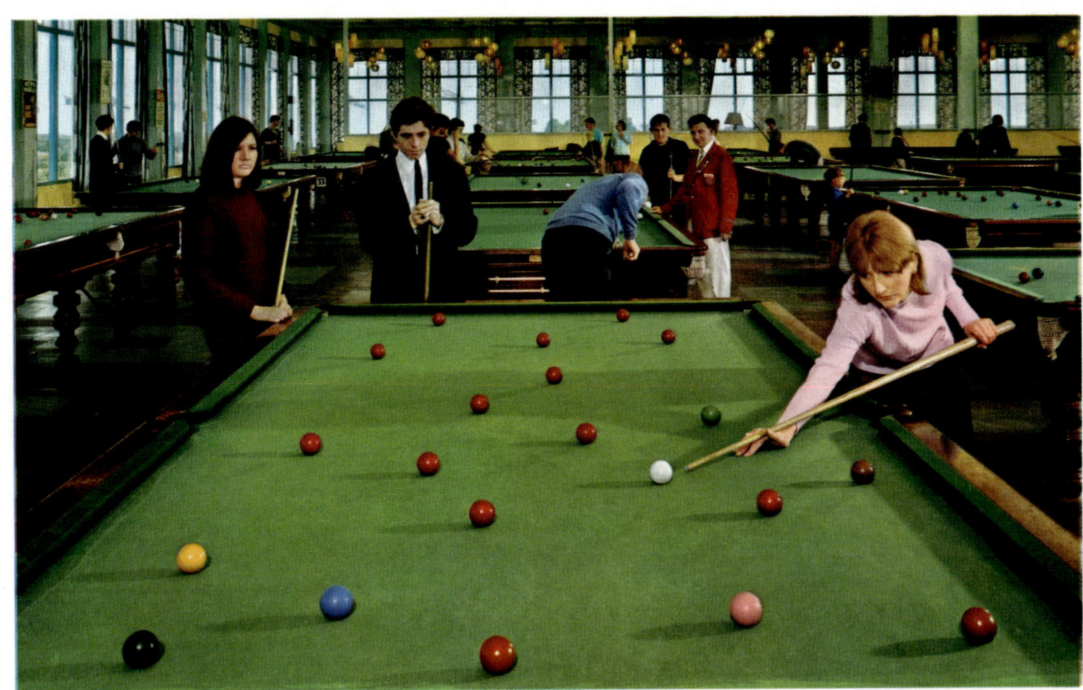

BUTLIN'S FILEY—*A Billiard Room*

Photo: E. Nägele, John Hinde Studios.

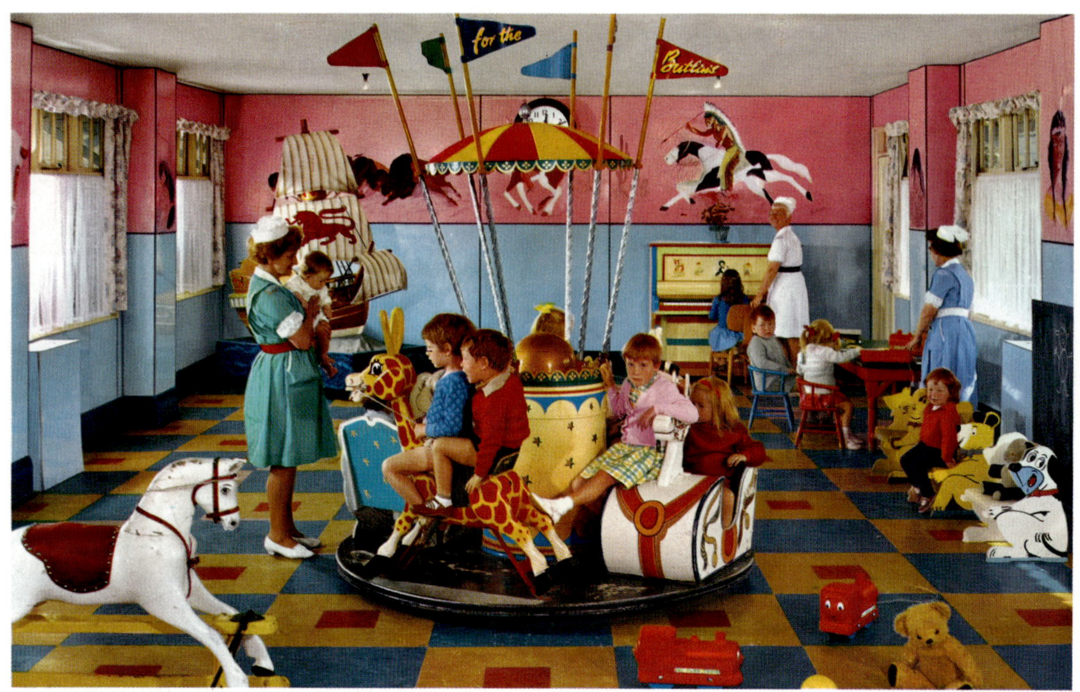

BUTLIN'S FILEY—*The Nursery*

Photo: E. Nägele, John Hinde Studios.

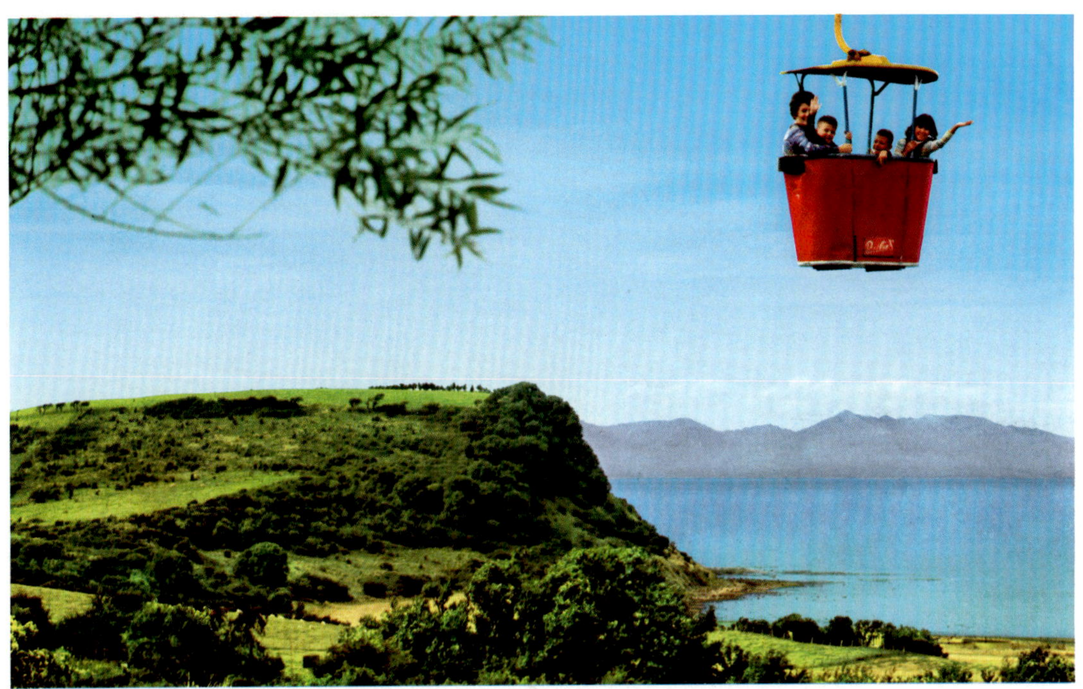

BUTLIN'S AYR—*Chairlift and Heads of Ayr*

Photo: D. Noble, John Hinde Studios.

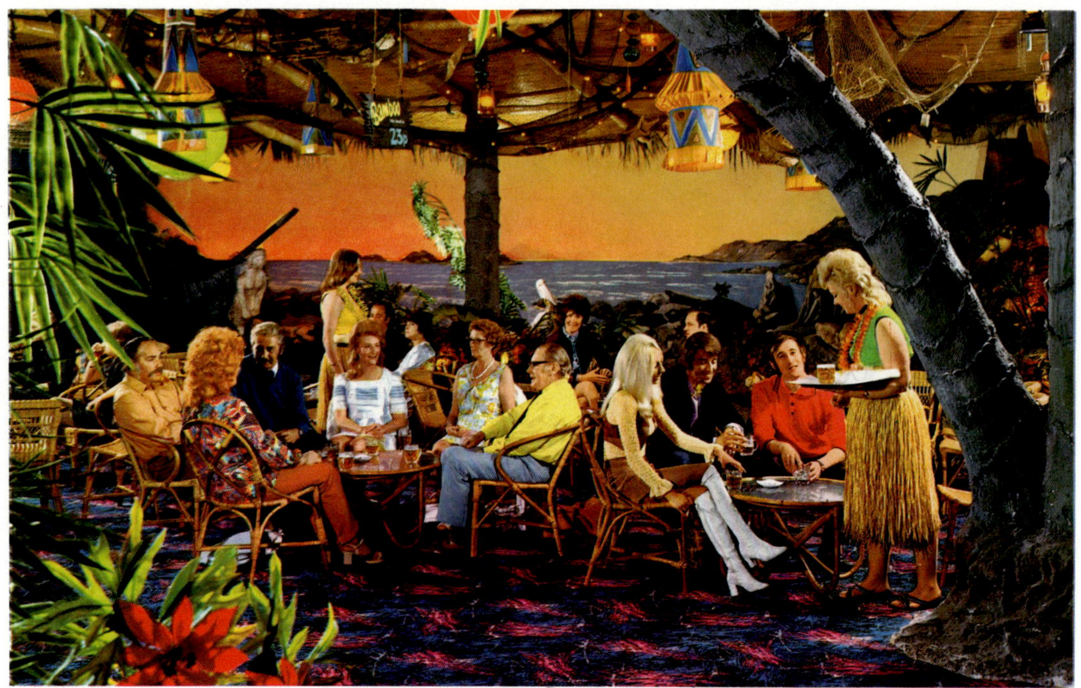

BUTLIN'S SKEGNESS—*The Beachcomber Bar.* Photo: D. Noble, John Hinde Studios.

"The wiring alone would take three hours to prepare and then the people would have to be warned that we were going to take a picture. Inevitably nothing happened the first time, or only half the bulbs would go off so you didn't really have anything. You usually needed three or four takes to get it right. The worst part was that all the drinkers in the Beachcombers were boozed up so they were tripping over your wires and pulling them out. All the Butlin's pictures were done live, no staging. Every surface was sticky with beer and dirt in the Beachcombers. What doesn't come over in the photograph is how tacky these places were, covered with dust and swimming in beer. Also, the bars were much darker than the photographs make them look, so you couldn't see how bad it was. I suppose we didn't make them look that much better. We used to move things around in the foreground but, if you like, it was the same as when you take pictures underwater. Those underwater pictures only look so bright because somebody's got a light on them. It's the same in the Beachcomber. You whack all that flash on to it and they've got all this plastic foliage, orchids and trees and Easter Island statues. So the colour is actually there. And then of course the separations were intensified as well."
David Noble

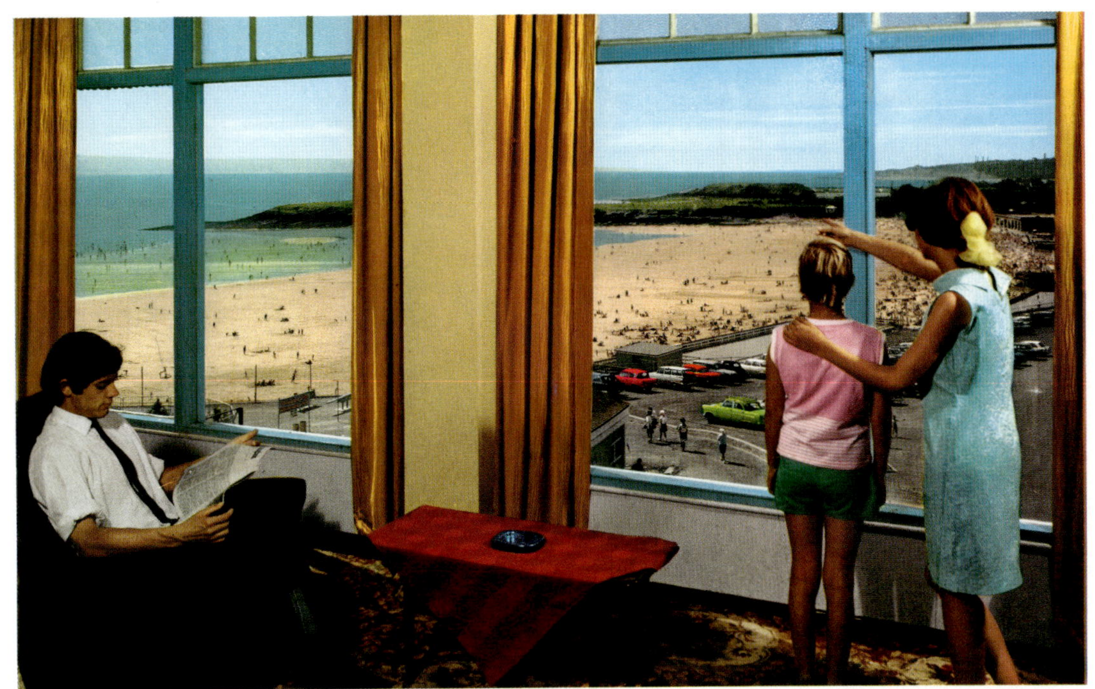

BUTLIN'S BARRY ISLAND—*A View from the Quiet Lounge.* Photo: E. Nägele, John Hinde Studios.

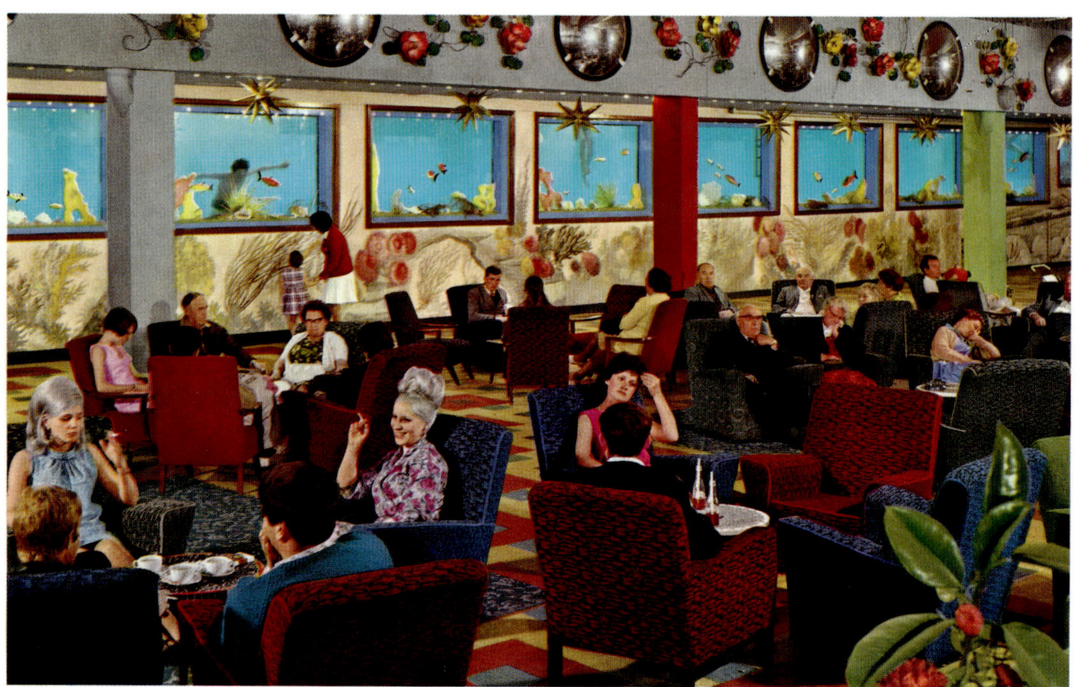

BUTLIN'S BOGNOR REGIS—*Lounge Adjoining Indoor Heated Pool.* Photo : E. Nägele, John Hinde Studios.

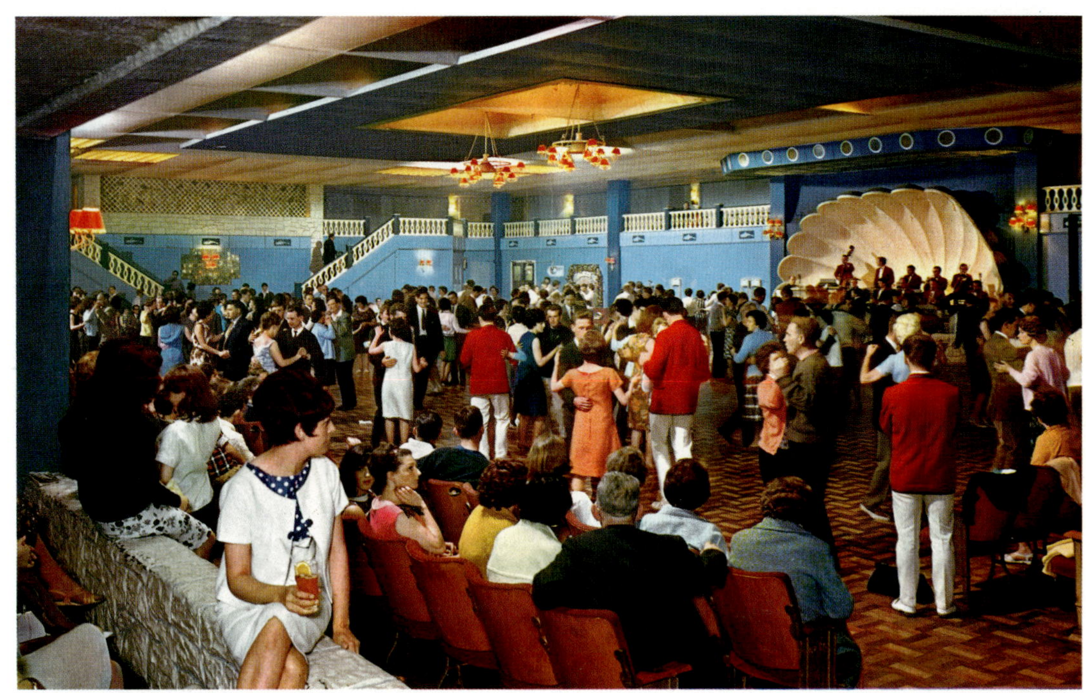

BUTLINLAND MOSNEY —*The Ballroom.* Photo: E. Ludwig, John Hinde Studios.

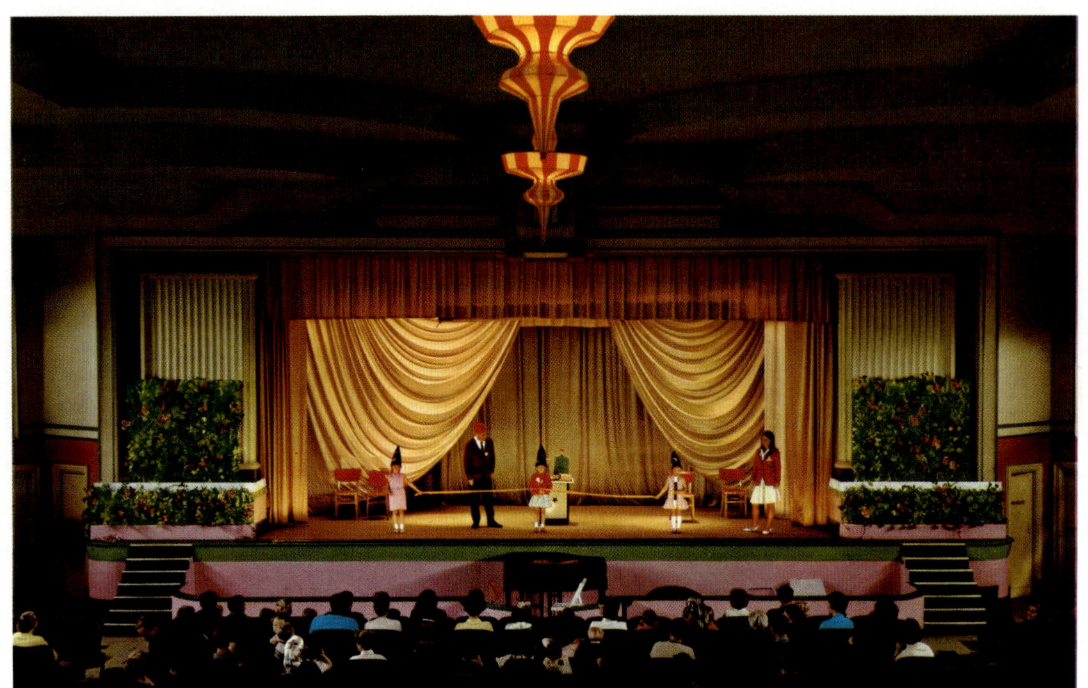

BUTLIN'S FILEY—*The Children's Theatre*

Photo: E. Nägele, John Hinde Studios.

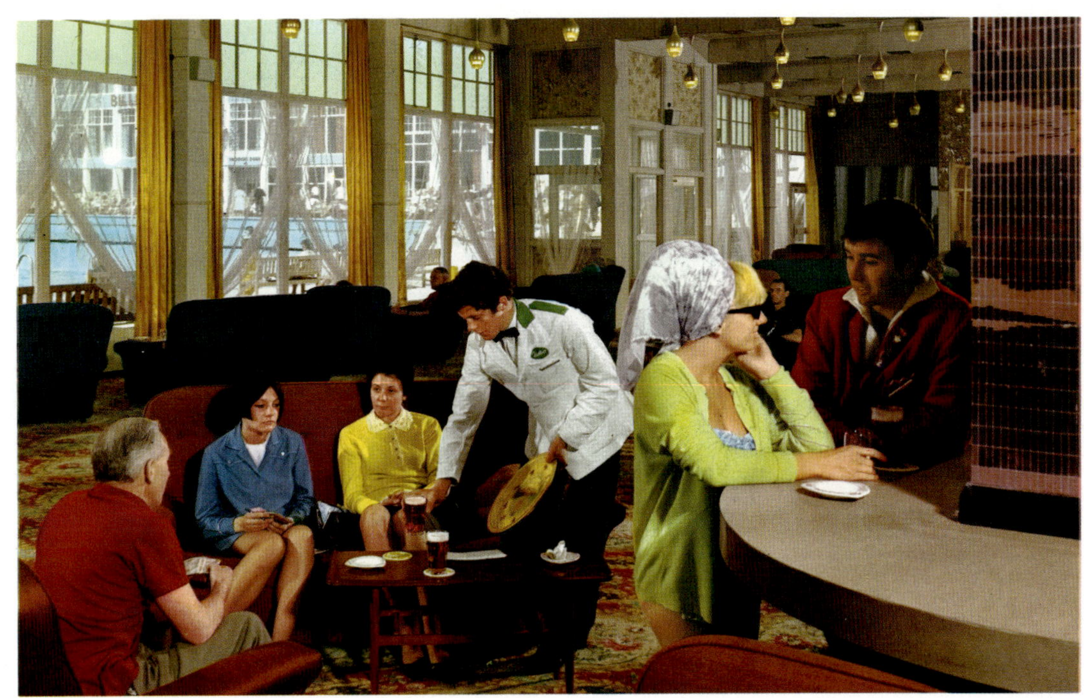

BUTLIN'S BARRY ISLAND—*The Gaiety Lounge*

Photo: E. Nägele, John Hinde Studios.

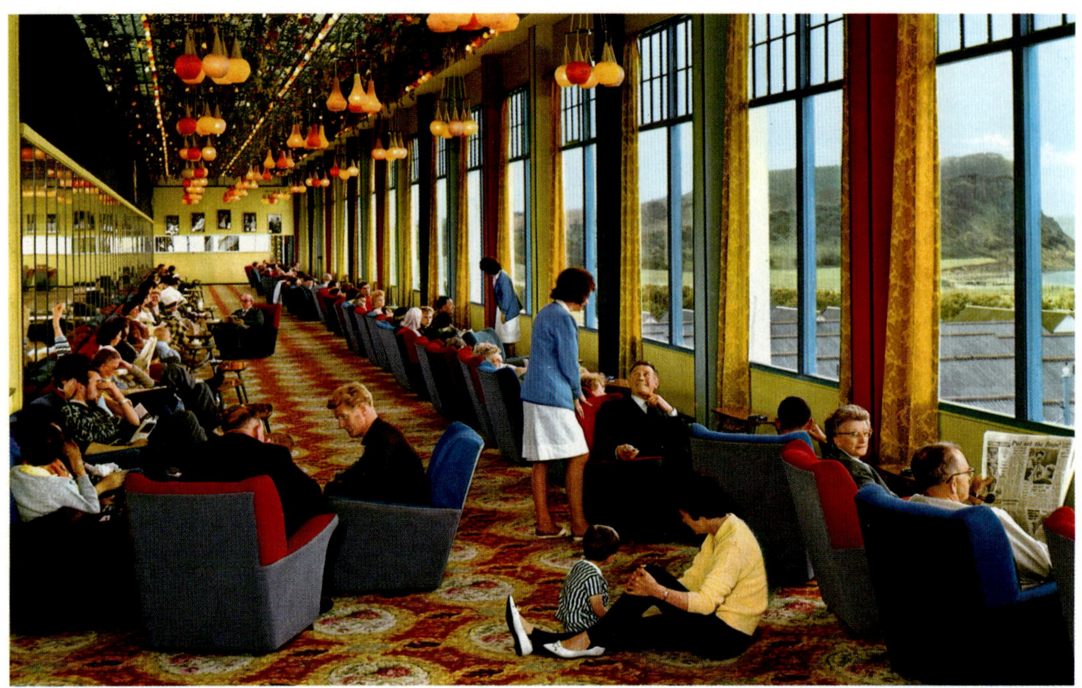

BUTLINLAND AYR— *A Quiet Lounge.* Photo: E. Ludwig, John Hinde Studios.

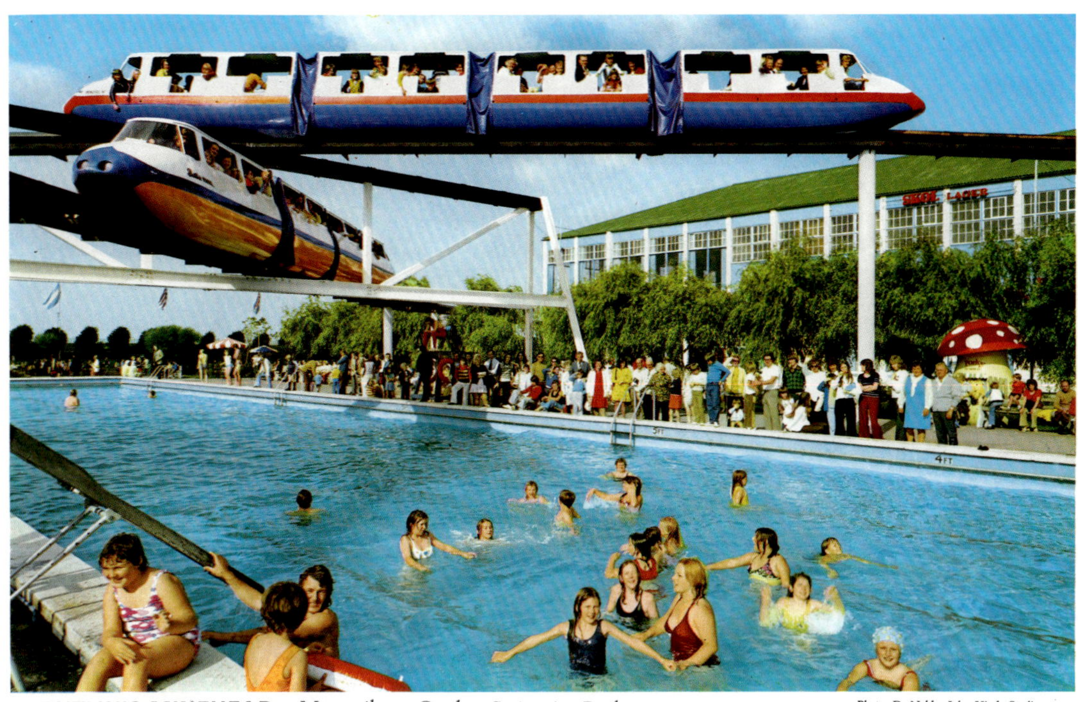

BUTLIN'S MINEHEAD – *Monorail over Outdoor Swimming Pool*

Photo: D. Noble, John Hinde Studios.

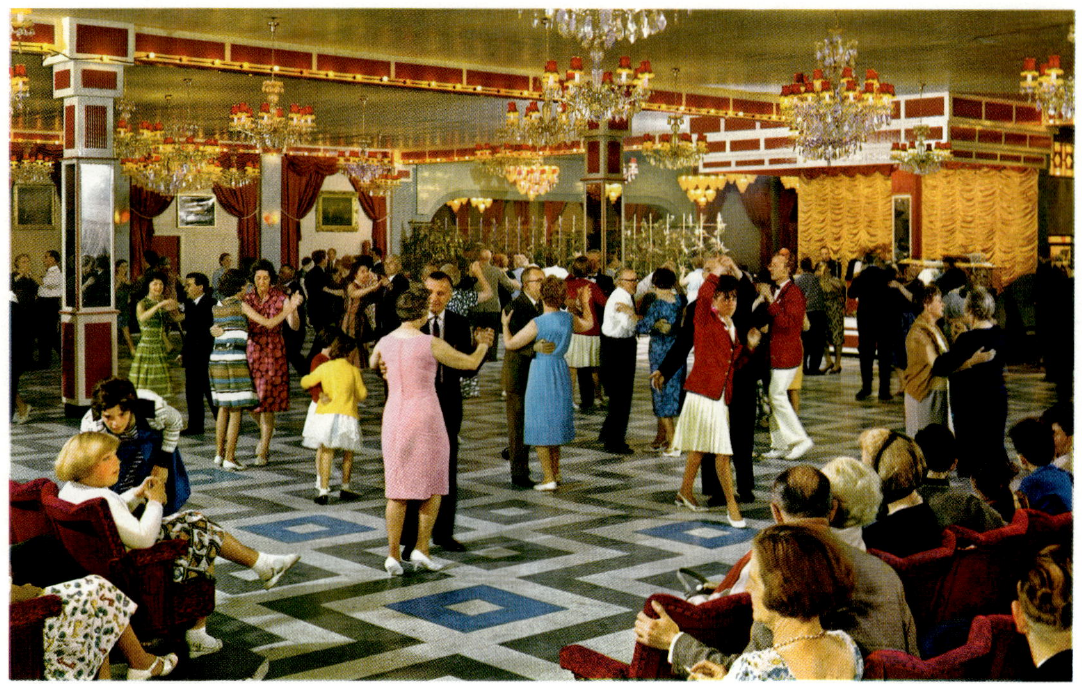

BUTLIN'S AYR—*The Modern Ballroom.* *Photo: E. Ludwig, John Hinde Studios.*

John Hinde, Biography

1916 - John Wilfrid Hinde born in Street, Somerset on May 17. Great grandson of James Clark, founder of Clark's Shoes.

1919 - Illness causes permanent disability in his left leg which necessitates spending much of the next eight years lying on his back.

1930 - Met Street local village chemist Carlos Pickering who encouraged Hinde's interest in photography.

1934 - During his last year in school he tries to make his first colour photograph.

1934-37 - Makes sporadic and mostly unsuccessful experiments with the colour carbro process of photographic printing.

1935 - On leaving school he entered the family business, Clark's Shoes, as an apprentice.

1936 - Becomes a student of Architecture and is articled to an architecture practice in Bristol.

1937 - Elected an Associate of the Royal Photographic Society, and a Fellow in 1943.

1937 - Enrols at the Reimann School to study photography, where Frank Newens tutors him in the production of carbro and wash-off relief prints. Newens is the foremost exponent of colour photographic printing in Britain.

1939 - January - Hinde sets up a photography studio in London in partnership with John Yerbury, son of architectural photographer Frank Yerbury.

1939 - Summer, visited Germany to investigate their techniques for taking and reproducing colour photographs.

1941 - December 6 - Lectured the Colour Group of the Royal Photographic Society on the Dufay colour process as applied to horticultural photography.

1941 - Started working for Adprint, a publisher's producer of the "Britain in Colour" series of books. Becomes absorbed in the reproduction of colour photographs.

1942 - Exhibited three colour prints - of flowers - at the annual exhibition of the Royal Photographic Society, and four the following year.

1942 - Began illustrating a series of horticultural dictionaries each containing 80 colour plates. They are:

"Aplines in Colour and Cultivation" (1942)
"Roses in Colour and Cultivation" (1943)
"The Border in Colour" (1944)
"Of Cabbages and Kings" (1945)
"Annuals in Colour and Cultivation" (1949)

(All edited and written by T.C. Mansfield and published by Collins). As Hinde himself observed: "These books were the first realisation that the process didn't stop with photography, but that it had to be supervised through to the end."

1943 - Worked for Illustrated magazine, and shot some of the first colour pictures used by them.

1944 - Completes a series of advertisements for Clark's Shoes featuring leading actresses.

1944- Cecil Beaton's British Photographers features a colour picture of a rose by Hinde.

1944/45 - Toured Britain with Reco's Circus.

1945 - Publication of "Citizens in War and After" by Stephen Spender, about the work of Civil Defence. Photography by John HInde.

1947 - Publication of Exmoor Village, about life in Luccombe, published by Harrap and Mass Observation. Also publication of The Small Canteen.

1947 - Goes to New York with the intention of staying in America to get involved with film. Doesn't like America.

1948 - Publication of "British Circus Life" co-authored with Lady Eleanor Smith.

1948 - Tours the West of Ireland showing cinema films in village halls.

1949-54 - Works as public relations manager for Chipperfields and Bertram Mills circuses, where he meets his wife, Jutta, a flying trapeze artiste.

1955 - Opens his own travelling variety show, the John Hinde Show, which closes after one season.

1956 - Starts John Hinde Ltd.

1957 - The first six postcards go on sale at Shannon Airport.

1960-70 Coincident with the increase in tourism the range of Irish postcards increased from roughly 30 to 300.

1963 - Moves to new factory at Cabinteely , Dublin. First export market opened in the UK, starting with London, Bournemouth and Blackpool.

1966 - Mr. Jack Lynch and other members of the Government officiate at the opening of "The John Hinde Story", an exhibition celebrating the company's 10th anniversary, held at the Intercontinental Hotel, Dublin.

1967 - Ceases taking photographs - except during annual working trips to Africa - to concentrate on the business.

1972 - Hinde sells the business at a time when the company is achieving 50 million postcard sales worldwide.

John Hinde now lives in Spain and France and paints landscapes in oils and gouache.

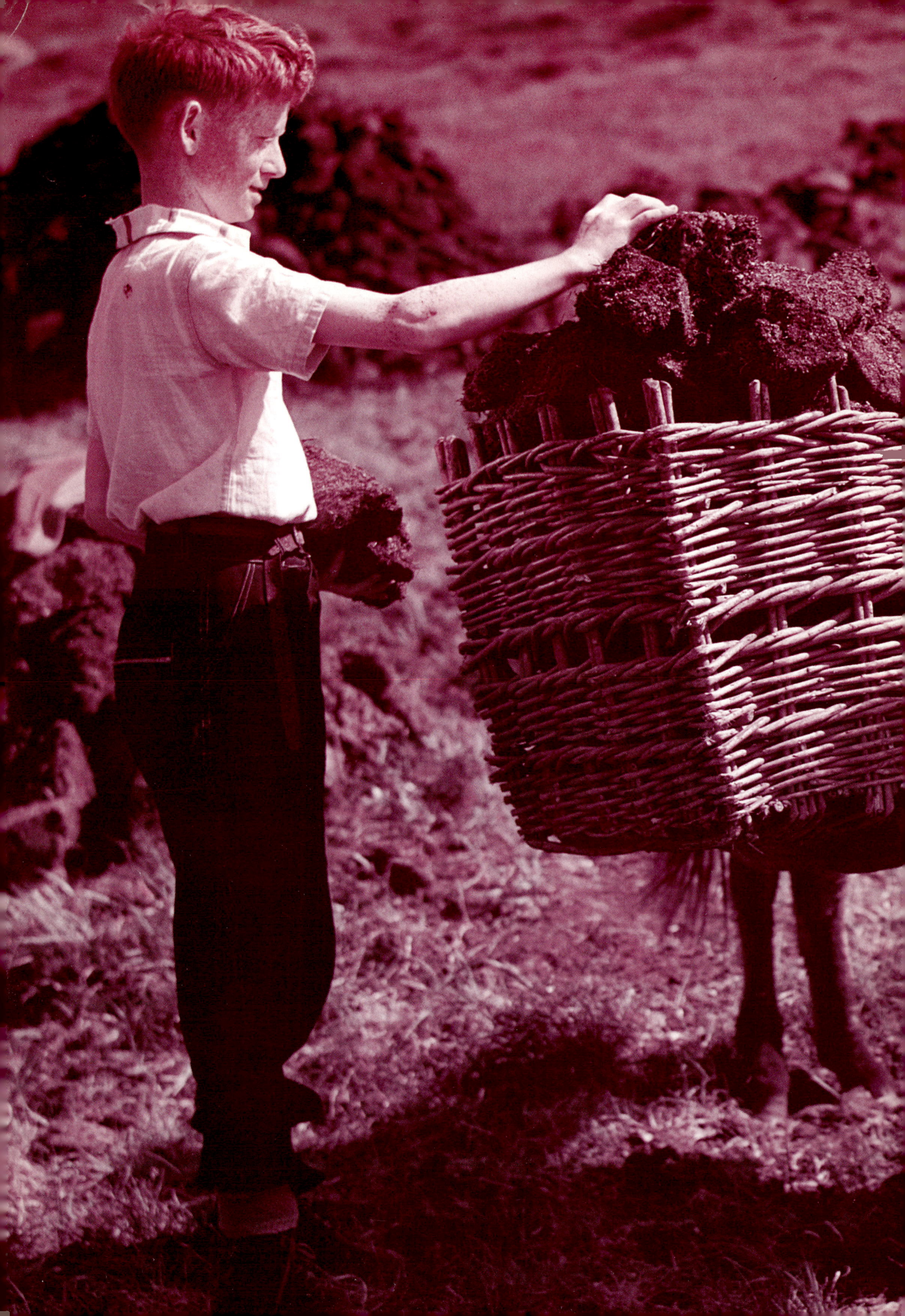